PORT ELIZABETH PLAYS

'MASTER HAROLD'
. . . AND THE BOYS

BLOOD KNOT
New Version

HELLO AND GOODBYE

BOESMAN AND LENA

ATHOL FUGARD

Edited with an Introduction by

Dennis Walder

OXFORD
UNIVERSITY PRESS

OXFORD
UNIVERSITY PRESS

Great Clarendon Street, Oxford OX2 6DP

Oxford University Press is a department of the University of Oxford.
It furthers the University's objective of excellence in research, scholarship,
and education by publishing worldwide in

Oxford New York

Auckland Cape Town Dar es Salaam Hong Kong Karachi Kuala Lumpur
Madrid Melbourne Mexico City Nairobi New Delhi Taipei Toronto
Shanghai

With offices in

Argentina Austria Brazil Chile Czech Republic France Greece
Guatemala Hungary Italy Japan South Korea Poland Portugal
Singapore Switzerland Thailand Turkey Ukraine Vietnam

Oxford is a registered trade mark of Oxford University Press
in the UK and in certain other countries

British Library Cataloguing in Publication Data
Data available

Library of Congress Cataloging in Publication Data
Fugard, Athol.
Selected plays
I. Title.
822   PR9369.3.F8
ISBN-13: 978-0-19-282529-2

10

Printed in Great Britain by
Clays Ltd, St Ives plc

PREFACE

At the best of times, labelling is a very frustrating experience for a writer, but there is one label that I live very happily with and have no hesitation in using when talking about my work: I am a Regional Writer. Unlike all the other labels—the most irksome being 'political playwright'—it has the virtue of being completely accurate.

Virtually all my plays are rooted in the specifics of one place and time: that little corner of South Africa centred round Port Elizabeth. That is where I grew up, where I have spent the major part of my life, and where my imagination has flourished. When I stand on a street corner in Port Elizabeth, I can put together a very plausible scenario for any one of the faces passing in front of me on the pavement: the old black woman exhausted after her day bent over a washing tub in the back yard of the middle-class white suburb, hurrying now to the black bus terminus and the long queue and wait for the bus that will carry her back to the township and her hungry children, who in turn are waiting for the leftovers she carries home in that plastic shopping bag . . . and in similar fashion, a scenario is there without any real effort for the Indian woman in her sari, the barefooted coloured man with a bag of empty bottles clinking on his back, or the white businessman in his suit, the keys for his luxury German motorcar in his hand. I can place them in their worlds, and I can do that without even thinking about it because I have mastered the code of that time and place; I can 'read' the motley flow of life on that pavement. That street corner is 'home' in the profoundest sense of the word . . . I belong there, and because of that, because it is mine in a way that no other place in this world can ever be, I have a sense of authority when I write about it. The four plays in this volume are the most intense and passionately felt expression of that regionalism. They defined me and my voice irrevocably, and because of that are the watershed from which all my other work has come.

But just as these plays are dressed in the physical specificity of that world—the mud flats of the Swartkops river where Lena sits shivering through the darkest night of her life, the Jubilee Boarding House where Hally found a haven in the black servants' quarters, the statue of Queen Victoria in Port Elizabeth's Market Square where Johnnie waited for sunsets, and the stinking cesspool of water, Korsten 'lake', outside the door of Morrie and Zach's little shack—they also occupy a very specific psychological region: The Family. In each of these four plays it is the nexus of family ties—parent to parent (man and woman), parent to child, brother to sister, brother to brother—and the tensions and antagonisms they generate that provide the material out of which I have fashioned their drama. During the formative years of my playwrighting, the 'family' was a psychological region as important to me as Port Elizabeth was at a physical level.

ATHOL FUGARD

October 1999

CONTENTS

Notes to the texts of the plays can be found on page 249
and are cued by asterisks.

INTRODUCTION

I

Athol Fugard is widely acknowledged as one of the best dramatists of our time. His plays command audiences the world over, despite their manifestly local origins and accent. He has transformed the unfamiliar situations and landscape of his small corner of South Africa into work of profound and lasting significance. He has done this by creating drama which, typically, engages our sympathies for the fate of two or three characters closely entangled by ties of blood, love, or friendship, struggling to survive in an arbitrary, bleak, and almost meaningless universe. 'Almost' meaningless: because his dark vision of pain never totally excludes the possibility of a flicker of light, of compassion, or dignity.

The effects of the unique system of racial oppression known as apartheid may seem familiar enough. But there is a level and quality of suffering, humiliation, despair and, occasionally, hope, present in the lives of millions of ordinary South Africans —mostly, but not exclusively, black—which demands recognition. Fugard's plays help obtain that recognition. In a favourite phrase, they 'bear witness'. If they did nothing more, that might be enough. But they go further: they reach out and touch the secret pain we all inflict upon each other in the private recesses of our closest relationships. This is why his plays make us feel, with an intensity almost unbearable; yet they also offer a shape, a meaning for those feelings. This meaning emerges as the climax of a shifting pattern of emotions of gradually increasing strength—harsh, pathetic, banal, comic and, even, poetic, in turn; a climax expressed as a revelatory 'living moment', or 'image', on stage.

Words are only part of what Fugard defines—in terms borrowed from Ezra Pound—as his crucial 'image': the 'presentation of a psychological and emotional complex in a moment of time'. Movement, gesture, the 'sub-textual' penumbra of dialogue: all contribute to a theatrical language often most eloquent when it is silent. Despite the subsequent assimilation of Fugard's work into the mainstream consumer theatre with which we are all too familiar—the theatre of purpose-built auditoria, revolving sets, carpeted foyers—all that he has ever *required* is 'the actor and the stage, the actor *on* the stage'.[1] This helps explain his reliance upon his chosen performers, as well as his determination to have a controlling hand in at least the first run of his plays—in which he has also often acted himself.

Some of Fugard's most well-known and memorable work has testified directly to the effects of specific apartheid laws, such as the notorious influx control laws (which controlled all black people's lives in South Africa), the laws forbidding opposition, and the so-called 'Immorality Act' (which prohibited miscegenation, long repealed. These *Statements* plays (including *Sizwe Bansi is Dead*) are available elsewhere; as are his more introspective, psycho-mythological works (such as *Dimetos* and *The Road to Mecca*). The plays selected for this volume embody a blend or mixture of these contrary impulses—towards explicitness of surface reference on the one hand (e.g. Sam's remarks about the race laws in *'Master Harold'* . . . *and the boys*), and inwardness on the other (as in Johnnie's monologues in *Hello and goodbye*). All four plays are set among the people and in the place Fugard knows most intimately—Port Elizabeth. They are, in that sense, 'Port Elizabeth' plays. They are also 'family' plays, in that each deals with a family situation or relationship from a different but clearly discernible perspective. The order of the plays in this edition is designed to reinforce their thematic interconnectedness: moving from a focus upon the son alone in *'Master Harold'* . . . *and the boys*, to the two brothers in *Blood Knot*, to brother and sister in *Hello and Goodbye* to, finally (after parents have hovered invisibly offstage in all of these), the parents, beyond childbearing, in *Boesman and Lena*. There is also a shift from the didactic naturalism which dominates the first play, towards a more radical, modernist, and symbolic mode in the last.

The texts reprinted here are the most recent approved by the author, and have been carefully checked. This may not seem

[1] Athol Fougard [*sic*], 'The Blood Knot' (foreword to an extract), *Contrast* (Cape Town), ii (Autumn 1969), 29.

very important for a playwright who emphasizes performance rather than publication, theatrical 'image' rather than verbal detail; but apart from the obvious desirability of establishing consistently accurate published texts, there is the point that Fugard himself has long thought *The Blood Knot* (original title) 'monstrously overwritten',[2] and has been directing it since the early sixties in a much reduced version. So *Blood Knot*, as he now calls it, appears here for the first time in print in this authoritative form (the main change in comparison with previous printed texts consists of substantial cuts in Morris's speeches). And numerous errors and inconsistencies in the four plays have been corrected (e.g. Lena's plea in Act One of *Boesman and Lena*, 'I want somebody to listen' has long been printed as 'I was somebody to listen').

II

Probably the stature of great artists comes from some critical coincidence between their personal life and the life of their times, a coincidence which finds objective expression in their works. Athol Fugard has often said that all his plays come directly from personal experience and encounters with actual people. His biography is therefore of peculiar interest and significance—as, too, are the accounts in his private notebooks of the secret, slow and painful germination of those plays.

Harold Athol Lannigan Fugard was born on 11 June 1932, on a farm near Middelburg, Cape Province—a dry, dusty little town in the semi-desert Karroo region of South Africa. His parents ran a small, general dealer's 'cash store' in Middelburg, with little success. His father, Harold, a crippled former jazz pianist, was descended from Manchester immigrants, possibly Irish–Huguenot in origin. His mother, Elizabeth, née Potgieter, carried the name of one of the foremost Voortrekker (pioneering) families, long settled in the Karroo. He thinks of himself as of 'mixed descent' in white South African terms, inheriting both the Afrikaans, narrowly Calvinist but independent

[2] Jonathan Marks, 'Interview with Athol Fugard', *Yale/Theater*, iv (Winter 1973), 66.

attitudes of his mother's background; and the broadly Christian, more 'liberal' attitudes of his father's English culture. In fact, his mother was the more tolerant, as well as the stronger parent. Yet he was brought up and educated in an English-speaking environment, and chose to write in English—or, more accurately, in a uniquely South African idiom, which reflects both the uncertainty and the potential of his culture by mingling English, Afrikaans and, sometimes, African speech. All the characters in the plays reprinted here, apart from '*Master Harold*' (and Outa in *Boesman and Lena*) would normally speak Afrikaans; but Fugard has 'translated' their speech into his own Eastern Cape idiom—thus reaching a world audience without sacrificing what he calls his local 'specifics'.

In 1935 the family (including an older brother, Royal, and sister, Glenda) moved to Port Elizabeth, where they lived to begin with in a boarding-house run by Mrs Fugard. Port Elizabeth has been the dramatist's home ever since, despite spells in larger centres such as Cape Town or Johannesburg, or abroad (mainly America), and the purchase of a second home in New Bethesda, a small village not far from Middelburg. Fugard finds it painful to continue living where he does; but, apparently, he cannot function as a writer anywhere else. He has 'acquired the code' there, that 'degree of familiarity which is necessary for me . . . I must know the textures I'm going to deal with'.[3] It is hard to imagine a less propitious place for the production of works of art or literature. Situated on the eastern coast between Cape Town and Durban, Port Elizabeth (which was founded by the 1820 British settlers) is known mainly for its winds, motor car factories, and snake park. Two-thirds of the population of half a million are obliged by law to live in 'locations' or 'townships' (such as Korsten or New Brighton) near the factories which rely on their labour: they are mostly Xhosa-speaking Africans, but also Chinese, Indians, and a substantial number of 'Coloureds' (persons of mixed-race). The poorer whites, generally Afrikaans-speaking, reside in suburbs adjoining the factories and 'non-white' areas; wealthy whites, both Afrikaans- and English-speaking, live luxuriously

---

[3] Dennis Walder, *Athol Fugard* (Macmillan, 1984), p. 20 (from an interview).

in the tree-lined southern suburbs, near the beach. Apart from their servants (average two per household), garden 'boys', clerks, and messengers, whites have little personal contact with blacks, and less understanding of their aspirations. As for 'culture': the whites watch (heavily-censored) television, attend drive-in cinemas and occasional overseas theatrical productions; the blacks make their own entertainment, in church or community halls. Everyone enjoys sport. 'Liberals' are conspicuously absent, and most whites support the government. Blacks are left to extra-parliamentary opposition, such as (increasingly) trade unions, and underground resistance; many have died in recent disturbances.

While his mother continued to keep the family, taking over the St George's Park Tea Room in the city centre, 'Hally'—as he was called until his teens—began his secondary education on a council scholarship at the local technical college. There he had his first experience of amateur dramatics, as actor and director (although Glenda Fugard remembers dancing the Apache with her brother for the troops in the local Opera House). The young Fugard read omnivorously; he had begun writing, before a scholarship took him to the University of Cape Town—one of South Africa's 'liberal', English-language universities. Here his lifelong interest in Camus began, partly under the influence of a remarkable teacher of philosophy, Martin Versfeld, a Catholic existentialist. Fugard also studied French literature and social anthropology. Shortly before his final exams, he set off with a fellow student to hitch-hike up Africa. They reached Juba, Sudan, where they separated, and Fugard signed on as a deck-hand with the British tramp steamer SS *Graigaur*. He found time to write a novel (his second attempt), which he threw into the sea at Fiji. Within a year he was back home, working freelance for the Port Elizabeth *Evening Post*.

The inspiration to become directly involved in drama came when Fugard met Sheila Meiring, at the time an actress in Cape Town. They married in September 1956. Small acting parts led to the Fugards forming a theatre workshop ('Circle Players'), for which Sheila did the writing until her husband began to contribute 'some rather pretentious little pieces' (now lost), including *Klaas and the Devil* and *The Cell*, the latter under the influence of J. M. Synge.[4] Like other writers to whom Fugard was attracted at the time, such as Tennessee Williams and William Faulkner, Synge helped confirm a growing sense that his work should be, above all, rooted in the local.

It was not until 1958, when the Fugards were attracted by the possibility of work in Johannesburg, that his instinct to make his work 'local' bore fruit. The only job the playwright could find was as clerk in a 'Native Commissioner's Court', where pass-law offenders were tried. If he thought he knew his society was evil before, 'seeing the machinery in operation taught me how it works and in fact what it does to people'. Few white South Africans have seen or are aware of what happens in such places. 'I think my basic pessimism was born there, watching that procession of faces and being unable to relate to them.'[5] Yet, at the same time, the Fugards began an African Theatre Workshop in the multiracial ghetto Sophiatown, where they had met a remarkable group of people, including the critic Lewis Nkosi, the writer Can Themba, and one extraordinary acting talent, in the person of jazz musician Zakes Mokae, for whom Fugard was to create the part of Zach, in *The Blood Knot*. But first he conceived his earliest successful plays: *No-Good Friday* (1958) and *Nongogo* (1959), both written for and performed by black amateur casts in rough, makeshift conditions, using 'Method' acting techniques. The key to the 'township' life portrayed in these works was *survival*: and this became a central theme.

Fugard and Mokae met through the non-racial artists' equity association, the Union of South African Artists—or Union Artists, as it became when it acquired Dorkay House, the factory warehouse where 'township' talent was presented before mainly white audiences in Johannesburg during the late fifties. The huge success of the jazz opera *King Kong* (1959) enabled Union Artists to initiate the African Music and Drama Association and to sponsor the Rehearsal Room, the private, experimental 'theatre' in which Fugard and Mokae first performed *The Blood Knot* on 3 September 1961. The idea for the

[4] 'Keeping an Appointment with the Future' (interview with Mary Benson), *Theatre Quarterly*, vii (Winter 1977/8), 78.

[5] Marks 'Interview', 72; 'Afrikaner Humanist' (interview), *Observer*, 18 July 1971.

play came to Fugard in London during 1960. The small local success of his 'Sophiatown' plays had enabled him—with the help of a visiting Belgian director, Tone Brulin—to obtain his first work in professional theatre, as stage manager with the (all-white) National Theatre Organisation. At the NTO's experimental *Kamertoneel* theatre, Fugard had a 'crash course' in modern drama—Beckett, Ionesco, Shaw—which whetted his appetite for further experience, until he and Sheila saved enough to leave for Europe. In London they resorted to odd jobs to keep going, and pay for theatre tickets. Tone Brulin, back in Belgium, invited them over to help form an acting group which successfully presented South African David Herbert's 'try for white' play (about a black passing for white), *A Kakamas Greek*, with Fugard in the title role, at a Festival of Avant-Garde Theatre. By the end of 1960, with Sheila pregnant, and no further work in prospect, the Fugards had returned to Port Elizabeth, where *The Blood Knot* was completed.

The South African theatre director Barney Simon, a year younger than Fugard and from a similarly near-poor-white background (in Johannesburg), had met the playwright before the Fugards left for Europe; he had himself already visited London, where he had worked with Joan Littlewood and developed a strong passion for her small-scale, 'workshop' approach. His help in being the 'third eye' (with Fugard) in overseeing the opening of *The Blood Knot* was invaluable, and Fugard has acknowledged his influence—the only local talent (apart from performers) he has thus admitted. Fugard has ignored South African contemporaries such as James Ambrose Brown or Lewis Sowden—the latter also wrote a 'try for white' play, *Kimberley Train* (1958). Instead, he has looked to Europe or America for theoretical or intellectual stimulus, while drawing practical inspiration from local people and their conditions.

The Blood Knot explores the South African obsession with race, and the use of it to define relations of power and dependence; although with a subtlety, humour, and resonance which ensured both immediate and lasting success. Two months after its Rehearsal Room opening, and cut from its original four to two-and-a-half hours, it reopened under professional management, and a tour was set up. 'South Africa has produced a playwright', announced a correspondent in *The Times* (Mary Benson). In March 1962 the final (140th) performance took place in New Brighton, Port Elizabeth. The following year it was launched at the New Arts Theatre, Hampstead, London, with Zakes Mokae and Ian Bannen, directed by John Berry. Audiences were good, but Kenneth Tynan all but destroyed the play by remarking (in the *Observer*) that it merely reflected white guilt. The American response (to the Cricket Theatre production in New York, with James Earl Jones and J. D. Cannon) was more sympathetic: the *New York Times* voted it the best play of the year. Fugard's international career had begun.

The Blood Knot established the essentials of Fugard drama: a small cast of 'marginal' characters in a passionately close relationship embodying the tensions of their society, and first performed by actors involved in its creation, in a makeshift, 'fringe', or at least non-establishment venue. Plot was minimal; dialogue and setting sparely suggestive. During the following years Fugard wrote three more plays along the same lines: *Hello and Goodbye*, which was first directed by Barney Simon, with Fugard as Johnnie and Molly Seftel as Hester, in the Library Theatre, Johannesburg, after 'previews' in Dorkay House; *People are Living There* (set in Braamfontein, Johannesburg), which, after failing to find a local sponsor, opened at the Close Theatre, Glasgow, in March 1968, directed by Robin Midgley, who had impressed Fugard with his direction of *The Blood Knot* for BBC TV the previous year; and *Boesman and Lena*, an early version of which opened in the Rhodes University Little Theatre, Grahamstown, on 10 July 1969, directed by Fugard, with himself as Boesman and Yvonne Bryceland as Lena. Earlier that year Bryceland, already one of the country's most experienced actresses, had been cast for what became an acclaimed production of *People are Living There*. In her, Fugard had found another creative co-performer, who was to become a vital resource.

The playwright's passport was taken away in 1967, 'for reasons of state safety and security', the day after *The Blood Knot* appeared on British television, apparently because of the effect the play was presumed to have. He did not stop work; nor leave the country on a one-way 'exit permit', which is what the authorities probably desired. He had initiated an international playwright's boycott of South Africa in 1963, to provoke a response from local theatre managements who had accepted segregated audiences before being forced to do so by law; but when such legislation was introduced he reversed his decision because, he said, keeping South Africans isolated from liberal ideas was just what the government wanted. More recently, theatres have been desegregated. Fugard, most of whose plays first appear in 'unofficial' venues (or abroad, nowadays), has always allowed them to be produced within his country as long as all races might have access to them. This has involved him in compromise; to him the choice is between that or silence.

In 1971, after a public petition helped secure the return of his passport, he accepted an invitation to direct *Boesman and Lena* at the Royal Court Theatre Upstairs, with Bryceland as Lena and Mokae as Boesman. The production was a triumph, and the interest of Ross Devenish, a young South African television film maker, was aroused. He persuaded Fugard to collaborate on a film version, with the playwright himself and Bryceland in the title roles. This led to further filmwork together, and the televising of other Fugard plays. The Royal Court subsequently offered a 'South African Season' (1973–4), including the three *Statements* plays, which increased Fugard's reputation, and established that of his co-creators and actors, John Kani and Winston Ntshona. This is not the place to recall the background of those plays; but it is worth mentioning that the initial impetus behind Serpent Players, whose collaborative work resulted in *Sizwe Bansi is Dead* and *The Island* (amongst other plays), derived from Fugard and Mokae's performance of *The Blood Knot* in New Brighton, which prompted the request for Fugard's help in setting up a drama workshop in the 'township'. Serpent Players survived police harassment and the imprisonment of most members until the mid-seventies. By then the combined effect of political pressure and personal exhaustion had led Fugard towards the almost entirely private emphasis of the film *The Guest at Steenkampskraal* and his play *Dimetos* (both 1975).

Unable to deal directly with the present—which, since the Soweto rising of 1976, has taken a newly bloody and extreme turn—Fugard has retreated to the past, his own past. Yet he seems to want to *address* the present: evident in a certain didacticism, for example in the very title of *A Lesson from Aloes* (1978), or in the 'hell of a lot of teaching' which, in Sam's words, has been 'going on' in *'Master Harold'* . . . *and the boys* (1982). *Aloes*, set in Port Elizabeth in 1963, was premiered at Barney Simon's Market Theatre in Johannesburg, situated in an old fruit market (a site excluded from the Group Areas Act, and so, too, from theatre segregation). But this play was eclipsed by its successor, which goes back to its author's teens. The autobiographical emphasis led Fugard to open *'Master Harold'* abroad, at the Yale Repertory Theatre in New Haven; but he also chose Yale because, as he anticipated, there was initially adverse response at home to *'Master Harold'*'s explicitness of action and dialogue—indeed, the play was banned in South Africa before its first performance (at the Market), and then hastily unbanned when it was realized who the author was. Not long after, the Cape school board ordered that copies of *Boesman and Lena* should be burnt, fearing its 'corrupting' effect upon white youth.

But these are little more than the passing fancies of a power which is coming to admit a more serious and immediate threat than any artist can provide: the growing, undeclared, but irresistible war within its borders. As the conclusion of *'Master Harold'* suggests, the whites are faced with a choice: to join the blacks in brotherhood, or to try and remain 'master' in isolation and impending darkness.

III

Fugard has often remarked that the ten-month experience of living and working side by side with men of all races on the SS *Graigaur* liberated him from the prejudice endemic among those with his background. Nadine Gordimer claims that every white South African needs to be born twice: the second time into an awareness of racialism. But, unlike other white South African liberal writers, such as Gordimer (or Alan Paton or Dan Jacobson), for Fugard this has meant turning against his own people, becoming a 'traitor' to his mother's, if not his father's race. This helps explain the painful, guilt-ridden intensity of his work. He has called himself 'the classic example of the impotent white liberal'. And yet such feelings generate his plays. He once traced his sense of guilt and remorse to a specific incident in his childhood: 'I spat in the face of a black man. I cannot talk about it to this day.'[6] Years later, that painful incident found its place as the central, climactic 'image' of *'Master Harold'* . . . *and the boys*.

The genesis of this 'image' has been recorded in the *Notebooks* Fugard edited and revised for publication with the aid of Mary Benson:[7]

March [1961]
Sam Semela—Basuto—with the family fifteen years. Meeting him again when he visited Mom set off a string of memories.

The kite which he produced for me one day during those early years when Mom ran the Jubilee Hotel and he was a waiter there. He had made it himself: brown paper, its ribs fashioned from thin strips of tomato-box plank which he had smoothed down, a paste of flour and water for glue. I was surprised and bewildered that he had made it for me.

I vaguely recall shyly 'haunting' the servants' quarters in the well of the hotel—cold, cement-grey world—the pungent mystery of the dark little rooms—a world I didn't understand. Frightened to enter any of the rooms. Sam, broad-faced, broader-based—he smelled of woodsmoke. The 'kaffir smell' of South Africa is the smell of poverty —woodsmoke and sweat.

Later, when he worked for her at the Park café, Mom gave him the sack: '. . . he became careless. He came late for work. His work went to hell. He didn't seem to care no more.' I was about thirteen and served behind the counter while he waited on table.

Realize now he was the most significant—the only—friend of my boyhood years. On terrible windy days when no-one came to swim or walk in the park, we would sit together and talk. Or I was reading —Introductions to Eastern Philosophy or Plato and Socrates—and when I had finished he would take the book back to New Brighton.

Can't remember now what precipitated it, but one day there was a rare quarrel between Sam and myself. In a truculent silence we closed the café, Sam set off home to New Brighton on foot and I followed a

[6] Colin Smith, 'White man on a Tightrope' (interview). *Observer*, 6 January 1974; programme note, *Dimetos*, Edinburgh International Festival, 1975.
[7] *Athol Fugard: Notebooks 1960–1977*, ed. Mary Benson (Faber, 1983), 25–7. In the extracts which follow this one I have drawn on the earlier, unedited version of his Notebooks reprinted by Fugard in his Introduction to *Three Port Elizabeth Plays* (OUP, 1974), pp. x–xxiv.

INTRODUCTION

few minutes later on my bike. I saw him walking ahead of me and, coming out of a spasm of acute loneliness, as I rode up behind him I called his name, he turned in mid-stride to look back and, as I cycled past, I spat in his face. Don't suppose I will ever deal with the shame that overwhelmed me the second after I had done that.

Now he is thin. We had a long talk. He told me about the old woman ('Ma') whom he and his wife have taken in to look after their house while he goes to work—he teaches ballroom dancing. 'Ma' insists on behaving like a domestic—making Sam feel guilty and embarrassed . . .

Sam's incredible theory about the likeness of those 'with the true seed of love'. Starts with Plato and Socrates—they were round. 'Man is being shrinking all the time. An Abe Lincoln, him, too, taller, but that's because man is shrinking.' Basically, those with the true seed of love look the same—'It's in the eyes.'

He spoke admiringly of one man, a black lawyer in East London, an educated man—university background—who was utterly without snobbery, looking down on no-one—any man, educated or ignorant, rich or poor, was another *man* to him, another human being, to be respected, taken seriously, to be talked to, listened to.

'They' won't allow Sam any longer to earn a living as a dancing teacher. 'You must get a job!' One of his fellow teachers was forced to work at Fraser's quarries.

It is a sad but instructive irony that Sam Semela died in his poor New Brighton home shortly before John Kani arrived to take him to see the South African première of *'Master Harold'* in Johannesburg in 1983—in which Kani played the former waiter. The published play was dedicated to Sam and 'H. D. F.'—Fugard's father.

The opening entry of Fugard's first notebook, begun in London in 1960, is an evocation of place, and provides the germ of *The Blood Knot*:

Korsten: The Berry's Corner bus, then up the road past the big motor assembly and rubber factories. Turn right down a dirt road—badly potholed, full of stones, donkeys wandering loose, Chinese and Indian grocery shops—down this road until you come to the lake. Dumping ground for waste products from the factories. Terrible smell. On the far side, like a scab, Korsten location. A collection of shanties, pondoks, lean-to's. No streets, names, or numbers. A world where anything goes.

When the wind blows in from the east the inhabitants of Korsten live with the terrible smell of the lake.

In one of these shacks the two brothers—Morrie and Zach. Morrie is a light-skinned Coloured who has found out that to ignore the temptations to use his lightness is the easiest way to live. Rather than live with the fear and uncertainty that would have come from 'trying for white', he has settled for being Coloured. He has some education —can read and write. In contrast, his brother Zach—dark-skinned Coloured, virtually African in appearance. Zach has no education, has made no attempt to acquire any, will never have any. Zach can never be anything other than what he is—a black man. There are no choices for him.

The appearance of Ethel in their lives. Morrie wants to have nothing to do with her. He is frightened of her. Zach wants her but can't have her. It is masochism and revenge that make Zach insist that his brother meet her. Zach could in the beginning, and eventually does, envy Morrie the lightness of his skin.

Their relationship as brothers . . . Zach is confused. Suspicion and envy. The question haunting him . . . Why? It was the same mother! Why?

The blood tie linking them has chained them. They are dead or dying because of it.

The situation of the two brothers (imprisonment in a blood tie) cannot continue after the appearance of Ethel. Too much has surfaced—Zach's envy and hate, Morrie's crippling sense of guilt and responsibility.

A last confrontation.

Hello and Goodbye explores another 'blood knot': like Morris, Hester Smit has returned to her brother (whom she finds alone), at least partly out of guilt for leaving; but this time it is the one who has stayed at home who is the introspective neurotic, unable to take on work, while she is the unreflecting, 'spontaneous', less educated sibling. The racial complication is absent: both are 'poor white' Afrikaners, in their cramped family cottage at 57a Valley Road, Port Elizabeth—a run-down part of the city centre. Fugard's compulsive return to 'family matters' may be explained by the notes he later recognized as the seeds of this play. The illness of his father (alluded to in *'Master Harold'*) had now become very serious: he was to die a few months later, shortly after the birth of the Fugards' daughter.

11/5/61
Dad's pain . . . The habit of suffering. The inward wait and watch for pain. The Lesson of a life. He knows it, the anatomy of pain, the way other old people know their pets. The secret places where it plays —the chest, toe-nails, stump, cramp in the good leg. This and the habit of dependence, the habit of humiliation, of loneliness. A man withdrawn, marooned finally on the last unassailable island of the individual consciousness . . . pain.

Fugard began work on *Hello and Goodbye* towards the end of 1963.

19/5/63
From time to time I keep remembering, and still see occasionally on the streets, one face from my youth. That of a man who, for as long as I can remember, could be seen at night standing motionless against the wall on the corner of Jetty and Main Streets. Large unsmiling eyes, heavy lids. Bitter mouth. Must have seen him a hundred times, yet I have no recollection of any expression other than this one of morbid withdrawal. Saw him about a week ago—entrance to the public lavatory behind the Town Hall. Has taken to standing there these days. I watched him for a few minutes. He stood motionless, staring at nothing. Face is now bloated, eyes glazed, shabbily dressed. Next to him stood a young Coloured boy, watching the white man with amused contempt. My man said something to the boy (without looking at him), then lurched away down the street. He was dead drunk.

Remember my father. He had the same way of telling people, even strangers, the next move in their enormously trivial game of life, and then doing it. 'Well, better be on my way.' 'Think I'll make it an early night.'

When I think of the places where this man could live, I get excited. The Valley for example.

Johnnie (Boetie to his family).

Johnnie Smit.

Johnnie Le Gransie.

19/6/63
Still thinking about Johnnie. A Port Elizabeth story. I see and feel him in terms of Jetty Street, the Valley, South End and his tireless vigil on the Union Castle Corner at night, and beside Queen Victoria's statue during the day. Not to forget of course that that is where the bus drivers gather with their tin boxes of tickets and time-sheets.

16/9/63

Last night before sleep found myself thinking about Johnnie—the local street-corner derelict I made a few notes about some months back. I remembered a thought I had about a sister and suddenly I saw very clearly the germinal situation of a play. Thinking about it this morning I am again excited.

Johnnie living with his father in a two-room shack in Valley Road. The father is blind and a cripple . . . victim of a blasting accident when he worked for the South African Railways. Johnnie looks after him—feeding, washing, dressing, carrying. They exist on the old man's pension—old age or disability. One night, after ten or fifteen years absence, his sister arrives back unexpectedly at the little house. All she possesses in the world she has with her in an old and battered suitcase. Her purpose is revealed. She believes the old man was paid 'hundreds of pounds compensation' by the S. A. R. for the accident. It is in a box under his bed. She wants the money. Is ready to steal. Eventually even prepared to kill the old man to get it. None of these possibilities happens. She leaves Johnnie and the old man together.

First problem. Do we see the old man? Or only Johnnie and his sister? (Her name?) Even if not seen, the old man's presence must be felt . . . a bigotry and meanness of spirit as twisted and misshapen as his physical reality.

The sister a common prostitute. Even before leaving home for Johannesburg she had men. Sailors (war years). In fact the reason for her leaving home—her father found out. Her past fifteen years in Johannesburg an experience that has taken her to the limits of physical violence and crudity. Carnal reality.

'I'm not a woman any more. What's a woman? Not me. They fuck me but I'm not a woman.' All that is left for her is the 'happiness' in the box 'under daddy's bed'. What does she mean by happiness?

What defeats her?

Johnnie does not recognize his sister when she walks in with her old suitcase. She has to tell him, 'I'm . . .'

The sister: All hope (blind) and meaning in 'the box under daddy's bed'. An obsession that allows of neither right nor wrong, yes or no. She must get it. This is what life has come down to. Apart from that there are only memories, and most of them provoke her to either anger, hate, or disgust. One other reality—her bruises, her physical self. Flesh that has said fuck-you to the spirit.

The old man: His cries, pain, plight—a drug which keeps Johnnie numb.

25/9/63

Almost certain now that the next play is going to be about Johnnie and Hester Smit. Central images becoming increasingly obsessional. How many themes does a writer really have? How few can he have? This play—the idea—is in one sense a fusion of elements in *The Blood Knot* and *People Are Living There*. If I can realize my intentions though, it should be closer to the former in style and structure—tense and tight. Main problem remains whether to have only two characters, or whether the father should also be seen.

29/9/63

Certain now that there will only be two characters—Johnnie and Hester. At one level this worries me a little because it means the inevitable comparison with *The Blood Knot*. Once I get past this fear though and concern myself only with what is real, it seems so pointless to even consider 'adding' another character. In Hester and Johnnie I find a *complete* expression of the complex of ideas and images that have generated this play.

Two acts, one interval.

The First Act—Hester's arrival, her reason for returning, the first suitcase.

The Second Act—suitcase after suitcase, box after box, their contents spilling out onto the floor. A growing chaos in which Hester flounders, almost drowns, as she finds her past, her promise, her life, and finally sees clearly their ruin in the present. And leaves.

19/12/63

Thinking and making notes almost continuously now about the Valley play. Difficulty in the mechanics of the climax, when Hester 'loses hope' and 'learns she must die'. Suspicious of what I feel is a stock pattern or formula in my resolution of the climactic moment, i.e. *growing desperation*, leading to *emotional crisis*, leading to *the leap*.

Thinking about it for a moment I realize that I am wrong to see this as a formula common to all my other plays. *The Blood Knot* doesn't have it. Far from leaping, Morrie and Zach wake up heavy and hopeless, almost prostrate on the earth.

Yes, that is it! What I am searching for in the new play is the moment when Hester 'wakes up'. Three experiences: Loss of hope, knowledge of death, and finally the only certainty, the flesh . . . 'truths the hand can touch'.[8]

---

[8] A favourite phrase, borrowed from Camus: see, e.g., *The Myth of Sisyphus* (Engl. transl. 1955), *passim*.

What could be more obvious than that I should be drawn to, overwhelmed by Camus. Wasn't I trying to do that to Morrie and Zach at the end of *The Blood Knot*—two men who were going to try to live without hope, without appeal. In effect Morrie is trying to say, in that final beat of the play: Now we Know.

After a break, Fugard returned to intense work on *Hello and Goodbye* in early September 1964. By late February 1965, he was asking himself a 'question I cannot fully answer' in relation to the play's conclusion:

What is it that draws Johnnie to the crutches? Any number of 'little' answers. Tantalized by the thought that there is one 'final' answer that still eludes my thinking? Do I need to know it? Because I *feel* the absolute reality of his fascination with his father's crutches, I see him so clearly drawing closer and closer to the moment when he goes onto them permanently.

When Johnnie struggles up on to his father's crutches at the end of the play, he assumes the dead man's story even as he tries to assume his identity: 'Let's face it, a man on his own two legs is a shaky proposition!' We are left with this macabre image of the man, standing facing us, and uttering a last bitter word, as darkness descends: 'Resurrection'.

The religious resonance is important in all Fugard's plays. Here, Johnnie's failed rebirth suggests a larger failure: the failure of the Afrikaner to escape his own distorted faith, his Calvinist version of history. This faith, this history, is shared by those he denies, the 'Coloureds': hence Morris's absurdly futile attempts to inject meaning into his world by means of the word of the Bible, in *Blood Knot*. But somehow Johnnie's sister Hester—like other women in the plays which follow (especially Miss Helen in *The Road to Mecca*, 1985)—is able to reject or at least overcome the strain of morbid self-pity which afflicts Fugard's male protagonists. In *Boesman and Lena*, the woman represents an extreme of suffering, of pain; yet she, too, despite herself, is able to survive—even, at one transcendent moment, to sing, to dance, to stamp defiantly down on the earth to which her poor body will soon return. This possibility is present from the first of Fugard's thoughts about *Boesman and Lena*, on which he began working in October 1967:

Boesman—self-hatred and shame, focused on Lena, who is, after all, his life . . . tangible and immediate enough to be beaten, derided, and, worst of all, needed. His jealousy and bewilderment in her relationship with the old man. Her discovery of value, of herself as having value. Boesman's loneliness at that moment.

Boesman and Lena facing each other across the scraps and remnants of their life.

'I'll carry my share.'

'This is all we are . . . all we've got.'

Love. Desertion.

After another break in his playwriting, Fugard returned to his Notebooks to rediscover this opening entry and its 'images':

2/6/68

. . . These, plus a sudden realization of personal parallels, of the possibility of making a personal statement, make the thought of these two reject characters very provocative.

A little surprised to find how fully realized the Boesman and Lena story already is, how much of it is implicit in those early images. Why had I shelved it? Boesman shouldering all they have, and then Lena taking her share and joining him! Will see what happens.

4/7/68

First Act down in the roughest of rough drafts, skeleton for the second. More difficulty than I expected in finding the substance to this man–woman relationship. Struggling for objectivity and distance. For example: Boesman's hatred and abuse of Lena. Easy enough to formulate this as an 'idea' but a struggle to reveal the full carnal reality of it in incident and dialogue.

Unrelieved squalor of their situation demands that I write this one very carefully. Flowers on the dung-heap. Where has all my 'joy' gone? Morrie and Zach had it. Hester and Johnnie had it. Realized that the genesis of this play lies possibly in an image from over ten years ago—Coloured man and woman, burdened with all their belongings, whom I passed somewhere on the road near Laingsburg. It was sunset and they were miles from the nearest town. Then of course also the old woman near Cradock on the drive back from Norman's trial.[9] 'Put your life on your head and walk.'

---

[9] Norman Ntshinga, former member of Serpent Players, on trial for allegedly belonging to the banned African National Congress.

Again: Brecht's 'ease' (*Messingkauf Dialogues*). Lightness and laughter.

6/7/68

A Lena on the banks of the Swartkops River yesterday while fishing with Don.[10]

Saw her as we were leaving our spot on the Canal wall. Either drunk or hung-over—number of bait-diggers and Coloured fishermen had spent the night here. Bitterly cold. Bottles of cheap wine to help them live through it.

Scarf on her head, faded maroon blouse, and an old blue skirt. Barefoot. Unseeing eyes, focused if anything on the ground just ahead. We were merely 'whitemen'—nothing could have been more remote from her life, from her experience of herself, at that moment. Walked like a somnambulist. Face shrivelled and distorted by dissipation, resentment, regrets. Strangely no surprise at seeing her.

To Don: '. . . just a sense of the possibility of the sacrilegious and the sacred, of the demand that the truth be told, that I must not bear false witness'.

Physical texture of the place—mud.

13/7/68

Memory of another Coloured woman who gives weight to my image of Lena. Lived somewhere in the bush along the Glendore Road. Worked for us for a short period about two years ago. Sense of terrible physical and spiritual destitution, of servility. Did the housework without a sound, without the slightest flicker of 'self'. For some reason left us after about two months, then came back some time later to see if we had any work. Stiflingly hot day—Berg wind blowing. In the course of the few words I had with her she seemed in an even more desperate condition—not so much physically as in a sense of her disorientation, almost derangement, as if only a fraction of herself was committed to and involved in the world around her.

After our telling the woman we had no work she left to try a few other houses. Last sight of her about two hours later. Heat even more fierce. Obviously unsuccessful in her search for work, she was trudging up the hill on her way back to the Glendore bush.

That hill, that sun, that walk! Possibly even a walk that my Lena had not yet made, but *will* one day in the course of the little time that lies ahead of her as she takes up her load and follows the frightened

---

[10] Don MacLennan, close friend of Fugard's, playwright and Senior Lecturer in English, Rhodes University, Grahamstown.

Boesman across the mudflats. A walk beyond the moment of rebellion
—that possibility past, even forgotten—a walk beyond the battles,
the refusals, the last few tears. A walk into the final ignominy of
silence, burdened at that moment as never before by those unanswer-
able little words . . . Why? How? Who? What?

16/7/68

Floundering in first Act, specifically Lena's first long soliloquy when
she tries to unravel and order her memories of the past, tries to work
out how she got to where she is. Very clear on the function and 'feel'
of this moment, but can't get it down on paper. Same in a sense true
for the whole first movement of the play . . . from their arrival to the
appearance of Outa. Sure I experienced the same problem with *Hello
and Goodbye*—made a note about skating on a hard surface reality,
waiting for it to break somewhere, somehow, so that I could fall in and
be forced to survive in 'depth'.

19/7/68

To be careful that I do not pitch Boesman at a level of monotonous
hatred and abuse. Not just the technical problem of variety of tone
and tempo—the more basic issue that it is not as simple as Lena being
the victim and Boesman the oppressor. Both are ultimately victims of
a common, a shared predicament, and of each other. Which of course
makes it some sort of love story. They are each other's fate.

So for Boesman as total a statement as for Lena. What is mutilated
and why? The key I am sure is to reveal and dramatize his self-hatred
as focused on Lena. What he really hates is himself.

Thus:

Lena . . . sense of injustice, implying therefore a value of self.

Boesman . . . no value, or rather a denial of value as the price of his
uneasy and violent acceptance of the world he finds himself in. His
fear and loneliness when Lena chooses the old man at the end of Act
One . . . *because Boesman's greatest fear is discovering he has value.*

Must do something about a decent title.

23/7/68

The complex of central images survives the frequent assault of my
doubts about validity, significance, etc. On top of this they have now
also become obsessional—increasingly impatient with any time spent
away from them. Now also working in the afternoons. Any number of
blanks remain though. Lena and the old man . . . I do not yet have any
image of her 'choice'. Why does she choose to sit out there in the cold
with him? Any number of ideas as answers, but still no image.

21/8/68

Good work on Boesman and Lena (must find title).

Strong and clear sense of the dynamics to the first Act. Most important consequence is that Lena now has a drive, is 'moving' and not just sitting there in the mud floundering in her predicament. Reading Laing's *Politics of Experience* and *Bird of Paradise* has added new dimensions to my thinking about Boesman and Lena. Ontological insecurity: Lena in her demand that her life be witnessed. Not just a sense of injustice and abuse.

Growing sense also of the pattern of the whole of being able to find the right (and only) moment for images and actions.

23/8/68

. . . Sorting out my ideas and images for the ending of Act One—Lena at the fire with Outa, sharing her mug of tea and piece of bread, kept hearing her say, 'This mug . . .' 'This bread' . . . 'My life . . .' Suddenly, and apparently irrelevantly, remembered Lisa[11] the other day reading a little book on the Catholic Mass. There it was. Lena's Mass—the moment and its ingredients became sacramental, the whole a celebration of her life.

9/9/68

Two or three more days and I should have a skeleton outline for the second Act. Two fulcrums in the dynamic of Lena's predicament.

1) Calling Outa into her life—her sense of her life, her feeling for it, involvement in it, demand that it be witnessed.

2) Outa's death—her alienation. 'I'm alone.' 'So that is all. Hold on tight, and then let go.' She lets go. But you can't be dead before you die, so . . . 'Give me mine.' She takes herself back for another walk, possibly her last.

Do I know what this means!!!

The naïveté of these notes. Like maps of the world before they discovered the earth was round.

Title: *Boesman and Lena*.

With the completion of the play, Fugard wrote that he felt 'nagging doubts' about the insufficiency of its 'social content'. Confronting himself with the 'Marxist notion' that the artist is 'commissioned by his society', he asked: 'How do I align myself

[11] Fugard's daughter.

with a future, a possibility, in which I believe but of which I have no clear image? A failure of imagination.'

With rueful honesty, he thus revealed the dilemma of his position, as a white liberal, English-speaking Afrikaner: striving to proclaim the possibility of human dignity in a situation of widespread suffering and oppression; yet unable to anticipate how that dignity may be attained, or to participate in the movement which may make it possible. In the behaviour of Boesman, Fugard shows the depths to which the human spirit can sink in South Africa: when the man realizes that the African stranger who has come to share his fire poses more of a threat to him dead than alive. 'How do you throw away a dead *kaffer*?', Lena asks him. Yet the whole play suggests that people can survive, despite everything. How? Fugard does not claim to know. The two outcasts take up their meagre belongings and trail off into the darkness.

DENNIS WALDER

London 1986

'MASTER HAROLD'

. . . AND THE BOYS

CHARACTERS

HALLY, *a seventeen-year-old white boy*
SAM, *a black man in his mid-forties*
WILLIE, *also black and about the same age*

'MASTER HAROLD' . . . AND THE BOYS was first performed at the Yale Repertory Theatre, New Haven, on 12 March 1982, directed by the author, with the following cast:

HALLY	Željko Ivanek
SAM	Zakes Mokae
WILLIE	Danny Glover

The play transferred to the Lyceum Theatre, New York, on 5 May, when Lonny Price replaced Željko Ivanek. In November Zakes Mokae was replaced by James Earl Jones. The designer was Jane Clark.

'MASTER HAROLD' . . . AND THE BOYS was originally produced on Broadway by the Shubert Organization, Freydberg/Bloch Productions, Dasha Epstein, Emmanuel Azenberg and David Geffen.

'MASTER HAROLD' . . . AND THE BOYS was performed at the Market Theatre, Johannesburg, on 22 March 1983, directed by the author, with the following cast:

HALLY	Duart Sylwain
SAM	John Kani
WILLIE	Ramolao Makhene

The Market Theatre Production first appeared at the Cottesloe Theatre in the National Theatre, London, on 24 November 1983, directed by the author, assisted by Mannie Manim. The designer was Douglas Heap.

The St George's Park Tea Room on a wet and windy Port Elizabeth afternoon.

Tables and chairs have been cleared and are stacked on one side except for one which stands apart with a single chair. On this table a knife, fork, spoon, and side plate in anticipation of a simple meal, together with a pile of comic books.

Other elements: a serving counter with a few stale cakes under glass and a not very impressive display of sweets, cigarettes and cool drinks, etc.; a few cardboard advertising handouts—Cadbury's Chocolate, Coca-Cola —and a blackboard on which an untrained hand has chalked up the prices of Tea, Coffee, Scones, Milkshakes—all flavours—and Cool Drinks; a few sad ferns in pots; a telephone; an old-style jukebox.

There is an entrance on one side and an exit into a kitchen on the other.

Leaning on the solitary table, his head cupped in one hand as he pages through one of the comic books, is Sam. *He wears the white coat of a waiter. Behind him on his knees, mopping down the floor with a bucket of water and a rag, is* Willie. *He has his sleeves and trousers rolled up. The year:* 1950

WILLIE. [*Singing as he works.*]
> 'She was scandalizin' my name,
> She took my money
> She called me honey
> But she was scandalizin' my name.
> Called it love but was playin' a game . . .'

[*He gets up and moves the bucket. Stands thinking for a moment, then, raising his arms to hold an imaginary partner, he launches into an intricate ballroom dance step. Although a mildly comic figure, he reveals a reasonable degree of accomplishment.*]

Hey, Sam.

[*Sam, absorbed in the comic book, does not respond.*]

Hey, *Boet* Sam!

[*Sam looks up.*]

I'm getting it. The quickstep. Look now and tell me. [*He repeats the step.*] Well?

SAM. [*Encouragingly.*] Show me again.

WILLIE. Okay, count for me.

SAM. Ready?

WILLIE. Ready.

SAM. Five, six, seven, eight . . . [*Willie starts to dance.*] A-n-d one two three four . . . and one two three four . . . [*Ad libbing as Willie dances.*] Your shoulders, Willie . . . your shoulders! Don't look down! Look happy, Willie! Relax, Willie!

WILLIE. [*Desperate but still dancing.*] I am relax.

SAM. No, you're not.

WILLIE. [*He falters.*] *Ag* no man, Sam! Mustn't talk. You make me make mistakes.

SAM. But you're too stiff.

WILLIE. Yesterday I'm not straight . . . today I'm too stiff!

SAM. Well, you are. You asked me and I'm telling you.

WILLIE. Where?

SAM. Everywhere. Try to glide through it.

WILLIE. Glide?

SAM. *Ja*, make it smooth. And give it more style. It must look like you're enjoying yourself.

WILLIE. [*Emphatically.*] I wasn't.

SAM. Exactly.

WILLIE. How can I enjoy myself? Not straight, too stiff and now it's also glide, give it more style, make it smooth . . . *Haai!* Is hard to remember all those things, *Boet* Sam.

SAM. That's your trouble. You're trying too hard.

WILLIE. I try hard because it *is* hard.

SAM. But don't let me see it. The secret is to make it look easy. Ballroom must look happy, Willie, not like hard work. It must . . . *Ja!* . . . it must look like romance.

WILLIE. Now another one! What's romance?

SAM. Love story with happy ending. A handsome man in tails, and in his arms, smiling at him, a beautiful lady in evening dress!

WILLIE. Fred Astaire, Ginger Rogers.

SAM. You got it. Tapdance or ballroom, it's the same. Romance. In two weeks' time when the judges look at you and Hilda, they must see a man and a woman who are dancing their way to a happy ending. What I saw was you holding her like you were frightened she was going to run away.

WILLIE. *Ja!* Because that is what she wants to do! I got no romance left for Hilda anymore, *Boet* Sam.

SAM. Then pretend. When you put your arms around Hilda, imagine she is Ginger Rogers.

WILLIE. With no teeth? You try.

SAM. Well, just remember, there's only two weeks left.

WILLIE. I know, I know! [*To the jukebox.*] I do it better with music. You got sixpence for Sarah Vaughan?

SAM. That's a slow foxtrot. You're practising the quickstep.

WILLIE. I'll practise slow foxtrot.

SAM. [*Shaking his head.*] It's your turn to put money in the jukebox.

WILLIE. I only got bus fare to go home. [*He returns disconsolately to his work.*] Love story and happy ending! She's doing it all right, *Boet* Sam, but is not me she's giving happy endings. Fuckin' whore! Three nights now she doesn't come practise. I wind up gramophone, I get record ready and I sit and wait. What happens? Nothing. Ten o'clock I start dancing with my pillow. You try and practise romance by yourself, *Boet* Sam. 'Struesgod, she doesn't come tonight I take back my dress and ballroom shoes and I find me new partner. Size twenty-six. Shoes size seven. And now she's also making trouble for me with the baby again. Reports me to Child Wellfed, that I'm not giving her money. She lies! Every week I am giving her money for milk. And how do I know is my baby? Only his hair looks like me. She's fucking around all the time I turn my back. Hilda Samuels is a bitch! [*Pause.*] Hey, Sam!

SAM. *Ja.*

WILLIE. You listening?

SAM. *Ja.*

WILLIE. So what you say?

SAM. About Hilda?

WILLIE. *Ja.*

SAM. When did you last give her a hiding?

WILLIE. [*Reluctantly.*] Sunday night.

SAM. And today is Thursday.

WILLIE. [*He knows what's coming.*] Okay.

SAM. Hiding on Sunday night, then Monday, Tuesday and Wednesday she doesn't come to practise . . . and you are asking me why?

WILLIE. I said okay, *Boet* Sam!

SAM. You hit her too much. One day she's going to leave you for good.

WILLIE. So? She makes me the hell-in too much.

SAM. [*Emphasizing his point.*] *Too* much and *too* hard. You had the same trouble with Eunice.

WILLIE. Because she also make the hell-in, *Boet* Sam. She never got the steps right. Even the waltz.

SAM. Beating her up every time she makes a mistake in the waltz? [*Shaking his head.*] No, Willie! That takes the pleasure out of ballroom dancing.

WILLIE. Hilda is not too bad with the waltz, *Boet* Sam. Is the quickstep where the trouble starts.

SAM. [*Teasing him gently.*] How's your pillow with the quickstep?

WILLIE. [*Ignoring the tease.*] Good! And why? Because it got no legs. That's her trouble. She can't move them quick enough, *Boet* Sam. I start the record and before halfway Count Basie is already winning. Only time we catch up with him is when gramophone runs down.

[*Sam laughs.*]

Haaikona, Boet Sam, is not funny.

SAM. [*Snapping his fingers.*] I got it! Give her a handicap.

WILLIE. What's that?

SAM. Give her a ten-second start and then let Count Basie go. Then I put my money on her. Hot favourite in the Ballroom Stakes: Hilda Samuels ridden by Willie Malopo.

WILLIE. [*Turning away.*] I'm not talking to you no more.

SAM. [*Relenting.*] Sorry, Willie . . .

WILLIE. It's finish between us.

SAM. Okay, okay . . . I'll stop.

WILLIE. You can also fuck off.

6

SAM. Willie, listen! I want to help you!

WILLIE. No more jokes?

SAM. I promise.

WILLIE. Okay. Help me.

SAM. [*His turn to hold an imaginary partner.*] Look and learn. Feet together. Back straight. Body relaxed. Right hand placed gently in the small of her back and wait for the music. Don't start worrying about making mistakes or the judges or the other competitors. It's just you, Hilda and the music, and you're going to have a good time. What Count Basie do you play?

WILLIE. 'You the cream in my coffee, you the salt in my stew.'

SAM. Right. Give it to me in strict tempo.

WILLIE. Ready?

SAM. Ready.

WILLIE. A-n-d . . . [*Singing.*]
'You the cream in my coffee.
You the salt in my stew.
You will always be my
    necessity.
I'd be lost without
    you. . . .' [*etc.*]

[*Sam launches into the quickstep. He is obviously a much more accomplished dancer than Willie. Hally enters. Wet raincoat and school case. He stops and watches Sam. The demonstration comes to an end with a flourish. Applause from Hally and Willie.*]

HALLY. Bravo! No question about it. First place goes to Mr. Sam Semela.

WILLIE. [*In total agreement.*] You was gliding with style, *Boet* Sam.

HALLY. [*Cheerfully.*] How's it, chaps?

SAM. Okay, Hally.

WILLIE. [*Springing to attention like a soldier and saluting.*] At your service, Master Harold!

HALLY. Not long to the big event, hey!

SAM. Two weeks.

HALLY. You nervous?

7

SAM. No.

HALLY. Think you stand a chance?

SAM. Let's just say I'm ready to go out there and dance.

HALLY. It looked like it. What about you, Willie?

[*Willie groans.*]

What's the matter?

SAM. He's got leg trouble.

HALLY. [*Innocently.*] Oh, sorry to hear that, Willie.

WILLIE. *Boet* Sam! You promised. [*Willie returns to his work.*]

[*Hally deposits his school case and takes off his raincoat. His clothes are a little neglected and untidy: black blazer with school badge, grey flannel trousers in need of an ironing, khaki shirt and tie, black shoes. Sam has fetched a towel for Hally to dry his hair.*]

HALLY. God, what a lousy bloody day. It's coming down cats and dogs out there. Bad for business, chaps . . . [*Conspiratorial whisper.*] . . . but it also means we're in for a nice quiet afternoon.

SAM. You can speak loud. Your Mom's not here.

HALLY. Out shopping?

SAM. No. The hospital.

HALLY. But it's Thursday. There's no visiting on Thursday afternoons. Is my Dad okay?

SAM. Sounds like it. In fact, I think he's going home.

HALLY. [*Stopped short by Sam's remark.*] What do you mean?

SAM. The hospital phoned.

HALLY. To say what?

SAM. I don't know. I just heard your Mom talking.

HALLY. So what makes you say he's going home?

SAM. It sounded as if they were telling her to come and fetch him.

[*Hally thinks about what Sam has said for a few seconds.*]

HALLY. When did she leave?

SAM. About an hour ago. She said she would phone you. Want to eat?

[*Hally doesn't respond.*]

8

Hally, want your lunch?

HALLY. I suppose so. [*His mood has changed.*] What's on the menu? . . . as if I don't know.

SAM. Soup, followed by meat pie and gravy.

HALLY. Today's?

SAM. No.

HALLY. And the soup?

SAM. Nourishing pea soup.

HALLY. Just the soup. [*The pile of comic books on the table.*] And these?

SAM. For your Dad. Mr. Kempston brought them.

HALLY. You haven't been reading them, have you?

SAM. Just looking.

HALLY. [*Examining the comics.*] *Jungle Jim* . . . *Batman and Robin* . . . *Tarzan* . . . God, what rubbish! Mental pollution. Take them away.

[*Sam exits waltzing into the kitchen. Hally turns to Willie.*]

HALLY. Did you hear my Mom talking on the telephone, Willie?

WILLIE. No, Master Hally. I was at the back.

HALLY. And she didn't say anything to you before she left?

WILLIE. She said I must clean the floors.

HALLY. I mean about my Dad.

WILLIE. She didn't say nothing to me about him, Master Hally.

HALLY. [*With conviction.*] No! It can't be. They said he needed at least another three weeks of treatment. Sam's definitely made a mistake. [*Rummages through his school case, finds a book and settles down at the table to read.*] So, Willie!

WILLIE. Yes, Master Hally! Schooling okay today?

HALLY. Yes, okay. . . . [*He thinks about it.*] . . . No, not really. *Ag*, what's the difference? I don't care. And Sam says you've got problems.

WILLIE. Big problems.

HALLY. Which leg is sore?

[*Willie groans.*]

9

Both legs.

WILLIE. There is nothing wrong with my legs. Sam is just making jokes.

HALLY. So then you *will* be in the competition.

WILLIE. Only if I can find me a partner.

HALLY. But what about Hilda?

SAM. [*Returning with a bowl of soup.*] She's the one who's got trouble with her legs.

HALLY. What sort of trouble, Willie?

SAM. From the way he describes it, I think the lady has gone a bit lame.

HALLY. Good God! Have you taken her to see a doctor?

SAM. I think a vet would be better.

HALLY. What do you mean?

SAM. What do you call it again when a racehorse goes very fast?

HALLY. Gallop?

SAM. That's it!

WILLIE. *Boet* Sam!

HALLY. 'A gallop down the homestretch to the winning post.' But what's that got to do with Hilda?

SAM. Count Basie always gets there first.

[*Willie lets fly with his slop rag. It misses Sam and hits Hally.*]

HALLY. [*Furious.*] For Christ's sake, Willie! What the hell do you think you're doing!

WILLIE. Sorry, Master Hally, but it's him. . . .

HALLY. Act your bloody age! [*Hurls the rag back at Willie.*] Cut out the nonsense now and get on with your work. And you too, Sam. Stop fooling around.

[*Sam moves away.*]

No. Hang on. I haven't finished! Tell me exactly what my Mom said.

SAM. I have. 'When Hally comes, tell him I've gone to the hospital and I'll phone him.'

HALLY. She didn't say anything about taking my Dad home?

SAM. No. It's just that when she was talking on the phone . . .

HALLY. [*Interrupting him.*] No, Sam. They can't be discharging him. She would have said so if they were. In any case, we saw him last night and he wasn't in good shape at all. Staff nurse even said there was talk about taking more X-rays. And now suddenly today he's better? If anything, it sounds more like a bad turn to me . . . which I sincerely hope it isn't. Hang on . . . how long ago did you say she left?

SAM. Just before two . . . [*His wrist watch.*] . . . hour and a half.

HALLY. I know how to settle it. [*Behind the counter to the telephone. Talking as he dials.*] Let's give her ten minutes to get to the hospital, ten minutes to load him up, another ten, at the most, to get home and another ten to get him inside. Forty minutes. They should have been home for at least half an hour already. [*Pause—he waits with the receiver to his ear.*] No reply, chaps. And you know why? Because she's at his bedside in hospital helping him pull through a bad turn. You definitely heard wrong.

SAM. Okay.

[*As far as Hally is concerned, the matter is settled. He returns to his table, sits down and divides his attention between the book and his soup. Sam is at his school case and picks up a textbook.*]

Modern Graded Mathematics for Standards Nine and Ten. [*Opens it at random and laughs at something he sees.*] Who is this supposed to be?

HALLY. Old fart-face Prentice.

SAM. Teacher?

HALLY. Thinks he is. And believe me, that is not a bad likeness.

SAM. Has he seen it?

HALLY. Yes.

SAM. What did he say?

HALLY. Tried to be clever, as usual. Said I was no Leonardo da Vinci and that bad art had to be punished. So, six of the best, and his are bloody good.

SAM. On your bum?

HALLY. Where else? The days when I got them on my hands are gone forever, Sam.

SAM. With your trousers down!

11

HALLY. No. He's not quite that barbaric.

SAM. That's the way they do it in jail.

HALLY. [*Flicker of morbid interest.*] Really?

SAM. *Ja.* When the magistrate sentences you to 'strokes with a light cane'.

HALLY. Go on.

SAM. They make you lie down on a bench. One policeman pulls down your trousers and holds your ankles, another one pulls your shirt over your head and holds your arms . . .

[*Sam and Willie demonstrate.*]

HALLY. Thank you! That's enough.

SAM. . . . and the one that gives you the strokes talks to you gently and for a long time between each one. [*He laughs.*]

HALLY. I've heard enough, Sam! Jesus! It's a bloody awful world when you come to think of it. People can be real bastards.

SAM. That's the way it is, Hally.

HALLY. It doesn't *have* to be that way. There is something called progress, you know. We don't exactly burn people at the stake anymore.

SAM. Like Joan of Arc.

HALLY. Correct. If she was captured today, she'd be given a fair trial.

SAM. And then the death sentence.

HALLY. [*A world-weary sigh.*] I know, I know! I os-killate between hope and despair for this world as well, Sam. But things will change, you wait and see. One day somebody is going to get up and give history a kick up the backside and get it going again.

SAM. Like who?

HALLY. [*After thought.*] They're called social reformers. Every age, Sam, has got its social reformer. My history book is full of them.

SAM. So where's ours?

HALLY. Good question. And I hate to say it, but the answer is: I don't know. Maybe he hasn't even been born yet. Or is still only a babe in arms at his mother's breast. God, what a thought.

SAM. So we just go on waiting.

HALLY. *Ja*, looks like it. [*Back to his soup and the book.*]

SAM. [*Reading from the textbook.*] 'Introduction: In some mathematical problems only the magnitude . . .' [*He mispronounces the word 'magnitude'.*]

HALLY. [*Correcting him without looking up.*] Magnitude.

SAM. What's it mean?

HALLY. How big it is. The size of the thing.

SAM. [*Reading.*] '. . . magnitude of the quantities is of importance. In other problems we need to know whether these quantities are negative or positive. For example, whether there is a debit or credit bank balance . . .'

HALLY. Whether you're broke or not.

SAM. '. . . whether the temperature is above or below Zero . . .'

HALLY. Nought degrees. Cheerful state of affairs! No cash and you're freezing to death. Mathematics won't get you out of that one.

SAM. 'All these quantities are called . . .' [*Spelling the word.*] . . . s-c-a-l . . .

HALLY. Scalars.

SAM. Scalars! [*Shaking his head with a laugh.*] You understand all that?

HALLY. [*Turning a page.*] No. And I don't intend to try.

SAM. So what happens when the exams come?

HALLY. Failing a maths exam isn't the end of the world, Sam. How many times have I told you that examination results don't measure intelligence?

SAM. I would say about as many times as you've failed one of them.

HALLY. [*Mirthlessly.*] Ha, ha, ha.

SAM. [*Simultaneously.*] Ha, ha, ha.

HALLY. Just remember Winston Churchill didn't do particularly well at school.

SAM. You've also told me that one many times.

HALLY. Well, it just so happens to be the truth.

SAM. [*Enjoying the word.*] Magnitude! Magnitude! Show me how to use it.

HALLY. [*After thought.*] An intrepid social reformer will not be daunted by the magnitude of the task he has undertaken.

SAM. [*Impressed.*] Couple of jaw-breakers in there!

HALLY. I gave you three for the price of one. Intrepid, daunted and magnitude. I did that once in an exam. Put five of the words I had to explain in one sentence. It was half a page long.

SAM. Well, I'll put my money on you in the English exam.

HALLY. Piece of cake. Eighty percent without even trying.

SAM. [*Another textbook from Hally's case.*] And history?

HALLY. So-so. I'll scrape through. In the fifties if I'm lucky.

SAM. You didn't do too badly last year.

HALLY. Because we had World War One. That at least had some action. You try to find that in the South African Parliamentary system.

SAM. [*Reading from the history textbook.*] 'Napoleon and the principle of equality.' Hey! This sounds interesting. 'After concluding peace with Britain in 1802, Napoleon used a brief period of calm to in-sti-tute . . .'

HALLY. Introduce.

SAM. '. . . many reforms. Napoleon regarded all people as equal before the law and wanted them to have equal opportunities for advancement. All ves-ti-ges of the feu-dal system with its oppression of the poor were abolished.' Vestiges, feudal system and abolished. I'm all right on oppression.

HALLY. I'm thinking. He swept away . . . abolished . . . the last remains . . . vestiges . . . of the bad old days . . . feudal system.

SAM. Ha! There's the social reformer we're waiting for. He sounds like a man of some magnitude.

HALLY. I'm not so sure about that. It's a damn good title for a book, though. A man of magnitude!

SAM. He sounds pretty big to me, Hally.

HALLY. Don't confuse historical significance with greatness. But maybe I'm being a bit prejudiced. Have a look in there and you'll see he's two chapters long. And hell! . . . has he only

14

got dates, Sam, all of which you've got to remember! This campaign and that campaign, and then, because of all the fighting, the next thing is we get Peace Treaties all over the place. And what's the end of the story? Battle of Waterloo, which he loses. Wasn't worth it. No, I don't know about him as a man of magnitude.

SAM. Then who would you say was?

HALLY. To answer that, we need a definition of greatness, and I suppose that would be somebody who . . . somebody who benefited all mankind.

SAM. Right. But like who?

HALLY. [*He speaks with total conviction.*] Charles Darwin. Remember him? That big book from the library. *The Origin of the Species.*

SAM. Him?

HALLY. Yes. For his Theory of Evolution.

SAM. You didn't finish it.

HALLY. I ran out of time. I didn't finish it because my two weeks was up. But I'm going to take it out again after I've digested what I read. It's safe. I've hidden it away in the Theology section. Nobody ever goes in there. And anyway who are you to talk? You hardly even looked at it.

SAM. I tried. I looked at the chapters in the beginning and I saw one called 'The Struggle for an Existence.' Ah ha, I thought. At last! But what did I get? Something called the mistiltoe which needs the apple tree and there's too many seeds and all are going to die except one . . . ! No, Hally.

HALLY. [*Intellectually outraged.*] What do you mean, No! The poor man had to start somewhere. For God's sake, Sam, he revolutionized science. Now we know.

SAM. What?

HALLY. Where we come from and what it all means.

SAM. And that's a benefit to mankind? Anyway, I still don't believe it.

HALLY. God, you're impossible. I showed it to you in black and white.

SAM. Doesn't mean I got to believe it.

HALLY. It's the likes of you that kept the Inquisition in business. It's called bigotry. Anyway, that's my man of magnitude. Charles Darwin! Who's yours?

SAM. [*Without hesitation.*] Abraham Lincoln.

HALLY. I might have guessed as much. Don't get sentimental, Sam. You've never been a slave, you know. And anyway we freed your ancestors here in South Africa long before the Americans.* But if you want to thank somebody on their behalf, do it to Mr. William Wilberforce. Come on. Try again. I want a real genuis. [*Now enjoying himself, and so is Sam. Hally goes behind the counter and helps himself to a chocolate.*]

SAM. William Shakespeare.

HALLY. [*No enthusiasm.*] Oh. So you're also one of them, are you? You're basing that opinion on only one play, you know. You've only read my *Julius Caesar* and even I don't understand half of what they're talking about. They should do what they did with the old Bible: bring the language up to date.

SAM. That's all you've got. It's also the only one *you've* read.

HALLY. I know. I admit it. That's why I suggest we reserve our judgement until we've checked up on a few others. I've got a feeling, though, that by the end of this year one is going to be enough for me, and I can give you the names of twenty-nine other chaps in the Standard Nine class of the Port Elizabeth Technical College who feel the same. But if you want him, you can have him. My turn now. [*Pacing.*] This is a damned good exercise, you know! It started off looking like a simple question and here it's got us really probing into the intellectual heritage of our civilization.

SAM. So who is it going to be?

HALLY. My next man . . . and he gets the title on two scores: social reform and literary genius . . . is Leo Nikolaevich Tolstoy.

SAM. That Russian.

HALLY. Correct. Remember the picture of him I showed you?

SAM. With the long beard.

HALLY. [*Trying to look like Tolstoy.*] And those burning, visionary eyes. My God, the face of a social prophet if ever I saw one!

16

And remember my words when I showed it to you? Here's a *man*, Sam!

SAM. Those were words, Hally.

HALLY. Not many intellectuals are prepared to shovel manure with the peasants and then go home and write a 'little book' called *War and Peace*. Incidentally, Sam, he was somebody else who, to quote, '. . . did not distinguish himself scholastically.'

SAM. Meaning?

HALLY. He was also no good at school.

SAM. Like you and Winston Churchill.

HALLY. [*Mirthlessly.*] Ha, ha, ha.

SAM. [*Simultaneously.*] Ha, ha, ha.

HALLY. Don't get clever, Sam. That man freed his serfs of his own free will.

SAM. No argument. He was a somebody, all right. I accept him.

HALLY. I'm sure Count Tolstoy will be very pleased to hear that. Your turn. Shoot. [*Another chocolate from behind the counter.*] I'm waiting, Sam.

SAM. I've got him.

HALLY. Good. Submit your candidate for examination.

SAM. Jesus.

HALLY. [*Stopped dead in his tracks.*] Who?

SAM. Jesus Christ.

HALLY. Oh, come on, Sam!

SAM. The Messiah.

HALLY. *Ja*, but still . . . No, Sam. Don't let's get started on religion. We'll just spend the whole afternoon arguing again. Suppose I turn around and say Mohammed?

SAM. All right.

HALLY. You can't have them both on the same list!

SAM. Why not? You like Mohammed, I like Jesus.

HALLY. I *don't* like Mohammed. I never have. I was merely being hypothetical. As far as I'm concerned, the Koran is as bad as the Bible. No. Religion is out! I'm not going to waste my time again arguing with you about the existence of God.

You know perfectly well I'm an atheist . . . and I've got homework to do.

SAM. Okay, I take him back.

HALLY. You've got time for one more name.

SAM. [*After thought.*] I've got one I know we'll agree on. A simple straightforward great Man of Magnitude . . . and no arguments. And *he* really *did* benefit all mankind.

HALLY. I wonder. After your last contribution I'm beginning to doubt whether anything in the way of an intellectual agreement is possible between the two of us. Who is he?

SAM. Guess.

HALLY. Socrates? Alexandre Dumas? Karl Marx? Dostoevsky? Nietzsche?

[*Sam shakes his head after each name.*]

Give me a clue.

SAM. The letter P is important . . .

HALLY. Plato!

SAM. . . . and his name begins with an F.

HALLY. I've got it. Freud and Psychology.

SAM. No. I didn't understand him.

HALLY. That makes two of us.

SAM. Think of mouldy apricot jam.

HALLY. [*After a delighted laugh.*] Penicillin and Sir Alexander Fleming! And the title of the book: *The Microbe Hunters.* [*Delighted.*] Splendid, Sam! Splendid. For once we are in total agreement. The major breakthrough in medical science in the Twentieth Century. If it wasn't for him, we might have lost the Second World War. It's deeply gratifying, Sam, to know that I haven't been wasting my time in talking to you. [*Strutting around proudly.*] Tolstoy may have educated his peasants, but I've educated you.

SAM. Standard Four to Standard Nine.

HALLY. Have we been at it as long as that?

SAM. Yep. And my first lesson was geography.

HALLY. [*Intrigued.*] Really? I don't remember.

SAM. My room there at the back of the old Jubilee Boarding

18

House. I had just started working for your Mom. Little boy in short trousers walks in one afternoon and asks me seriously: 'Sam, do you want to see South Africa?' Hey man! Sure I wanted to see South Africa!

HALLY. Was that me?

SAM. . . . So the next thing I'm looking at a map you had just done for homework. It was your first one and you were very proud of yourself.

HALLY. Go on.

SAM. Then came my first lesson. 'Repeat after me, Sam: Gold in the Transvaal, mealies in the Free State, sugar in Natal and grapes in the Cape.' I still know it!

HALLY. Well, I'll be buggered. So that's how it all started.

SAM. And your next map was one with all the rivers and the mountains they came from. The Orange, the Vaal, the Limpopo, the Zambezi . . .

HALLY. You've got a phenomenal memory!

SAM. You should be grateful. That is why you started passing your exams. You tried to be better than me.

[*They laugh together. Willie is attracted by the laughter and joins them.*]

HALLY. The old Jubilee Boarding House. Sixteen rooms with board and lodging, rent in advance and one week's notice. I haven't thought about it for donkey's years . . . and I don't think that's an accident. God, was I glad when we sold it and moved out. Those years are not remembered as the happiest ones of an unhappy childhood.

WILLIE. [*Knocking on the table and trying to imitate a woman's voice.*] 'Hally, are you there?'

HALLY. Who's that supposed to be?

WILLIE. 'What you doing in there, Hally? Come out at once!'

HALLY. [*To Sam.*] What's he talking about?

SAM. Don't you remember?

WILLIE. 'Sam, Willie . . . is he in there with you boys?'

SAM. Hiding away in our room when your mother was looking for you.

HALLY. [*Another good laugh.*] Of course! I used to crawl and hide under your bed! But finish the story, Willie. Then what used to happen? You chaps would give the game away by telling her I was in there with you. So much for friendship.

SAM. We couldn't lie to her. She knew.

HALLY. Which meant I got another rowing for hanging around the 'servants' quarters'. I think I spent more time in there with you chaps than anywhere else in that dump. And do you blame me? Nothing but bloody misery wherever you went. Somebody was always complaining about the food, or my mother was having a fight with Micky Nash because she'd caught her with a petty officer in her room. Maud Meiring was another one. Remember those two? They were . . . prostitutes, you know. Soldiers and sailors from the troopships. Bottom fell out of the business when the war ended. God, the flotsam and jetsam that life washed up on our shores! No joking, if it wasn't for your room, I would have been the first certified ten-year-old in medical history. *Ja*, the memories are coming back now. Walking home from school and thinking: 'What can I do this afternoon?' Try out a few ideas, but sooner or later I'd end up in there with you fellows. I bet you I could still find my way to your room with my eyes closed. [*He does exactly that.*] Down the corridor . . . telephone on the right, which my Mom keeps locked because somebody is using it on the sly and not paying . . . past the kitchen and unappetizing cooking smells . . . around the corner into the backyard, hold my breath again because there are more smells coming when I pass your lavatory, then into that little passageway, first door on the right and into your room. How's that?

SAM. Good. But, as usual, you forgot to knock.

HALLY. Like that time I barged in and caught you and Cynthia . . . at it. Remember? God, was I embarrassed! I didn't know what was going on at first.

SAM. *Ja*, that taught you a lesson.

HALLY. And about a lot more than knocking on doors, I'll have you know, and I don't mean geography either. Hell, Sam, couldn't you have waited until it was dark?

SAM. No.

HALLY. Was it that urgent?

SAM. Yes, and if you don't believe me, wait until your time comes.

HALLY. No, thank you. I am not interested in girls. [*Back to his memories . . . Using a few chairs he recreates the room as he lists the items.*] A gray little room with a cold cement floor. Your bed against that wall . . . and I now know why the mattress sags so much! . . . Willie's bed . . . it's propped up on bricks because one leg is broken . . . that wobbly little table with the wash-basin and jug of water . . . Yes! . . . stuck to the wall above it are some pin-up pictures from magazines. Joe Louis . . .

WILLIE. Brown Bomber. World Title. [*Boxing pose.*] Three rounds and knockout.

HALLY. Against who?

SAM. Max Schmeling.

HALLY. Correct. I can also remember Fred Astaire and Ginger Rogers, and Rita Hayworth in a bathing costume which always made me hot and bothered when I looked at it. Under Willie's bed is an old suitcase with all his clothes in a mess, which is why I never hide there. Your things are neat and tidy in a trunk next to your bed, and on it there is a picture of you and Cynthia in your ballroom clothes, your first silver cup for third place in a competition and an old radio which doesn't work anymore. Have I left out anything?

SAM. No.

HALLY. Right, so much for the stage directions. Now the characters. [*Sam and Willie move to their appropriate positions in the bedroom.*] Willie is in bed, under his blankets with his clothes on, complaining non-stop about something, but we can't make out a word of what he's saying because he's got his head under the blankets as well. You're on your bed trimming your toenails with a knife—not a very edifying sight—and as for me . . . What am I doing?

SAM. You're sitting on the floor giving Willie a lecture about being a good loser while you get the checker board and pieces ready for a game. Then you go to Willie's bed, pull off the blankets and make him play with you first because you know you're going to win, and that gives you the second game with me.

HALLY. And you certainly were a bad loser, Willie!

WILLIE. *Haai!*

HALLY. Wasn't he, Sam? And so slow! A game with you almost took the whole afternoon. Thank God I gave up trying to teach you how to play chess.

WILLIE. You and Sam cheated.

HALLY. I never saw Sam cheat, and mine were mostly 'the mistakes of youth'.

WILLIE. Then how is it you two was always winning?

HALLY. Have you ever considered the possibility, Willie, that it was because we were better than you?

WILLIE. Every time better?

HALLY. Not every time. There were occasions when we deliberately let you win a game so that you would stop sulking and go on playing with us. Sam used to wink at me when you weren't looking to show me it was time to let you win.

WILLIE. So then you two didn't play fair.

HALLY. It was for your benefit, Mr. Malopo, which is more than being fair. It was an act of self-sacrifice. [*To Sam.*] But you know what my best memory is, don't you?

SAM. No.

HALLY. Come on, guess. If your memory is so good, you must remember it as well.

SAM. We got up to a lot of tricks in there, Hally.

HALLY. This one was special, Sam.

SAM. I'm listening.

HALLY. It started off looking like another of those useless nothing-to-do afternoons. I'd already been down to Main Street looking for adventure, but nothing had happened. I didn't feel like climbing trees in the Donkin Park or pretending I was a private eye and following a stranger . . . so as usual: See what's cooking in Sam's room. This time it was you on the floor. You had two thin pieces of wood and you were smoothing them down with a knife. It didn't look particularly interesting, but when I asked you what you were doing, you just said, 'Wait and see, Hally. Wait . . . and see' . . . in that secret sort of way of yours, so I knew there was a surprise coming. You teased me, you bugger, by being deliberately slow and not answering my questions!

[*Sam laughs.*]

And whistling while you worked away! God, it was infuriating! I could have brained you! It was only when you tied them together in a cross and put that down on the brown paper that I realized what you were doing. 'Sam is making a kite?' And when I asked you and you said 'Yes' . . . ! [*Shaking his head with disbelief.*] The sheer audacity of it took my breath away. I mean, seriously, what the hell does a black man know about flying a kite? I'll be honest with you, Sam, I had no hopes for it. If you think I was excited and happy, you got another guess coming. In fact, I was shit-scared that we were going to make fools of ourselves. When we left the boarding house to go up onto the hill, I was praying quietly that there wouldn't be any other kids around to laugh at us.

SAM. [*Enjoying the memory as much as Hally.*] Ja, I could see that.

HALLY. I made it obvious, did I?

SAM. *Ja.* You refused to carry it.

HALLY. Do you blame me? Can you remember what the poor thing looked like? Tomato-box wood and brown paper! Flour and water for glue! Two of my mother's old stockings for a tail, and then all those bits and pieces of string you made me tie together so that we could fly it! Hell, no, that was now only asking for a miracle to happen.

SAM. Then the big argument when I told you to hold the string and run with it when I let go.

HALLY. I was prepared to run, all right, but straight back to the boarding house.

SAM. [*Knowing what's coming.*] So what happened?

HALLY. Come on, Sam, you remember as well as I do.

SAM. I want to hear it from you.

[*Hally pauses. He wants to be as accurate as possible.*]

HALLY. You went a little distance from me down the hill, you held it up ready to let it go. . . . 'That is it,' I thought. 'Like everything else in my life, here comes another fiasco.' Then you shouted, 'Go, Hally!' and I started to run. [*Another pause.*] I don't know how to describe it, Sam. *Ja!* The miracle

23

happened! I was running, waiting for it to crash to the ground, but instead suddenly there was something alive behind me at the end of the string, tugging at it as if it wanted to be free. I looked back . . . [*Shakes his head.*] . . . I still can't believe my eyes. It was flying! Looping around and trying to climb even higher into the sky. You shouted to me to let it have more string. I did, until there was none left and I was just holding that piece of wood we had tied it to. You came up and joined me. You were laughing.

SAM. So were you. And shouting, 'It works, Sam! We've done it!'

HALLY. And we had! I was so proud of us! It was the most splendid thing I had ever seen. I wished there were hundreds of kids around to watch us. The part that scared me, though, was when you showed me how to make it dive down to the ground and then just when it was on the point of crashing, swoop up again!

SAM. You didn't want to try yourself.

HALLY. Of course not! I would have been suicidal if anything had happened to it. Watching you do it made me nervous enough. I was quite happy just to see it up there with its tail fluttering behind it. You left me after that, didn't you? You explained how to get it down, we tied it to the bench so that I could sit and watch it, and you went away. I wanted you to stay, you know. I was a little scared of having to look after it by myself.

SAM. [*Quietly.*] I had work to do, Hally.

HALLY. It was sort of sad bringing it down, Sam. And it looked sad again when it was lying there on the ground. Like something that had lost its soul. Just tomato-box wood, brown paper and two of my mother's old stockings! But, hell, I'll never forget that first moment when I saw it up there. I had a stiff neck the next day from looking up so much.

[*Sam laughs. Hally turns to him with a question he never thought of asking before.*]

Why did you make that kite, Sam?

SAM. [*Evenly.*] I can't remember.

HALLY. Truly?

SAM. Too long ago, Hally.

HALLY. *Ja*, I suppose it was. It's time for another one, you know.

SAM. Why do you say that?

HALLY. Because it feels like that. Wouldn't be a good day to fly it, though.

SAM. No. You can't fly kites on rainy days.

HALLY. [*He studies Sam. Their memories have made him conscious of the man's presence in his life.*] How old are you, Sam?

SAM. Two score and five.

HALLY. Strange, isn't it?

SAM. What?

HALLY. Me and you.

SAM. What's strange about it?

HALLY. Little white boy in short trousers and a black man old enough to be his father flying a kite. It's not every day you see that.

SAM. But why strange? Because the one is white and the other black?

HALLY. I don't know. Would have been just as strange, I suppose, if it had been me and my Dad . . . cripple man and a little boy! Nope! There's no chance of me flying a kite without it being strange. [*Simple statement of fact—no self-pity.*] There's a nice little short story there. 'The Kite-Flyers.' But we'd have to find a twist in the ending.

SAM. Twist?

HALLY. Yes. Something unexpected. The way it ended with us was too straightforward . . . me on the bench and you going back to work. There's no drama in that.

WILLIE. And me?

HALLY. You?

WILLIE. Yes me.

HALLY. You want to get into the story as well, do you? I got it! Change the title: 'Afternoons in Sam's Room' . . . expand it and tell all the stories. It's on its way to being a novel. Our days in the old Jubilee. Sad in a way that they're over. I almost wish we were still in that little room.

SAM. We're still together.

HALLY. That's true. It's just that life felt the right size in there . . . not too big and not too small. Wasn't so hard to work up a bit of courage. It's got so bloody complicated since then.

[*The telephone rings. Sam answers it.*]

SAM. St. George's Park Tea Room . . . Hello, Madam . . . Yes, Madam, he's here . . . Hally, it's your mother.

HALLY. Where is she phoning from?

SAM. Sounds like the hospital. It's a public telephone.

HALLY. [*Relieved.*] You see! I told you. [*The telephone.*] Hello, Mom . . . Yes . . . Yes no fine. Everything's under control here. How's things with poor old Dad? . . . Has he had a bad turn? . . . What? . . . Oh, God! . . . Yes, Sam told me, but I was sure he'd made a mistake. But what's this all about, Mom? He didn't look at all good last night. How can he get better so quickly? . . . Then very obviously you must say no. Be firm with him. You're the boss. . . . You know what it's going to be like if he comes home. . . . Well then, don't blame me when I fail my exams at the end of the year. . . . Yes! How am I expected to be fresh for school when I spend half the night massaging his gammy leg? . . . So am I! . . . So tell him a white lie. Say Dr. Colley wants more X-rays of his stump. Or bribe him. We'll sneak in double tots of brandy in future. . . . What? . . . Order him to get back into bed at once! If he's going to behave like a child, treat him like one. . . . All right, Mom! I was just trying to. . . . I'm sorry. . . . I said I'm sorry. . . . Quick, give me your number. I'll phone you back. [*He hangs up and waits a few seconds.*] Here we go again! [*He dials.*] I'm sorry, Mom. . . . Okay . . . But now listen to me carefully. All it needs is for you to put your foot down. Don't take no for an answer. . . . Did you hear me? And whatever you do, don't discuss it with him. . . . Because I'm frightened you'll give in to him. . . . Yes, Sam gave me lunch. . . . I ate all of it! . . . No, Mom, not a soul. It's still raining here. . . . Right, I'll tell them. I'll just do some homework and then lock up. . . . But remember now, Mom. Don't listen to anything he says. And phone me back and let me know what happens. . . . Okay. Bye, Mom. [*He hangs up. The men are staring at him.*] My Mom says that when you're finished with the floors you must do the windows.

[*Pause.*] Don't misunderstand me, chaps. All I want is for him to get better. And if he was, I'd be the first person to say: 'Bring him home.' But he's not, and we can't give him the medical care and attention he needs at home. That's what hospitals are there for. [*Brusquely.*] So don't just stand there! Get on with it!

[*Sam clears Hally's table.*]

You heard right. My Dad wants to go home.

SAM. Is he better?

HALLY. [*Sharply.*] No! How the hell can he be better when last night he was groaning with pain? This is not an age of miracles!

SAM. Then he should stay in hospital.

HALLY. [*Seething with irritation and frustration.*] Tell me something I don't know, Sam. What the hell do you think I was saying to my Mom? All I can say is fuck-it-all.

SAM. I'm sure he'll listen to your Mom.

HALLY. You don't know what she's up against. He's already packed his shaving kit and pajamas and is sitting on his bed with his crutches, dressed and ready to go. I know him when he gets in that mood. If she tries to reason with him, we've had it. She's no match for him when it comes to a battle of words. He'll tie her up in knots. [*Trying to hide his true feelings.*]

SAM. I suppose it gets lonely for him in there.

HALLY. With all the patients and nurses around? Regular visits from the Salvation Army? Balls! It's ten times worse for him at home. I'm at school and my mother is here in the business all day.

SAM. He's at least got you at night.

HALLY. [*Before he can stop himself.*] And we've got him! Please! I don't want to talk about it anymore. [*Unpacks his school case, slamming down books on the table.*] Life is just a plain bloody mess, that's all. And people are fools.

SAM. Come on, Hally.

HALLY. Yes, they are! They bloody well deserve what they get.

SAM. Then don't complain.

HALLY. Don't try to be clever, Sam. It doesn't suit you.

27

Anybody who thinks there's nothing wrong with this world needs to have his head examined. Just when things are going along all right, without fail someone or something will come along and spoil everything. Somebody should write that down as a fundamental law of the Universe. The principle of perpetual disappointment. If there is a God who created this world, he should scrap it and try again.

SAM. All right, Hally, all right. What you got for homework?

HALLY. Bullshit, as usual. [*Opens an exercise book and reads.*] 'Write five hundred words describing an annual event of cultural or historical significance.'

SAM. That should be easy enough for you.

HALLY. And also plain bloody boring. You know what he wants, don't you? One of their useless old ceremonies. The commemoration of the landing of the 1820 Settlers, or if it's going to be culture, Carols by Candlelight every Christmas.

SAM. It's an impressive sight. Make a good description, Hally. All those candles glowing in the dark and the people singing hymns.

HALLY. And it's called religious hysteria. [*Intense irritation.*] Please, Sam! Just leave me alone and let me get on with it. I'm not in the mood for games this afternoon. And remember my Mom's orders . . . you're to help Willie with the windows. Come on now, I don't want any more nonsense in here.

SAM. Okay, Hally, okay.

[*Hally settles down to his homework; determined preparations . . . pen, ruler, exercise book, dictionary, another cake . . . all of which will lead to nothing.*]

[*Sam waltzes over to Willie and starts to replace tables and chairs. He practises a ballroom step while doing so. Willie watches. When Sam is finished, Willie tries.*] Good! But just a little bit quicker on the turn and only move in to her after she's crossed over. What about this one?

[*Another step. When Sam is finished, Willie again has a go.*]

Much better. See what happens when you just relax and enjoy yourself? Remember that in two weeks' time and you'll be all right.

WILLIE. But I haven't got partner, *Boet* Sam.

SAM. Maybe Hilda will turn up tonight.

WILLIE. No, *Boet* Sam. [*Reluctantly.*] I gave her a good hiding.

SAM. You mean a bad one.

WILLIE. Good bad one.

SAM. Then you mustn't complain either. Now you pay the price for losing your temper.

WILLIE. I also pay two pounds ten shilling entrance fee.

SAM. They'll refund you if you withdraw now.

WILLIE. [*Appalled.*] You mean, don't dance?

SAM. Yes.

WILLIE. No! I wait too long and I practise too hard. If I find me new partner, you think I can be ready in two weeks? I ask Madam for my leave now and we practise every day.

SAM. Quickstep non-stop for two weeks. World record, Willie, but you'll be mad at the end.

WILLIE. No jokes, *Boet* Sam.

SAM. I'm not joking.

WILLIE. So then what?

SAM. Find Hilda. Say you're sorry and promise you won't beat her again.

WILLIE. No.

SAM. Then withdraw. Try again next year.

WILLIE. No.

SAM. Then I give up.

WILLIE. *Haaikona, Boet* Sam, you can't.

SAM. What do you mean, I can't? I'm telling you: I give up.

WILLIE. [*Adamant.*] No! [*Accusingly.*] It was you who start me ballroom dancing.

SAM. So?

WILLIE. Before that I use to be happy. And is you and Miriam who bring me to Hilda and say here's partner for you.

SAM. What are you saying, Willie?

WILLIE. You!

SAM. But me what? To blame?

WILLIE. Yes.

SAM. Willie . . . ? [*Bursts into laughter.*]

WILLIE. And now all you do is make jokes at me. You wait. When Miriam leaves you is my turn to laugh. Ha! Ha! Ha!

SAM. [*He can't take Willie seriously any longer.*] She can leave me tonight! I know what to do. [*Bowing before an imaginary partner.*] May I have the pleasure? [*He dances and sings.*]
'Just a fellow with his pillow . . .
Dancin' like a willow . . .
In an autumn breeze . . .'

WILLIE. There you go again!

[*Sam goes on dancing and singing.*]

Boet Sam!

SAM. There's the answer to your problem! Judges' announcement in two weeks' time: 'Ladies and gentlemen, the winner in the open section . . . Mr. Willie Malopo and his pillow!'

[*This is too much for a now really angry Willie. He goes for Sam, but the latter is too quick for him and puts Hally's table between the two of them.*]

HALLY. [*Exploding.*] For Christ's sake, you two!

WILLIE. [*Still trying to get at Sam.*] I *donner* you, Sam! 'Struesgod!

SAM. [*Still laughing.*] Sorry, Willie . . . Sorry . . .

HALLY. Sam! Willie! [*Grabs his ruler and gives Willie a vicious whack on the bum.*] How the hell am I supposed to concentrate with the two of you behaving like bloody children!

WILLIE. Hit him too!

HALLY. Shut up, Willie.

WILLIE. He started jokes again.

HALLY. Get back to your work. You too, Sam. [*His ruler.*] Do you want another one, Willie?

[*Sam and Willie return to their work. Hally uses the opportunity to escape from his unsuccessful attempt at homework. He struts around like a little despot, ruler in hand, giving vent to his anger and frustration.*]

Suppose a customer had walked in then? Or the Park Superintendent. And seen the two of you behaving like a pair of hooligans. That would have been the end of my mother's licence, you know. And your jobs! Well, this is the end of it.

From now on there will be no more of your ballroom nonsense in here. This is a business establishment, not a bloody New Brighton dancing school. I've been far too lenient with the two of you. [*Behind the counter for a green cool drink and a dollop of ice cream. He keeps up his tirade as he prepares it.*] But what really makes me bitter is that I allow you chaps a little freedom in here when business is bad and what do you do with it? The foxtrot! Specially you, Sam. There's more to life than trotting around a dance floor and I thought at least you knew it.

SAM. It's a harmless pleasure, Hally. It doesn't hurt anybody.

HALLY. It's also a rather simple one, you know.

SAM. You reckon so? Have you ever tried?

HALLY. Of course not.

SAM. Why don't you? Now.

HALLY. What do you mean? Me dance?

SAM. Yes. I'll show you a simple step—the waltz—then you try it.

HALLY. What will that prove?

SAM. That it might not be as easy as you think.

HALLY. I didn't say it was easy. I said it was simple—like in simple-minded, meaning mentally retarded. You can't exactly say it challenges the intellect.

SAM. It does other things.

HALLY. Such as?

SAM. Make people happy.

HALLY. [*The glass in his hand.*] So do American cream sodas with ice cream. For God's sake, Sam, you're not asking me to take ballroom dancing serious, are you?

SAM. Yes.

HALLY. [*Sigh of defeat.*] Oh, well, so much for trying to give you a decent education. I've obviously achieved nothing.

SAM. You still haven't told me what's wrong with admiring something that's beautiful and then trying to do it yourself.

HALLY. Nothing. But we happen to be talking about a foxtrot, not a thing of beauty.

SAM. But that is just what I'm saying. If you were to see two champions doing it, two masters of the art . . . !

31

HALLY. Oh, God, I give up. So now it's also art!

SAM. *Ja*.

HALLY. There's a limit, Sam. Don't confuse art and entertainment.

SAM. So then what is art?

HALLY. You want a definition?

SAM. *Ja*.

HALLY. [*He realizes he has got to be careful. He gives the matter a lot of thought before answering.*] Philosophers have been trying to do that for centuries. What is Art? What is Life? But basically I suppose it's . . . the giving of meaning to matter.

SAM. Nothing to do with beautiful?

HALLY. It goes beyond that. It's the giving of form to the formless.

SAM. *Ja*, well, maybe it's not art, then. But I still say it's beautiful.

HALLY. I'm sure the word you mean to use is entertaining.

SAM. [*Adamant.*] No. Beautiful. And if you want proof, come along to the Centenary Hall in New Brighton in two weeks' time.

[*The mention of the Centenary Hall draws Willie over to them.*]

HALLY. What for? I've seen the two of you prancing around in here often enough.

SAM. [*He laughs.*] This isn't the real thing, Hally. We're just playing around in here.

HALLY. So? I can use my imagination.

SAM. And what do you get?

HALLY. A lot of people dancing around and having a so-called good time.

SAM. That all?

HALLY. Well, basically it is that, surely?

SAM. No, it isn't. Your imagination hasn't helped you at all. There's a lot more to it than that. We're getting ready for the championships, Hally, not just another dance. There's going to be a lot of people, all right, and they're going to have a good time, but they'll only be spectators, sitting around and watch-

ing. It's just the competitors out there on the dance floor.
Party decorations and fancy lights all around the walls! The
ladies in beautiful evening dresses!

HALLY. My mother's got one of those, Sam, and, quite frankly,
it's an embarrassment every time she wears it.

SAM. [*Undeterred.*] Your imagination left out the excitement.

[*Hally scoffs.*]

Oh, yes. The finalists are not going to be out there just to have
a good time. One of those couples will be the 1950 Eastern
Province Champions. And your imagination left out the
music.

WILLIE. Mr. Elijah Gladman Guzana and his Orchestral
Jazzonions.

SAM. The sound of the big band, Hally. Trombone, trumpet,
tenor and alto sax. And then, finally, your imagination
also left out the climax of the evening when the dancing is
finished, the judges have stopped whispering among
themselves and the Master of Ceremonies collects their
scorecards and goes up on to the stage to announce the
winners.

HALLY. All right. So you make it sound like a bit of a do. It's an
occasion. Satisfied?

SAM. [*Victory.*] So you admit that!

HALLY. Emotionally yes, intellectually no.

SAM. Well, I don't know what you mean by that. All I'm telling
you is that it is going to be *the* event of the year in New
Brighton. It's been sold out for two weeks already. There's
only standing room left. We've got competitors coming from
Kingwilliamstown, East London, Port Alfred.

[*Hally starts pacing thoughtfully.*]

HALLY. Tell me a bit more.

SAM. I thought you weren't interested . . . intellectually.

HALLY. [*Mysteriously.*] I've got my reasons.

SAM. What do you want to know?

HALLY. It takes place every year?

SAM. Yes. But only every third year in New Brighton. It's East
London's turn to have the championships next year.

HALLY. Which, I suppose, makes it an even more significant event.

SAM. Ah ha! We're getting somewhere. Our 'occasion' is now a 'significant event'.

HALLY. I wonder.

SAM. What?

HALLY. I wonder if I would get away with it.

SAM. But what?

HALLY. [*To the table and his exercise book.*] 'Write five hundred words describing an annual event of cultural or historical significance.' Would I be stretching poetic licence a little too far if I called your ballroom championships a cultural event?

SAM. You mean . . . ?

HALLY. You think we could get five hundred words out of it, Sam?

SAM. Victor Sylvester has written a whole book on ballroom dancing.

WILLIE. You going to write about it, Master Hally?

HALLY. Yes, gentlemen, that is precisely what I am considering doing. Old Doc Bromely—he's my English teacher—is going to argue with me, of course. He doesn't like natives. But I'll point out to him that in strict anthropological terms the culture of a primitive black society includes its dancing and singing. To put my thesis in a nutshell: The war-dance has been replaced by the waltz. But it still amounts to the same thing: the release of primitive emotions through movement. Shall we give it a go?

SAM. I'm ready.

WILLIE. Me also.

HALLY. Ha! This will teach the old bugger a lesson. [*Decision taken.*] Right. Let's get ourselves organized. [*This means another cake on the table. He sits.*] I think you've given me enough general atmosphere, Sam, but to build the tension and suspense I need facts. [*Pencil poised.*]

WILLIE. Give him facts, *Boet* Sam.

HALLY. What you called the climax . . . how many finalists?

SAM. Six couples.

HALLY. [*Making notes.*] Go on. Give me the picture.

SAM. Spectators seated right around the hall. [*Willie becomes a spectator.*]

HALLY. . . . and it's a full house.

SAM. At one end, on the stage, Gladman and his Orchestral Jazzonions. At the other end is a long table with the three judges. The six finalists go onto the dance floor and take up their positions. When they are ready and the spectators have settled down, the Master of Ceremonies goes to the microphone. To start with, he makes some jokes to get the people laughing . . .

HALLY. Good touch! [*As he writes.*] '. . . creating a relaxed atmosphere which will change to one of tension and drama as the climax is approached.'

SAM. [*Onto a chair to act out the M.C.*] 'Ladies and gentlemen, we come now to the great moment you have all been waiting for this evening. . . . The finals of the 1950 Eastern Province Open Ballroom Dancing Championships. But first let me introduce the finalists! Mr. and Mrs. Welcome Tchabalala from Kingwilliamstown . . .'

WILLIE. [*He applauds after every name.*] Is when the people clap their hands and whistle and make a lot of noise, Master Hally.

SAM. 'Mr. Mulligan Njikelane and Miss Nomhle Nkonyeni of Grahamstown; Mr. and Mrs. Norman Ntshinga from Port Alfred; Mr. Fats Bokolane and Miss Dina Plaatjies from East London; Mr. Sipho Dugu and Mrs. Mabel Magada from Pedi; and from New Brighton our very own Mr. Willie Malopo and Miss Hilda Samuels.'

[*Willie can't believe his ears. He abandons his role as spectator and scrambles into position as a finalist.*]

WILLIE. Relaxed and ready to romance!

SAM. The applause dies down. When everybody is silent, Gladman lifts up his sax, nods at the Orchestral Jazzonions . . .

WILLIE. Play the jukebox please, *Boet* Sam!

SAM. I also only got bus fare, Willie.

HALLY. Hold it, everybody. [*Heads for the cash register behind the counter.*] How much is in the till, Sam?

35

SAM. Three shillings. Hally . . . your Mom counted it before she left.

[*Hally hesitates.*]

HALLY. Sorry, Willie. You know how she carried on the last time I did it. We'll just have to pool our combined imaginations and hope for the best. [*Returns to the table.*] Back to work. How are the points scored, Sam?

SAM. Maximum of ten points each for individual style, deportment, rhythm and general appearance.

WILLIE. Must I start?

HALLY. Hold it for a second, Willie. And penalties?

SAM. For what?

HALLY. For doing something wrong. Say you stumble or bump into somebody . . . do they take off any points?

SAM. [*Aghast.*] Hally . . . !

HALLY. When you're dancing. If you and your partner collide into another couple.

[*Hally can get no further. Sam has collapsed with laughter. He explains to Willie.*]

SAM. If me and Miriam bump into you and Hilda . . .

[*Willie joins him in another good laugh.*]

Hally, Hally . . . !

HALLY. [*Perplexed.*] Why? What did I say?

SAM. There's no collisions out there, Hally. Nobody trips or stumbles or bumps into anybody else. That's what that moment is all about. To be one of those finalists on that dance floor is like . . . like being in a dream about a world in which accidents don't happen.

HALLY. [*Genuinely moved by Sam's image.*] Jesus, Sam! That's beautiful!

WILLIE. [*Can endure waiting no longer.*] I'm starting! [*Willie dances while Sam talks.*]

SAM. Of course it is. That's what I've been trying to say to you all afternoon. And it's beautiful because that is what we want life to be like. But instead, like you said, Hally, we're bumping into each other all the time. Look at the three of us this afternoon: I've bumped into Willie, the two of us have

36

bumped into you, you've bumped into your mother, she bumping into your Dad. . . . None of us knows the steps and there's no music playing. And it doesn't stop with us. The whole world is doing it all the time. Open a newspaper and what do you read? America has bumped into Russia, England is bumping into India, rich man bumps into poor man. Those are big collisions, Hally. They make for a lot of bruises. People get hurt in all that bumping, and we're sick and tired of it now. It's been going on for too long. Are we never going to get it right? . . . Learn to dance life like champions instead of always being just a bunch of beginners at it?

HALLY. [*Deep and sincere admiration of the man.*] You've got a vision, Sam!

SAM. Not just me. What I'm saying to you is that everybody's got it. That's why there's only standing room left for the Centenary Hall in two weeks' time. For as long as the music lasts, we are going to see six couples get it right, the way we want life to be.

HALLY. But is that the best we can do, Sam . . . watch six finalists dreaming about the way it should be?

SAM. I don't know. But it starts with that. Without the dream we won't know what we're going for. And anyway I reckon there are a few people who have got past just dreaming about it and are trying for something real. Remember that thing we read once in the paper about the Mahatma Gandhi? Going without food to stop those riots in India?

HALLY. You're right. He certainly was trying to teach people to get the steps right.

SAM. And the Pope.

HALLY. Yes, he's another one. Our old General Smuts as well, you know. He's also out there dancing. You know, Sam, when you come to think of it, that's what the United Nations boils down to . . . a dancing school for politicians!

SAM. And let's hope they learn.

HALLY. [*A little surge of hope.*] You're right. We mustn't despair. Maybe there's some hope for mankind after all. Keep it up, Willie. [*Back to his table with determination.*] This is a lot bigger than I thought. So what have we got? Yes, our title: 'A World Without Collisions.'

SAM. That sounds good! 'A World Without Collisions.'

HALLY. Subtitle: 'Global Politics on the Dance Floor.' No. A bit too heavy, hey? What about 'Ballroom Dancing as a Political Vision'?

[*The telephone rings. Sam answers it.*]

SAM. St. George's Park Tea Room . . . Yes, Madam . . . Hally, it's your Mom.

HALLY. [*Back to reality.*] Oh, God, yes! I'd forgotten all about that. Shit! Remember my words, Sam? Just when you're enjoying yourself, someone or something will come along and wreck everything.

SAM. You haven't heard what she's got to say yet.

HALLY. Public telephone?

SAM. No.

HALLY. Does she sound happy or unhappy?

SAM. I couldn't tell. [*Pause.*] She's waiting, Hally.

HALLY. [*To the telephone.*] Hello, Mom . . . No, everything is okay here. Just doing my homework. . . . What's your news? . . . You've what? . . . [*Pause. He takes the receiver away from his ear for a few seconds. In the course of Hally's telephone conversation, Sam and Willie discreetly position the stacked tables and chairs. Hally places the receiver back to his ear.*] Yes, I'm still here. Oh, well, I give up now. Why did you do it, Mom? . . . Well, I just hope you know what you've let us in for. . . . [*Loudly.*] I said I hope you know what you've let us in for! It's the end of the peace and quiet we've been having. [*Softly.*] Where is he? [*Normal voice.*] He can't hear us from in there. But for God's sake, Mom, what happened? I told you to be firm with him. . . . Then you and the nurses should have held him down, taken his crutches away. . . . I know only too well he's my father! . . . I'm not being disrespectful, but I'm sick and tired of emptying stinking chamberpots full of phlegm and piss. . . . Yes, I do! When you're not there, he asks *me* to do it. . . . If you really want to know the truth, that's why I've got no appetite for my food. . . . Yes! There's a lot of things you don't know about. For your information, I still haven't got that science textbook

I need. And you know why? He borrowed the money you gave me for it. . . . Because I didn't want to start another fight between you two. . . . He says that every time. . . . All right, Mom! [*Viciously.*] Then just remember to start hiding your bag away again, because he'll be at your purse before long for money for booze. And when he's well enough to come down here, you better keep an eye on the till as well, because that is also going to develop a leak. . . . Then don't complain to me when he starts his old tricks. . . . Yes, you do. I get it from you on one side and from him on the other, and it makes life hell for me. I'm not going to be the peacemaker anymore. I'm warning you now: when the two of you start fighting again, I'm leaving home. . . . Mom, if you start crying, I'm going to put down the receiver. . . . Okay . . . [*Lowering his voice to a vicious whisper.*] Okay, Mom. I heard you. [*Desperate.*] No. . . . Because I don't want to. I'll see him when I get home! Mom! . . . [*Pause. When he speaks again, his tone changes completely. It is not simply pretence. We sense a genuine emotional conflict.*] Welcome home, chum! . . . What's that? . . . Don't be silly, Dad. You being home is just about the best news in the world. . . . I bet you are. Bloody depressing there with everybody going on about their ailments, hey! . . . How you feeling? . . . Good . . . Here as well, pal. Coming down cats and dogs. . . . That's right. Just the day for a kip and a toss in your old Uncle Ned. . . . Everything's just hunky-dory on my side, Dad. . . . Well, to start with, there's a nice pile of comics for you on the counter. . . . Yes, old Kempie brought them in. *Batman and Robin, Submariner* . . . just your cup of tea . . . I will. . . . Yes, we'll spin a few yarns tonight. . . . Okay, chum, see you in a little while. . . . No, I promise. I'll come straight home. . . . [*Pause—his mother comes back on the phone.*] Mom? Okay. I'll lock up now. . . . What? . . . Oh, the brandy . . . Yes, I'll remember! . . . I'll put it in my suitcase now, for God's sake. I know well enough what will happen if he doesn't get it. . . . [*Places a bottle of brandy on the counter.*] I *was* kind to him, Mom. I didn't say anything nasty! . . . All right. Bye. [*End of telephone conversation. A desolate Hally doesn't move. A strained silence.*]

SAM. [*Quietly.*] That sounded like a bad bump, Hally.

HALLY. [*Having a hard time controlling his emotions. He speaks carefully.*] Mind your own business, Sam.

SAM. Sorry. I wasn't trying to interfere. Shall we carry on? Hally? [*He indicates the exercise book. No response from Hally.*]

WILLIE. [*Also trying.*] Tell him about when they give out the cups, *Boet* Sam.

SAM. *Ja!* That's another big moment. The presentation of the cups after the winners have been announced. You've got to put that in.

[*Still no response from Hally.*]

WILLIE. A big silver one, Master Hally, called floating trophy, for the champions.

SAM. We always invite some big-shot personality to hand them over. Guest of honour this year is going to be His Holiness Bishop Jabulani of the All African Free Zionist Church.

[*Hally gets up abruptly, goes to his table and tears up the page he was writing on.*]

HALLY. So much for a bloody world without collisions.

SAM. Too bad. It was on its way to being a good composition.

HALLY. Let's stop bullshitting ourselves, Sam.

SAM. Have we been doing that?

HALLY. Yes! That's what all our talk about a decent world has been . . . just so much bullshit.

SAM. We did say it was still only a dream.

HALLY. And a bloody useless one at that. Life's a fuck-up and it's never going to change.

SAM. *Ja*, maybe that's true.

HALLY. There's no maybe about it. It's a blunt and brutal fact. All we've done this afternoon is waste our time.

SAM. Not if we'd got your homework done.

HALLY. I don't give a shit about my homework, so, for Christ's sake, just shut up about it. [*Slamming books viciously into his school case.*] Hurry up now and finish your work. I want to lock up and get out of here. [*Pause.*] And then go where? Home-sweet-fucking-home. Jesus, I hate that word.

[*Hally goes to the counter to put the brandy bottle and comics in his school case. After a moment's hesitation, he smashes the bottle of brandy. He abandons all further attempts to hide his feelings. Sam and Willie work away as unobtrusively as possible.*]

Do you want to know what is really wrong with your lovely little dream, Sam? It's not just that we are all bad dancers. That does happen to be perfectly true, but there's more to it than just that. You left out the cripples.

SAM. Hally!

HALLY. [*Now totally reckless.*] *Ja!* Can't leave them out, Sam. That's why we always end up on our backsides on the dance floor. They're also out there dancing . . . like a bunch of broken spiders trying to do the quickstep! [*An ugly attempt at laughter.*] When you come to think of it, it's a bloody comical sight. I mean, it's bad enough on two legs . . . but one and a pair of crutches! Hell, no, Sam. That's guaranteed to turn that dance floor into a shambles. Why you shaking your head? Picture it, man. For once this afternoon let's use our imaginations sensibly.

SAM. Be careful, Hally.

HALLY. Of what? The truth? I seem to be the only one around here who is prepared to face it. We've had the pretty dream, it's time now to wake up and have a good long look at the way things really are. Nobody knows the steps, there's no music, the cripples are also out there tripping up everybody and trying to get into the act, and it's all called the All-Comers-How-to-Make-a-Fuckup-of-Life Championships. [*Another ugly laugh.*] Hang on, Sam! The best bit is still coming. Do you know what the winner's trophy is? A beautiful big chamber-pot with roses on the side, and it's full to the brim with piss. And guess who I think is going to be this year's winner.

SAM. [*Almost shouting.*] Stop now!

HALLY. [*Suddenly appalled by how far he has gone.*] Why?

SAM. Hally! It's your father you're talking about.

HALLY. So?

SAM. Do you know what you've been saying?

[*Hally can't answer. He is rigid with shame. Sam speaks to him sternly.*]

No, Hally, you mustn't do it. Take back those words and ask for forgiveness! It's a terrible sin for a son to mock his father

41

with jokes like that. You'll be punished if you carry on. Your
father is your father, even if he is a . . . cripple man.

WILLIE. Yes, Master Hally. Is true what Sam say.

SAM. I understand how you are feeling, Hally, but even so . . .

HALLY. No, you don't!

SAM. I think I do.

HALLY. And I'm telling you you don't. Nobody does. [*Speaking
carefully as his shame turns to rage at Sam.*] It's your turn to be
careful, Sam. Very careful! You're treading on dangerous
ground. Leave me and my father alone.

SAM. I'm not the one who's been saying things about him.

HALLY. What goes on between me and my Dad is none of your
business!

SAM. Then don't tell me about it. If that's all you've got to say
about him, I don't want to hear.

[*For a moment Hally is at loss for a response.*]

HALLY. Just get on with your bloody work and shut up.

SAM. Swearing at me won't help you.

HALLY. Yes, it does! Mind your own fucking business and shut
up!

SAM. Okay. If that's the way you want it, I'll stop trying.

[*He turns away. This infuriates Hally even more.*]

HALLY. Good. Because what you've been trying to do is meddle
in something you know nothing about. All that concerns
you in here, Sam, is to try and do what you get paid for—keep
the place clean and serve the customers. In plain words, just
get on with your job. My mother is right. She's always
warning me about allowing you to get too familiar. Well, this
time you've gone too far. It's going to stop right now.

[*No response from Sam.*]

You're only a servant in here, and don't forget it.

[*Still no response. Hally is trying hard to get one.*]

And as far as my father is concerned, all you need to remember
is that he is your boss.

SAM. [*Needled at last.*] No, he isn't. I get paid by your mother.

HALLY. Don't argue with me, Sam!

SAM. Then don't say he's my boss.

HALLY. He's a white man and that's good enough for you.

[*Pause.*]

SAM. I'll try to forget you said that.

HALLY. Don't! Because you won't be doing me a favour if you do. I'm telling you to remember it.

[*A pause. Sam pulls himself together and makes one last effort.*]

SAM. Hally, Hally . . . ! Come on now. Let's stop before it's too late. You're right. We *are* on dangerous ground. If we're not careful, somebody is going to get hurt.

HALLY. It won't be me.

SAM. Don't be so sure.

HALLY. I don't know what you're talking about, Sam.

SAM. Yes, you do.

HALLY. [*Furious.*] Jesus, I wish you would stop trying to tell me what I do and what I don't know.

[*Sam gives up. He turns to Willie.*]

SAM. Let's finish up.

HALLY. Don't turn your back on me! I haven't finished talking.

[*He grabs Sam by the arm and tries to make him turn around. Sam reacts with a flash of anger.*]

SAM. Don't do that, Hally! [*Facing the boy.*] All right, I'm listening. Well? What do you want to say to me?

HALLY. [*Pause as Hally looks for something to say.*] To begin with, why don't you also start calling me Master Harold, like Willie.

SAM. Do you mean that?

HALLY. Why the hell do you think I said it?

SAM. And if I don't?

HALLY. You might just lose your job.

SAM. [*Quietly and very carefully.*] If you make me say it once, I'll never call you anything else again.

HALLY. So? [*The boy confronts the man.*] Is that meant to be a threat?

SAM. Just telling you what will happen if you make me do that. You must decide what it means to you.

43

HALLY. Well, I have. It's good news. Because that is exactly what Master Harold wants from now on. Think of it as a little lesson in respect, Sam, that's long overdue, and I hope you remember it as well as you do your geography. I can tell you now that somebody who will be glad to hear I've finally given it to you will be my Dad. Yes! He agrees with my Mom. He's always going on about it as well. 'You must teach the boys to show you more respect, my son.'

SAM. So now you can stop complaining about going home. Everybody is going to be happy tonight.

HALLY. That's perfectly correct. You see, you mustn't get the wrong idea about me and my Dad, Sam. We also have our good times together. Some bloody good laughs. He's got a marvellous sense of humour. Want to know what our favourite joke is? He gives out a big groan, you see, and says: 'It's not fair, is it, Hally?' Then I have to ask: 'What, chum?' And then he says: 'A kaffir's arse' . . . and we both have a good laugh.

[*The men stare at him with disbelief.*]

What's the matter, Willie? Don't you catch the joke? You always were a bit slow on the uptake. It's what is called a pun. You see, fair means both light in colour and to be just and decent. [*He turns to Sam.*] I thought *you* would catch it, Sam.

SAM. Oh *ja*, I catch it all right.

HALLY. But it doesn't appeal to your sense of humour.

SAM. Do you really laugh?

HALLY. Of course.

SAM. To please him? Make him feel good?

HALLY. No, for heaven's sake! I laugh because I think it's a bloody good joke.

SAM. You're really trying hard to be ugly, aren't you? And why drag poor old Willie into it? He's done nothing to you except show you the respect you want so badly. That's also not being fair, you know . . . and *I* mean just or decent.

WILLIE. It's all right, Sam. Leave it now.

SAM. It's me you're after. You should just have said 'Sam's arse' . . . because that's the one you're trying to kick. Anyway, how do you know it's not fair? You've never seen it. Do you want to? [*He drops his trousers and underpants and presents his*

44

backside for Hally's inspection.] Have a good look. A real Basuto arse . . . which is about as kaffir as they can come. Satisfied? [*Trousers up.*] Now you can make your Dad even happier when you go home tonight. Tell him I showed you my arse and he is quite right. It's not fair. And if it will give him an even better laugh next time, I'll also let *him* have a look. Come, Willie, let's finish up and go.

[*Sam and Willie start to tidy up the tea room. Hally doesn't move. He waits for a moment when Sam passes him.*]

HALLY. [*Quietly.*] Sam . . .

[*Sam stops and looks expectantly at the boy. Hally spits in his face. A long and heartfelt groan from Willie. For a few seconds Sam doesn't move.*]

SAM. [*Taking out a handkerchief and wiping his face.*] It's all right, Willie.

[*To Hally.*]

Ja, well, you've done it . . . Master Harold. Yes, I'll start calling you that from now on. It won't be difficult anymore. You've hurt yourself, Master Harold. I saw it coming. I warned you, but you wouldn't listen. You've just hurt yourself *bad*. And you're a coward, Master Harold. The face you should be spitting in is your father's . . . but you used mine, because you think you're safe inside your fair skin . . . and this time I don't mean just or decent. [*Pause, then moving violently towards Hally.*] Should I hit him, Willie?

WILLIE. [*Stopping Sam.*] No, *Boet* Sam.

SAM. [*Violently.*] Why not?

WILLIE. It won't help, *Boet* Sam.

SAM. I don't want to help! I want to hurt him.

WILLIE. You also hurt yourself.

SAM. And if he had done it to you, Willie?

WILLIE. Me? Spit at me like I was a dog? [*A thought that had not occurred to him before. He looks at Hally.*] *Ja*. Then I want to hit him. I want to hit him hard!

[*A dangerous few seconds as the men stand staring at the boy. Willie turns away, shaking his head.*]

But maybe all I do is go cry at the back. He's little boy, *Boet*

45

Sam. Little *white* boy. Long trousers now, but he's still little boy.

SAM. [*His violence ebbing away into defeat as quickly as it flooded.*] You're right. So go on, then: groan again, Willie. You do it better than me. [*To Hally.*] You don't know all of what you've just done . . . Master Harold. It's not just that you've made me feel dirtier than I've ever been in my life . . . I mean, how do I wash off yours and your father's filth? . . . I've also failed. A long time ago I promised myself I was going to try and do something, but you've just shown me . . . Master Harold . . . that I've failed. [*Pause.*] I've also got a memory of a little white boy when he was still wearing short trousers, and a black man, but they're not flying a kite. It was the old Jubilee days, after dinner one night. I was in my room. You came in and just stood against the wall, looking down at the ground, and only after I'd asked you what you wanted, what was wrong, I don't know how many times, did you speak and even then so softly I almost didn't hear you. 'Sam, please help me to go and fetch my Dad.' Remember? He was dead drunk on the floor of the Central Hotel Bar. They'd phoned for your Mom, but you were the only one at home. And do you remember how we did it? You went in first by yourself to ask permission for me to go into the bar. Then I loaded him on to my back like a baby and carried him back to the boarding house with you following behind carrying his crutches. [*Shaking his head as he remembers.*] A crowded Main Street with all the people watching a little white boy following his drunk father on a kaffir's back! I felt for that little boy . . . Master Harold. I felt for him. After that we still had to clean him up, remember? He'd messed in his trousers, so we had to clean him up and get him into bed.

HALLY. [*Great pain.*] I love him, Sam.

SAM. I know you do. That's why I tried to stop you from saying these things about him. It would have been so simple if you could have just despised him for being a weak man. But he's your father. You love him and you're ashamed of him. You're ashamed of so much! . . . And now that's going to include yourself. That was the promise I made to myself: to try and stop that happening. [*Pause.*] After we got him to bed you came back with me to my room and sat in a corner and carried on just looking down at the ground. And for days after that! You hadn't done anything wrong, but you went around as if you owed the world an apology for being alive. I didn't like seeing that! That's not the way a boy grows up to be a man! . . . But the one person who should have been teaching you what that means was the cause of your shame. If you really want to know, that's why I made you that kite. I wanted you to look up, be proud of something, of yourself . . . [*Bitter smile at the memory.*] . . . and you certainly were that when I left you with it up there on the hill. Oh, *ja* . . . something else! . . . If you ever do write it as a short story, there *was* a twist in our ending. I couldn't sit down there and stay with you. It was a 'Whites Only' bench. You were too young, too excited to notice then. But not anymore. If you're not careful . . . Master Harold . . . you're going to be sitting up there by yourself for a long time to come, and there won't be a kite in the sky. [*Sam has got nothing more to say. He exits into the kitchen, taking off his waiter's jacket.*]

WILLIE. Is bad. Is all all bad in here now.

HALLY. [*Books into his school case, raincoat on.*] Willie . . . [*It is difficult to speak.*] Will you lock up for me and look after the keys?

WILLIE. Okay.

[*Sam returns. Hally goes behind the counter and collects the few coins in the cash register. As he starts to leave . . .*]

SAM. Don't forget the comic books.

[*Hally returns to the counter and puts them in his case. He starts to leave again.*]

SAM. [*To the retreating back of the boy.*] Stop . . . Hally . . .

[*Hally stops, but doesn't turn to face him.*]

Hally . . . I've got no right to tell you what being a man means if I don't behave like one myself, and I'm not doing so well at that this afternoon. Should we try again, Hally?

HALLY. Try what?

SAM. Fly another kite, I suppose. It worked once, and this time I need it as much as you do.

HALLY. It's still raining, Sam. You can't fly kites on rainy days, remember.

47

SAM. So what do we do? Hope for better weather tomorrow?

HALLY. [*Helpless gesture.*] I don't know. I don't know anything anymore.

SAM. You sure of that, Hally? Because it would be pretty hopeless if that was true. It would mean nothing has been learnt in here this afternoon, and there was a hell of a lot of teaching going on . . . one way or the other. But anyway, I don't believe you. I reckon there's one thing you know. You don't *have* to sit up there by yourself. You know what that bench means now, and you can leave it any time you choose. All you've got to do is stand up and walk away from it.

[*Hally leaves. Willie goes up quietly to Sam.*]

WILLIE. Is okay, *Boet* Sam. You see. Is . . . [*He can't find any better words.*] . . . is going to be okay tomorrow. [*Changing his tone.*] Hey, *Boet* Sam! [*He is trying hard.*] You right. I think about it and you right. Tonight I find Hilda and say sorry. And make promise I won't beat her no more. You hear me, *Boet* Sam?

SAM. I hear you, Willie.

WILLIE. And when we practise I relax and romance with her from beginning to end. Non-stop! You watch! Two weeks' time: 'First prize for promising newcomers: Mr. Willie Malopo and Miss Hilda Samuels.' [*Sudden impulse.*] To hell with it! I walk home. [*He goes to the jukebox, puts in a coin and selects a record. The machine comes to life in the gray twilight, blushing its way through a spectrum of soft, romantic colours.*] How did you say it, *Boet* Sam? Let's dream. [*Willie sways with the music and gestures for Sam to dance.*]

[*Sarah Vaughan sings.*]

> 'Little man you're crying,
> I know why you're blue,
> Someone took your kiddy car away;
> Better go to sleep now,
> Little man you've had a busy day.' [*etc. etc.*]

You lead. I follow.

[*The men dance together.*]

> 'Johnny won your marbles,
> Tell you what we'll do;

Dad will get you new ones right away;
Better go to sleep now,
Little man you've had a busy day.'

BLOOD KNOT

A PLAY
IN SEVEN SCENES

CHARACTERS

MORRIS
ZACHARIAH

Zachariah is dark-skinned and Morris is light-skinned.

THE BLOOD KNOT (original title) was first performed at the
Rehearsal Room (African Music and Drama Association), Dorkay
House, Johannesburg, on 3 September 1961, with the following cast:

MORRIS	Athol Fugard
ZACHARIAH	Zakes Mokae

The production was directed by the author, as was the revised version
first performed at the Intimate Theatre, Johannesburg, on 8 November 1961, under Leon Gluckman's management (Union Artists), with
the same cast.

The 25th Anniversary Production of BLOOD KNOT was first
presented at Yale Repertory Theatre, New Haven, and opened at The
Golden Theatre in New York City on 10 December 1985, with the
original cast. The producers were James B. Freydberg, Max Weitz-
enhoffer, Lucille Lortel, Estrin Rose Berman Production in association with FWM Producing Group. The production was directed by
the author. Sets were designed by Rusty Smith. Costumes were
designed by Susan Hilferty. Lights were designed by William B.
Warfel.

BLOOD KNOT was first performed in the UK at the New Victoria
Theatre, Stoke-on-Trent, on 13 September 1988, directed by Peter
Cheeseman, with Winston Crooke (Zach) and Gary Lilburn
(Morris).

*All the action takes place in a one-room shack in the 'non-white location' of
Korsten, Port Elizabeth. The walls are a patchwork of scraps of
corrugated iron, packing-case wood, flattened cardboard boxes, and old
hessian bags. One door, one window (no curtains), two beds, a table, and
two chairs. Also in evidence is a cupboard of sorts with an oil-stove, a
kettle, and a few pots. The shack is tidy and swept, but this only enhances
the poverty of its furnishings. Over one of the beds is a shelf on which are a
few books (including a Bible) and an alarm-clock.*

SCENE ONE

Late afternoon.

Lying on his bed, the one with the shelf, and staring up at the ceiling, is Morris. *After a few seconds he stands up on the bed, looks at the alarm clock, and then lies down again in the same position. Time passes. The alarm rings and Morris jumps purposefully to his feet. He knows exactly what he is going to do. First, he winds and resets the clock, then lights the oil stove and puts on a kettle of water. Next, he places an enamel washbasin on the floor in front of the other bed and lays out a towel. He feels the kettle on the stove and then goes to the door and looks out. Nothing. He wanders aimlessly around the room for a few more seconds, pausing at the window for a long look at whatever lies beyond. Eventually he is back at the door again and, after a short wait, he sees someone coming. A second burst of activity. He places a packet of footsalts beside the basin and finally replaces the kettle.*

Zachariah *comes in through the door. Their meeting is without words.* Morris *nods and* Zachariah *grunts on his way to the bed, where he sits down, drags off his shoes, and rolls up his trousers. While he does this,* Morris *sprinkles footsalts into the basin and then sits back on his haunches and waits.* Zachariah *dips his feet into the basin, sighs with satisfaction, but stops abruptly when he sees* Morris *smile. He frowns, pretends to think, and makes a great business of testing the water with his foot.*

ZACHARIAH. Not as hot as last night, hey?

MORRIS. Last night you said it was too hot.

ZACHARIAH [*thinks about this*]. That's what I mean.

MORRIS. So what is it? Too hot or too cold?

ZACHARIAH. When?

MORRIS. Now.

ZACHARIAH. Luke-ish. [*Bends forward and smells.*] New stuff?

MORRIS. Yes.

ZACHARIAH. Let's see.

[*Morris hands him the packet. Zachariah first smells it, then takes out a pinch between thumb and forefinger.*]

It's also white.

MORRIS. Yes, but it is different stuff.

53

ZACHARIAH. The other lot was also white, but it didn't help, hey?

MORRIS. This is definitely different stuff, Zach. [*Pointing.*] See. There's the name. Radium Salts.

[*Zachariah is not convinced. Morris fetches a second packet.*]

Here's the other. Schultz's Foot Salts.

ZACHARIAH [*taking the second packet and looking inside*]. They look the same, don't they? [*Smells.*] But they smell different. You know something? I think the old lot smells nicest. What do you say we go back to the old lot?

MORRIS. But you just said it didn't help!

ZACHARIAH. But it smells better, man.

MORRIS. It's not the smell, Zach. You don't go by the smell, man.

ZACHARIAH. No?

MORRIS. No. It's the healing properties.

ZACHARIAH. Oh, maybe.

MORRIS [*taking back the new packet*]. Zach, listen to this . . . [*Reads.*] 'For all agonies of the joints: lumbago, rheumatism, tennis elbows, housemaid's knees; also ideal for bunions, corns, callouses'—that's what you got . . . 'and for soothing irritated skins.'

[*Zachariah lets him finish, examining the old packet while Morris reads.*]

ZACHARIAH. How much that new stuff cost?

MORRIS. Why?

ZACHARIAH. Tell me, man.

MORRIS [*aware of what is coming*]. Listen, Zach. It's the healing properties. Price has nothing . . .

ZACHARIAH [*insistent*]. How—much—does—that—cost?

MORRIS. Twenty-five cents.

ZACHARIAH [*with a small laugh*]. You know something?

MORRIS. Yes, yes, I know what you're going to say.

ZACHARIAH. This old stuff, which isn't so good, is thirty cents. Five cents more! [*He starts to laugh.*]

MORRIS So? Listen, Zach. Price . . . ZACH! Do you want to listen or don't you?

[*Zachariah is laughing loud in triumph.*]

PRICE HAS GOT NOTHING TO DO WITH IT!

ZACHARIAH. Then why is this more money?

MORRIS. Profit. He's making more profit on the old stuff. Satisfied?

ZACHARIAH. So?

MORRIS. So.

ZACHARIAH. Oh. [*Slowly.*] So he's making more profit on the old stuff. [*The thought comes.*] But that's what you been buying, man! *Ja*—and with my money, remember! So it happens to be my profit he's making. Isn't that so?

[*He is getting excited and now stands in the basin of water.*]

Hey. I see it now. I do the bloody work—all day long—in the sun. Not him. It's my stinking feet that got the hardnesses. But he goes and makes my profit.

[*Steps out of the basin.*]

I want to work this out, man. How long you been buying that old stuff?

MORRIS. Only four weeks.

ZACHARIAH. Four weeks?

MORRIS. Yes.

ZACHARIAH. That makes four packets, hey? So you say five cents profit . . . which comes to . . . twenty cents . . . isn't that so? Whose? Mine. Who's got it? Him . . . him . . . some dirty, rotting, stinking, creeping, little . . .

MORRIS. But we are buying the cheap salts now, Zach! [*Pause.*] He's not going to get the profits anymore. And what is more still, the new salts is better.

[*The thread of Zachariah's reasoning has been broken. He stares blankly at Morris.*]

ZACHARIAH. I still say the old smells sweeter.

MORRIS. Okay, okay, listen. I tell you what. I'll give you a double dose. One of the old and one of the new . . . together! That way you get the healing properties *and* the smell. Satisfied?

ZACHARIAH. Okay.

[*He goes to the bed, sits down and once again soaks his feet.*]

Hey! You got any more warm, Morrie?

[*Morris pours the last of the hot water into the basin. Zachariah now settles down to enjoy the luxury of his footbath. Morris helps him off with his tie, and afterwards puts away his shoes.*]

MORRIS. How did it go today?

ZACHARIAH. He's got me standing again.

MORRIS. At the gate?

ZACHARIAH. *Ja.*

MORRIS. But didn't you tell him, Zach? I told you to tell him that your feet are calloused and that you wanted to go back to pots.

ZACHARIAH. I did.

MORRIS. And then?

ZACHARIAH. He said: 'Go to the gate or go to hell.'

MORRIS. That's an insult.

ZACHARIAH. What's the other one?

MORRIS. Injury!

ZACHARIAH No, no. The long one.

MORRIS. Inhumanity!

ZACHARIAH. That's it. That's what I think it is. My inhumanity from him. 'Go to the gate or go to hell.' What do they think I am?

MORRIS. What about me?

ZACHARIAH. [*Anger*]. What do *you* think I am?

MORRIS. No, Zach! Good heavens! You got it all wrong. What do *they* think I am, when they think what you are.

ZACHARIAH. Oh.

MORRIS. Yes. I'm on your side, they're on theirs. I mean, I couldn't be living here with you and not be on yours, could I, Zach?

[*Morris is helping Zachariah off with his coat. When Zachariah is not looking, he smells it.*]

Zach, I think we must borrow Minnie's bath again.

ZACHARIAH. Okay, Morrie.

MORRIS. What about me? Do I smell?

ZACHARIAH. No. [*Pause.*] Hey! Have I started again?

[*Morris doesn't answer. Zachariah laughs.*]

Hey! What's that thing you say, Morrie? The one about smelling?

MORRIS [*quoting*]. 'The rude odours of manhood.'

ZACHARIAH. 'The rude odours of manhood.' What's the other one? The long one?

MORRIS. 'No smell'?

[*Zachariah nods.*]

> 'No smell doth stink as sweet as labour.
> 'Tis joyous times when man and man
> Do work and sweat in common toil,
> When all the world's my neighbour.'

ZACHARIAH. 'When all the world's my neighbour.'

[*Zachariah starts drying his feet with the towel. Morris empties the basin and puts it away.*]

Minnie.

MORRIS. What about Minnie?

ZACHARIAH. Our neighbour. You know, strange thing about Minnie. He doesn't come no more.

MORRIS. I don't miss him.

ZACHARIAH. No, you don't remember, man. I'm talking about before you. He came every night. *Ja!* Me and him used to go out—together, you know—quite a bit. [*Pause.*] Hey! How did I forget a thing like that!

MORRIS. What are you talking about?

ZACHARIAH. Me and Minnie going out! Almost every night . . . and I've forgotten. [*Pause.*] How long you been here, Morrie?

MORRIS. Oh, about a year now, Zach.

ZACHARIAH. Only one miserable year and I have forgotten just like that! Just like it might not have never happened!

MORRIS. Yes, Zach, the year has flown by.

ZACHARIAH. You never want to go out, Morrie.

MORRIS. So I don't want to go out. Ask me why and I'll

tell you. Come on.

ZACHARIAH. Why?

MORRIS. Because we got plans, remember? We're saving for a future, which is something Minnie didn't have.

ZACHARIAH. *Ja.* He doesn't come no more.

MORRIS. You said that already, Zach. I heard you the first time.

ZACHARIAH. I was just thinking. I remembered him today. I was at the gate. It was lunchtime, and I was eating my bread.

MORRIS. Hey—did you like the peanut butter sandwiches I made?

ZACHARIAH. I was eating my bread, and then it comes, the thought: What the hell has happened to old Minnie?

MORRIS. Zach, I was asking you—

ZACHARIAH. Wait, man! I'm remembering it now. He used to come, I thought to myself, with his guitar to this room, to me, to his friend, old Zachariah, waiting for him here. Friday nights it was, when an *ou*'s got pay in his pocket and there's no work tomorrow and Minnie's coming. Now there was a friend for a man! He could laugh, could Minnie, and drink! He knew the spots, I'm telling you . . . the places to be, the good times . . . and—*Ja*! [*Reverently.*] Minnie had music. Listen, he could do a *vastrap*, that man, non-stop, on all strings at once. He knew the lot. Polka, tickey-*draai*, *opskud en uitkap, ek sê* . . . Now that was jollification for you, with Minnie coming around. So, when I'm waiting in here, and I hear that guitar in the street, at my door, I'm happy! 'It's you!' I shout. He stops. 'I know it's you,' I say. He pretends he isn't there, you see. 'Minnie,' I call. 'Minnie!' So what does he do? He gives me a quick *chick-a-doem* in G. He knows I like G. 'It's Friday night, Minnie.' '*Chick-a-doem-doem, doem, doem*,' he says. And then I'm laughing. 'You bugger! You motherless bastard!' So I open the door. What do I see? Minnie! And what's he got in his hand? Golden Moments at fifty cents a bottle. Out there, Morrie, standing just right on that spot in the street with his bottle and his music and laughing with me. 'Zach,' he says, '*Ou pellie*, tonight is the night—' [*The alarm goes off.*] . . . is the night . . . is the night . . . is the night . . .

[*Zachariah loses the thread of his story. By the time the alarm stops, he has forgotten what he was saying. The moment the alarm goes off, Morris springs to his feet and busies himself at the table with their supper. Zachariah eventually goes back to the bed.*]

MORRIS [*watching Zachariah surreptitiously from the table*]. I been thinking, Zach. It's time we started making some definite plans. I mean . . . we've agreed on the main idea. The thing now is to find the right place. [*Pause.*] Zach? [*Pause.*] We have agreed, haven't we?

ZACHARIAH. About what?

MORRIS. Hell, man. The future. Is it going to be a small two-man farm, just big enough for me and you; or what is it going to be?

ZACHARIAH. *Ja*.

MORRIS. Right. We agree. Now, I'm saying we got to find the right place. [*Pause.*] Zach! What's the matter with you tonight?

ZACHARIAH. I was trying to remember what I was saying about Minnie. There was something else.

MORRIS. Now listen, Zach! You said yourself he doesn't come no more. So what are you doing thinking about him? Here am I putting our future to you and you don't even listen. The farm, Zach! Remember, man? The things we're going to do. Picture it! Picking our own fruit. Chasing those damned baboons helter-skelter in the *koppies*. Chopping the firewood trees . . . and a cow . . . and a horse . . . and little chickens. Isn't that exciting? Well, I haven't been sitting still.

[*Morris fetches an old map from the shelf over his bed.*]

Here, I want to show you something. You want to know what it is? A map . . . of Africa. Now, this is the point, Zach. Look—there . . . and there . . . and down here . . . Do you see it? Blank. Large, blank spaces. Not a town, not a road, not even those thin little red lines. And, notice, they're green. That means grass. I reckon we should be able to get a few acres in one of these blank spaces for next to nothing.

[*Zachariah, bored, goes to the window and looks out.*]

You listening, Zach?

ZACHARIAH. *Ja*.

MORRIS. This is not just talk, you know. It's serious. One fine day, you wait and see. We'll pack our things in something and get the hell and gone out of here. You say I don't want to get out? My reply is that I do, but I want to get right out. You think I like it here more than you? You should have been here this afternoon, Zach. The wind was blowing again. Coming this way it was, right across the lake. You should have smelt it, man. I'm telling you that water has gone bad. Really rotten! And what about the factories there on the other side? Hey? Lavatories all around us? They've left no room for a man to breathe in this world. But when we go, Zach, together, and we got a place to go, our farm in the future . . . that will be different.

[*Zachariah has been at the window all the time, staring out. He now sees something which makes him laugh. Just a chuckle to begin with, but with a suggestion of lechery.*]

What's so funny?

ZACHARIAH. Come here.

MORRIS. What's there?

ZACHARIAH. Two donkeys, man. You know.

[*Morris makes no move to the window. Zachariah stays there, laughing from time to time.*]

MORRIS. Yes. It's not just talk. When you bring your pay home tomorrow and we put away the usual, guess what we will have, Zach? Go on, guess. Forty-five rands. If it wasn't for me you wouldn't have nothing. Ever think about that? You talk about going out, but forty-five rands—

ZACHARIAH [*breaking off in the middle of a laugh*]. Hey! I remember now! By hell! About Minnie. [*His voice expresses vast disbelief.*] How did I forget a thing like that? It was . . . ja . . . ja . . . It was a woman! That's what we had when we went out at night. Woman!

[*Morris doesn't move. He stares at Zachariah blankly. When the latter pauses for a second, Morris speaks again in an almost normal voice.*]

MORRIS. Supper's ready.

[*Zachariah loses the train of his thought, as with the alarm clock, earlier. Morris sits down.*]

So . . . where were we? Yes. Our plans. When, Zach? That's the next thing we got to think about. Should we take our

chance with a hundred rands, one hundred and fifty? I mean
. . . we could even wait till there is three hundred, isn't that so?

[*Morris has already started on his supper. As if hypnotized by the sound of the other man's voice Zachariah fetches a chair and sits.*]

So what are we going to do, you ask? This. Find out what the deposit, cash, on a small two-man farm, in one of those blank spaces, is. Take some bread, man. [*Offering a slice.*]

ZACHARIAH. No! [*Hurls his slice of bread into a corner of the shack.*]

MORRIS. What's this?

[*Zachariah sweeps away the plate of food in front of him.*]

Zach!

ZACHARIAH. You're not going to make me forget. I won't. I'm not going to. We had woman I tell you. [*Pounding the table with his fists.*] Woman! Woman! Woman!

MORRIS. Do you still want the farm?

ZACHARIAH. Shut up! I won't listen.

[*Jumps up and rushes across to the other side of the room where his jacket is hanging, and begins to put it on.*]

What do you think I am, hey? Two legs and trousers. I'm a man. And in this world there is also woman, and the one has got to get the other. Even donkeys know that. What I want to know now, right this very now, is why me, Zach, a man, for a whole miserable year has had none. I was doing all right before that, wasn't I? Minnie used to come. He had a bottle, or I had a bottle, but we both had a good time, for a long time. And then you came . . . and then . . . and then . . . [*Pause.*]

MORRIS. Go on . . . say it.

ZACHARIAH. . . . . then you came. That's all.

[*Zachariah's violence is ebbing away. Perplexity takes its place.*]

You knocked on the door. Friday night. I remember, I got a fright. A knocking on my door on Friday night? On my door? Who? Not Minnie. Minnie's coming all right, but not like that. So I had a look, and it was you standing there, and you said something, hey? What did I say? 'Come in.' Didn't I? 'Come in,' I said. And when we had eaten I said, 'Come out with me and a friend of mine, called Minnie.' Then you said: 'Zach, let us spend tonight talking.' *Ja*, that's it. That's all. A whole year of spending tonights talking, talking. I'm sick of talking. I'm sick of this room.

MORRIS. I know, Zach. [*He speaks quietly, soothingly.*] That's why we got plans for the future.

ZACHARIAH. But I was in here ten years without plans and never needed them!

MORRIS. Time, Zach. It passes.

ZACHARIAH. I was in here ten years and didn't worry about my feet, or a future, or having supper on time! But I had fun and Minnie's music!

MORRIS. That's life for you, Zach. The passing of time, and worthless friends.

ZACHARIAH. I want woman.

MORRIS. I see. I see that, Zach. Believe me, I do. But let me think about it. Okay? Now have some supper and I'll think about it.

[*Morris puts his own plate of food in front of Zachariah and then moves around the room picking up the food that Zachariah swept to the floor.*]

You get fed up with talking, I know, Zach. But it helps, man. [*At the window.*] You find the answers to things, like we are going to find the answer to your problem. I mean . . . look what it's done for us already. Our plans! Our future! You should be grateful, man. And remember what I said. You're not the only one who's sick of this room. It also gets me down. [*Turning to Zachariah, leaving the window.*] Have you noticed, Zach, the days are getting shorter, the nights longer? Autumn is in our smelly air. It's the time I came back, hey! About a year ago! We should have remembered what day it was, though. Would have made a good birthday, don't you think? A candle on a cake for the day that Morris came back to Zach.

[*Zachariah leaves the table and goes to his bed.*]

You finished?

ZACHARIAH. *Ja.*

MORRIS. [*Pause. Morris makes the sandwiches.*] Has it helped, Zach?

ZACHARIAH. What?

MORRIS. The talking.

ZACHARIAH. Helped what?

MORRIS. About . . . woman.

ZACHARIAH. It's still there, Morrie. You said you was going to think about it and me.

MORRIS. I'm still busy, Zach. It takes time. Shall I talk some more?

ZACHARIAH. Let me!

[*He speaks eagerly. The first sign of life since the outburst.*]

Let me talk about . . . woman.

MORRIS. You think it wise?

ZACHARIAH. You said it helps. I want to help.

MORRIS. Go on.

ZACHARIAH. You know what I was remembering, Morrie? As I sat there?

MORRIS. No.

ZACHARIAH. Guess.

MORRIS. I can't.

ZACHARIAH. [*Soft, nostalgic smile.*] The first one. My very first one. You was already gone. It was in those years. [*Sigh.*] Her name was Connie.

MORRIS. That's a lovely name, Zach.

ZACHARIAH. Connie Ferreira.

MORRIS. You were happy, hey?

ZACHARIAH. *Ja.*

MORRIS. Don't be shy. Tell me more.

ZACHARIAH. We were young. Her mother did the washing. Connie used to buy blue soap from the Chinaman on the corner.

MORRIS. Your sweetheart, hey!

ZACHARIAH. I waited for her.

MORRIS. Was it true love?

ZACHARIAH. She called me a black *hotnot*, the bitch, so I waited for her. She had tits like fruits and I was waiting in the bushes.

MORRIS [*absolute loss of interest*]. Yes, Zach.

ZACHARIAH. She was coming along alone. Hell! Don't I remember Connie now! Coming along alone she was and I was
waiting in the bushes. [*Laugh.*] She got a fright, she did. She
tried to fight, to bite . . .

MORRIS. All right, Zach!

ZACHARIAH. She might have screamed, but when I had
her . . .

MORRIS. All right, Zach! [*Pause.*]

ZACHARIAH. That was Connie. [*He broods.*]

MORRIS. Feeling better?

ZACHARIAH. A little.

MORRIS. Talking helps, doesn't it? I said so. You find the
answers to things.

ZACHARIAH. Talking to one would help me even more.

MORRIS. [*Pause.*] You mean to a woman?

ZACHARIAH. I'm telling you, Morrie, I really mean it, man.
With all my heart.

MORRIS [*the idea is coming*]. There's a thought there, Zach.

ZACHARIAH. There is?

MORRIS. In fact I think I've got it.

ZACHARIAH. What?

MORRIS. The answer to your problem.

ZACHARIAH. Woman?

MORRIS. That's it! You said talking to one would help you,
didn't you? So what about writing? Just as good, isn't it, if she
writes back?

ZACHARIAH. Who . . . who you talking about?

MORRIS. A pen-pal. Zach! A corresponding pen-pal of the
opposite sex! Don't you know them? [*Zachariah's face is blank.*]
It's a woman, you see! [*Looking for newspaper.*] She wants a man
friend, but she's in another town, so she writes to him—to
you!

ZACHARIAH. No, I don't know her.

MORRIS. You will. You're her pen-pal!

ZACHARIAH. I don't write letters.

MORRIS. I will write them for you.

ZACHARIAH. Then it's your pen-pal.

MORRIS. No, Zach. You tell me what to say. You see, she writes to you. She doesn't even know about me. Can't you see it, man? A letter to Mr Zachariah Pietersen—from her.

ZACHARIAH. I don't read letters.

MORRIS. I'll read them to you.

ZACHARIAH. From a woman.

MORRIS. From a woman. You can take your pick.

ZACHARIAH [*now really interested*]. Hey!

MORRIS. There's so many.

ZACHARIAH. Is that so!

MORRIS. Big ones, small ones.

ZACHARIAH. What do you know about that!

MORRIS. Young ones, old ones.

ZACHARIAH. No. Not the old ones, Morrie. [*Excited.*] The young ones, on the small side.

MORRIS. Just take your pick.

ZACHARIAH. Okay. I will.

MORRIS. Now listen, Zach. When you get your pay tomorrow, go to a shop and ask for a newspaper with pen-pals.

ZACHARIAH. With pen-pals.

MORRIS. That's it. We'll study them and you can make your pick.

ZACHARIAH. And I can say what I like? Hey! What do you know! Pen-pals!

[*The alarm-clock rings.*]

Pen-pals!

[*Zachariah flops back on his bed laughing. Morris drifts to the window.*]

MORRIS. Wind's coming up. You sleepy?

ZACHARIAH. It's been a long day.

MORRIS. Okay, I'll cut it short. Your turn to choose the reading tonight, Zach.

[*Morris fetches the Bible from the shelf over his bed. He hands it to Zachariah who, with his eyes tightly closed, opens it and brings his finger down on the page.*]

Four?

[*Zachariah nods. Morris reads.*]

'And if thou bring an oblation of a meat offering baken in the oven, it shall be unleavened cakes of fine flour mingled with oil, or unleavened wafers anointed with oil; and if thy oblation be a meat offering baken in a pan, it shall be of fine flour, unleavened, mingled with oil. Thou shalt part it in pieces and pour oil thereon. It is a meat offering.'

ZACHARIAH. Sounds nice, hey?

MORRIS. You need an oven, Zach. Think of those you love. Ask for what you really want.

ZACHARIAH. Dear God, please bring back Minnie.

MORRIS. Is that all?

ZACHARIAH. Amen.

[*Morris replaces the Bible, finds needle and cotton, and then takes Zachariah's coat to the table.*]

MORRIS. I'm helping you, aren't I, Zach?

ZACHARIAH. *Ja.*

MORRIS. I want to believe that. You see . . . [*Pause.*] There was all those years, when I was away.

ZACHARIAH. Why did you come back?

MORRIS. I was passing this way.

ZACHARIAH. So why did you stay?

MORRIS. We are brothers, remember.

[*A few seconds pass in silence. Morris threads his needle and then starts working on a tear in Zachariah's coat.*]

That's a word, hey! Brothers! There's a broody sound for you if ever there was. I mean . . . take the others. Father. What is there for us in . . . Father? We never knew him. Even Mother. She died and we were young. That's the trouble with 'Mother'. We never said it enough.

[*He tries it.*]

Mother. Mother! Yes. Just a touch of sadness in it, and a grey dress on Sundays, soapsuds on brown hands. That's the lot. Father, Mother, and the sisters we haven't got. But brothers! Try it. Brotherhood. Brother-in-arms, each other's arms.

Brotherly love. That's a big one, hey, Zach? Zach?

[*He looks at Zachariah's bed.*]

Zachie? Zachariah!

[*He is asleep. Morris takes the lamp, goes to the bed, and looks down at the sleeping man. He returns to the table, picks up the Bible and after an inward struggle speaks in a solemn, 'Sunday' voice.*]

'And he said, what hast thou done? The voice of thy brother's blood crieth unto me from the ground. And now art thou cursed from the earth, which hath opened her mouth to receive thy brother's blood from thy hand. When thou tillest the ground it shall not henceforth yield unto thee her strength, a fugitive and a vagabond shalt thou be in the earth.'

[*Pause.*]

Oh Lord, Lord. So I turned around on the road, and came back. About this time, a year ago. It could have been today. I remember turning off the road and heading this way. I thought: it looks the same. It was. Because when I reached the first *pondokkies* and the thin dogs, the wind turned and brought the stink from the lake. No one recognized me after all those years. I could see they weren't sure, and wanting to say 'Sir' when I asked them the way. Six down, they said, pointing to the water's edge. So then there was only time left for a few short thoughts between counting doors. Will he be home? Will I be welcome? Be forgiven? Be brave, Morris! I held my breath . . . knocked . . . and waited . . .

[*Pause.*]

You were wearing this old coat . . .

[*Morris puts on Zachariah's coat. It is several sizes too large.*]

It's been a big help to me, this warm, old coat. You get right inside a man when you can wrap up in the smell of him. It prepared me for your flesh, Zach. Because your flesh, you see, has an effect on me. The sight of it, the feel of it . . . It feels, you see . . . I saw you again after all those years . . . and it hurt, man.

67

SCENE TWO

The next evening.

Zachariah sits disconsolately on the bed, his feet in the basin. Morris is studying a newspaper.

MORRIS. Well, Zach, you ready? There's three women here. The young ladies Ethel Lange, Nellie de Wet, and Betty Jones.

ZACHARIAH. So what do we do?

MORRIS. I'll get the ball rolling with this thought. They are all pretty good names. Ethel, Nellie, and Betty. Good, simple, decent, common names. About equal, I'd say.

ZACHARIAH [*hopefully*]. There's no Connie there, is there Morrie?

MORRIS. No. Now, before you decide, let me tell you about them.

ZACHARIAH. What do you know about them?

MORRIS. It's written down here. That's why you bought the paper. Listen . . . [*Reads.*] 'Ethel Lange, 10 de Villiers Street, Oudtshoorn. I am eighteen years old and well-developed and would like to correspond with a gent of sober habits and a good outlook on life. My interests are nature, rock-and-roll, swimming, and a happy future. My motto is, "Rolling stones gather no moss." Please note: I promise to reply faithfully.' How's that?

ZACHARIAH. Well-developed.

MORRIS. She gives you a clear picture, hey! Here's the next one. [*Reads.*] 'Nellie de Wet' . . . she's in Bloemfontein . . . 'Twenty-two and no strings attached. Would like letters from men of the same age or older. My interests are beauty contests and going out. A snap with the first letter, please.' [*Pause.*] That's all there is to her. I think I preferred Ethel.

ZACHARIAH. *Ja.* And what do I know how old I am?

MORRIS. Exactly, Zach! 'The same age or older?' Where does she think she comes from?

ZACHARIAH. Bloemfontein.

MORRIS. Yes. Last one. [*Reads.*] 'Betty Jones. Roodepoort.

Young and pleasing personality. I'd like to correspond with gentlemen friends of maturity. No teenagers need reply. My hobby at the moment is historical films, but I'm prepared to go back to last year's, which was autograph hunting. I would appreciate a photograph.' That one's got a education. Anyway . . . it's up to you. Ethel, Nellie, or Betty?

ZACHARIAH [*after thinking about it*]. Hey, hey, Morrie! Let's take all three.

MORRIS. No, Zach.

ZACHARIAH. *Ag*, come on, man.

MORRIS. You don't understand.

ZACHARIAH. Just once, just for sports.

MORRIS. I don't think they'd allow that.

ZACHARIAH. Oh.

MORRIS. No, they wouldn't.

[*Pause, emphatic.*]

Listen, Zach, you must take this serious.

ZACHARIAH. Okay.

MORRIS [*losing patience*]. Well, it's no good saying 'Okay' like that!

ZACHARIAH. Okay!

MORRIS. What's the use, Zach? You ask me to help you, and when I do, you're not interested no more. What's the matter, man?

ZACHARIAH. I can't get hot about a name on a piece of paper. It's not real to me.

MORRIS [*outraged*]. Not real! [*Reads.*] 'I am eighteen years old and well-developed' . . . eighteen years old and well-developed! If I called that Connie it would be real enough, wouldn't it?

ZACHARIAH [*his face lighting up*]. *Ja!*

MORRIS. So the only difference is a name. This is Ethel and not Connie . . . which makes no difference to being eighteen years old and well-developed! Think, man!

ZACHARIAH. [*Without hesitation.*] Look, Morrie, I'll take her.

MORRIS. That's better. So it's going to be Miss Ethel Lange

from Oudtshoorn, who would like to correspond with a gent of sober habits and a good outlook on life. [*Putting down the paper.*] Yes, she's the one for you all right. And I know what we do. How about asking Ethel to take a snapshot of herself? So we can see what her outlook is. Then—just think of it—you can see her, hear from her, write to her, correspond with her, post your letter off to her . . . Hell, man! What more do you want! [*Zachariah smiles.*] No! That's something else. This is pen-pals, and you got yourself Ethel in Oudtshoorn.

[*Morris moves to the table where he sorts out a piece of writing-paper, a pencil, and an envelope.*]

I've got everything ready. One day I must show you how. Maybe have a go at a letter yourself. Address in the top right-hand corner. Mr Zachariah Pietersen, Korsten, P. O. Port Elizabeth. Okay, now take aim and fire away. [*He waits for Zachariah.*] Well?

ZACHARIAH. What?

MORRIS. Speak to Ethel.

ZACHARIAH [*shy*]. Go jump in a lake, man.

MORRIS. No, listen, Zach. I'm sitting here ready to write. You must speak up.

ZACHARIAH. What?

MORRIS. To begin with, address her.

ZACHARIAH. What?

MORRIS. Address her.

ZACHARIAH. Oudtshoorn.

MORRIS. No, no, Zach. Look, imagine there was a woman, and you want to say something to her, what would you say? Go on.

ZACHARIAH. Hey! Cookie . . . or . . . *Bokkie* . . .

MORRIS [*quickly*]. Okay, Zach . . . You're getting hot, but that is what we call a personal address, you only use it later. This time you say: 'Dear Ethel'.

ZACHARIAH. Just like that?

MORRIS. You get her on friendly terms. Now comes the intro-duction. [*Writes.*] 'With reply to your advert for a pen-pal, I hereby write.' [*Holds up the writing paper.*] Now tell her who you are and where you are.

70

ZACHARIAH. How?

MORRIS. I am . . . and so on.

ZACHARIAH. I am Zach and I . . .

MORRIS. . . . ariah Pietersen . . .

ZACHARIAH. And I am at Korsten.

MORRIS. 'As you will see from the above.'

ZACHARIAH. What's that?

MORRIS. Something you must always add in letters, Zach. [*Newspaper.*] Now she says here: 'My interests are nature, rock-and-roll, swimming, and a happy future.' Well, what do you say to that?

ZACHARIAH. Shit! [*Pause, frozen stare from Morris.*] Oh, sorry, Morrie, sorry. 'Nature and a happy future.' *Ja*. Well, good luck! Good luck, Ethel. How's that?

MORRIS. Not bad. A little short, though. How about: I notice your plans, and wish you good luck with them.

ZACHARIAH. Sure, sure. Put that there.

MORRIS [*writes, then returns to the newspaper*]. '. . . plans, and wish you good luck with them.' Okay, next—'My motto is: "Rolling stones gather no moss".' [*Pause.*] That's tricky.

ZACHARIAH. *Ja*, I can see that.

MORRIS. What does she mean?

ZACHARIAH. I wonder.

MORRIS. Wait! I think I've got it. How about: 'Too many cooks spoil the broth'? That's my favourite.

ZACHARIAH. Why not? Why not, I ask?

MORRIS. Then it's agreed. [*Writes.*] 'Experience has taught me to make my motto: "Too many cooks spoil the broth".' Now let's get a little bit general, Zach.

ZACHARIAH [*yawning*]. Just as you say.

MORRIS [*after a pause*]. Well, it's your letter.

ZACHARIAH. Just a little bit general. Not too much, hey?

MORRIS [*not fooled by the feigned interest. Pause*]. I can make a suggestion.

ZACHARIAH. That's fine. Put that down there, too.

MORRIS. No, Zach. Here it is. How about: 'I have a brother who has seen Oudtshoorn twice.'

ZACHARIAH. You.

MORRIS. Yes.

ZACHARIAH. Maybe.

MORRIS. You mean you don't like it?

ZACHARIAH. Tell you what. Put down there: 'I'd like to see Oudtshoorn. I've heard about it from . . . someone. I'd like to see you, too. Send me a photo.'

MORRIS. '. . . please' . . . I'm near the bottom now.

ZACHARIAH. That's all.

MORRIS. 'Please write soon. Yours . . .'

ZACHARIAH. Hers?

MORRIS. '. . . faithfully. Zachariah Pietersen.'

[*Zachariah prepares for bed. Morris addresses and seals the envelope.*] I'll get this off tomorrow. Now remember, this is your letter, and what comes back is going to be your reply.

ZACHARIAH. And yours?

MORRIS. Mine?

ZACHARIAH. There's still Nellie or Betty. Plenty of big words there, as I remember.

MORRIS. One's enough, Zach. [*Alarm-clock rings.*] Bed time. [*Takes down his Bible.*] My turn to choose the reading tonight, Zach. [*Chooses a passage.*] Matthew. I like Matthew. [*Reads.*] 'And Asa begat Josaphat, and Josaphat begat Joram, and Joram begat Ozias; and Ozias begat Joatham, and Joatham begat Achaz, and Achaz begat Ezekias; and Ezekias begat Manassas, and Manassas begat Amon, and Amon begat . . .' [*Pause.*] That must have been a family. [*Puts away the Bible and prepares his own bed.*] Why you looking at me like that, Zach?

ZACHARIAH. I'm thinking.

MORRIS. Out with it. Let's hear!

ZACHARIAH. You ever had a woman, Morris?

[*Morris looks at Zachariah blankly, then pretends he hasn't heard.*]

MORRIS. What do you mean?

ZACHARIAH. Come on, you know what I mean.

72

MORRIS. Why?

ZACHARIAH. Have—you—ever—had—woman? Why have I never thought of that before? You been here a long time now, and never once did you go out, or speak to me about woman. Not like Minnie. Anything the matter with you?

MORRIS. Not like Minnie! What's that mean? Not like Minnie! Maybe it's not nice to be like Minnie. Or maybe I just don't want to be like Minnie! Ever thought about that? That there might be another way, a different way? Listen. You think I don't know there's women in this world, that I haven't got two legs and trousers too? That I haven't longed for beauty? Well, I do. But that's not what you're talking about, is it? That's not what Minnie means, hey! That's two bloody donkeys on a road full of stones and Connie crying in the bushes. Well, you're right about that, Zach. I am not interested. I touched something else once, with my life and these hands . . . just touched it and felt warmth and softness and wanted it like I've never wanted anything in my whole life. Ask me why I didn't take it when I touched it. That's the question. Do you want to know why, Zach? Do you? Zach? [*Pause, then softly.*] Zachariah?

[*Zachariah is asleep. Morris covers him with a blanket.*]

SCENE THREE

A few days later.

Morris is at the table counting their savings—banknotes and silver. The alarm-clock rings. He sweeps the money into a tin which he then carefully hides among the pots on the kitchen-dresser. Next he resets the clock and prepares the footbath as in the first scene. Zachariah appears, silent and sullen, goes straight to the bed, where he sits.

MORRIS. You look tired tonight, old fellow.

[*Zachariah looks at him askance.*]

Today too long?

ZACHARIAH. What's this 'old fellow' thing you got hold of tonight?

MORRIS. Just a figure of speaking, Zach. The Englishman would say 'old boy' . . . but we don't like that 'boy' business, hey?

ZACHARIAH. *Ja.* They call a man a boy. You got a word for that, Morrie?

MORRIS. Long or short?

ZACHARIAH. Squashed, like it didn't fit the mouth.

MORRIS. I know the one you mean.

ZACHARIAH. *Ja,* then say it.

MORRIS. Prejudice.

ZACHARIAH. Pre-ja-dis.

MORRIS. Injustice!

ZACHARIAH. That's all out of shape as well.

MORRIS. Inhumanity!

ZACHARIAH. No. That's when he makes me stand at the gate.

MORRIS. Am I right in thinking you were there again today?

ZACHARIAH. All day long.

MORRIS. You tried to go back to pots?

ZACHARIAH. I tried to go back to pots. 'My feet', I said, 'are killing me.'

MORRIS. And then?

ZACHARIAH. He said, 'Go to the gate or go to hell . . . Boy!'

MORRIS. He said 'boy' as well?

ZACHARIAH. He did.

MORRIS. In one sentence?

ZACHARIAH. Prejudice and inhumanity in one sentence!

[*He starts to work off one shoe with the other foot and then dips the bare foot into the basin of water. He will not get as far as taking off the other shoe.*]

When your feet are bad, you feel it, man.

[*Morris starts helping Zachariah take off his coat. At this point Morris finds an envelope in the inside pocket of Zachariah's coat. He examines it secretly. Zachariah broods on, one foot in the basin.*]

MORRIS. Zach, did you stop by the Post Office on your way back?

ZACHARIAH. *Ja*. There was a letter there.

MORRIS. I know there was. [*Holding up the envelope.*] I just found it.

ZACHARIAH. Good.

MORRIS. What do you mean, 'good'?

ZACHARIAH. Good, like 'okay'.

MORRIS [*excited and annoyed*]. What's the matter with you?

ZACHARIAH. What's the matter with me?

MORRIS. This is your pen-pal. This is your reply from Ethel!

ZACHARIAH. In Oudtshoorn.

MORRIS. But Zach! You must get excited, man! Don't you want to know what she said?

ZACHARIAH. Sure.

MORRIS. Shall we open it then?

ZACHARIAH. Why not!

MORRIS [*tears open the letter*]. By God, she did it! She sent you a picture of herself.

ZACHARIAH [*first flicker of interest*]. She did?

MORRIS. So this is Ethel!

ZACHARIAH. Morrie . . . ?

MORRIS. Eighteen years . . . and fully . . . developed.

ZACHARIAH. Let me see, man!

[*He grabs the photograph. The certainty and excitement fade from Morris's face. He is obviously perplexed by something.*]

Hey! Not bad. Now that's what I call a goosie. Good for old Oudtshoorn. You don't get them like this over here. That I can tell you. Not with a watch! Pretty smart, too. Nice hair. Just look at those locks. And how's that for a wall she's standing against? Ever seen a wall like that, as big as that, in Korsten? I mean it's made of bricks, isn't it!

MORRIS [*snatching the photograph out of Zachariah's hand and taking it to the window where he has a good look*]. Zach, let me have another look at her.

ZACHARIAH. Hey! What's the matter with you! It's my pen-pal, isn't it? It is!

MORRIS. Keep quiet, Zach!

ZACHARIAH. What's this 'keep quiet'?

[*Morris throws the photograph down on the bed and finds the letter, which he reads feverishly. Zachariah picks up the photograph and continues his study.*]

ZACHARIAH. You're acting like you never seen a woman in your life. Why don't you get a pen-pal? Maybe one's not enough.

MORRIS [*having finished the letter, his agitation is now even more pronounced*]. That newspaper, Zach. Where is that newspaper?

ZACHARIAH. How should I know?

MORRIS [*anguished*]. Think, man!

ZACHARIAH. You had it. [*Morris is scratching around frantically.*] What's the matter with you tonight? Maybe you threw it away.

MORRIS. No. I was keeping it in case . . . [*Finds it.*] Thank God! Oh, please, God, now make it that I am wrong!

[*He takes a look at the newspaper, pages through it, and then drops it. He stands quite still, unnaturally calm after the frenzy of the previous few seconds.*]

You know what you done, don't you?

ZACHARIAH. Me?

MORRIS. Who was it, then? Me?

ZACHARIAH. But what?

76

MORRIS. Who wanted woman?

ZACHARIAH. Oh. Me.

MORRIS. Right. Who's been carrying on about Minnie, and Connie, and good times? Not me.

ZACHARIAH. Morrie! What are you talking about?

MORRIS. That photograph.

ZACHARIAH. I've seen it.

MORRIS. Have another look.

ZACHARIAH [*he does*]. It's Ethel.

MORRIS. Miss Ethel Lange to you!

ZACHARIAH. Okay, I looked. Now what!

MORRIS. Can't you see, man! Ethel Lange is a white woman!

[*Pause. They look at each other in silence.*]

ZACHARIAH [*slowly*]. You mean that this Ethel . . . here . . .

MORRIS. Is a white woman!

ZACHARIAH. How do you know?

MORRIS. Oh for God's sake, Zach—use your eyes. Anyway, that paper you bought was white. There's no news about our sort.

ZACHARIAH [*studying the photo*]. Hey—you're right, Morrie. [*Delighted.*] You're damn well right. And this white woman has written to me, a *hot-not*, a *swartgat*. This white woman thinks I'm a white man. That I like!

[*Zachariah bursts into laughter. Morris jumps forward and snatches the photograph out of his hand.*]

Hey! What are you going to do?

MORRIS. What do you think?

ZACHARIAH. Read it.

MORRIS. I'm going to burn it.

ZACHARIAH. No!

MORRIS. Yes.

ZACHARIAH [*jumps up and comes to grips with Morris who, after a short struggle, is thrown violently to the floor. Zachariah picks up the letter and the photograph. He stands looking down at Morris for a few seconds, amazed at what he has done*]. No, Morrie. You're not going to burn it, Morrie.

MORRIS [*vehemently*]. Yes, burn the bloody thing! Destroy it!

ZACHARIAH. But it's my pen-pal, Morris. Now, isn't it? Doesn't it say here: 'Mr Zachariah Pietersen'? Well, that's me . . . isn't it? It is. My letter. You just don't go and burn another man's letter, Morrie.

MORRIS. But it's an error, Zach! Can't you see? The whole thing is an error.

ZACHARIAH. Read the letter, man. I don't know.

[*The alarm-clock rings.*]

MORRIS. Supper time.

ZACHARIAH. Later.

MORRIS. Listen—

ZACHARIAH. Letter first.

MORRIS. Then can I burn it?

ZACHARIAH. Read the letter first, man. Let's hear it, what it says. [*Handing Morris the letter.*] No funny business, hey!

MORRIS [*reading*]. 'Dear Zach, many thanks for your letter You asked me for a snap, so I'm sending you it. Do you like it? That's my brother's foot sticking in the picture behind the bench on the side—'

ZACHARIAH. Hey! She's right! Here it is.

MORRIS. 'Cornelius is a . . . policeman.' [*Pause.*] 'He's got a motor-bike, and I been with him to the dam, on the back. My best friend is Lucy van Tonder. Both of us hates Oudtshoorn, man. How is Port Elizabeth? There's only two movies here, so we don't know what to do on the other nights. That's why I want pen-pals. How about a picture of you? You got a car? All for now. Cheerio. Ethel. P.S. Please write soon.'

(*Morris folds the letter.*)

ZACHARIAH [*gratefully*]. Oh—thank you, Morrie.

[*Holds out his hand for the letter.*]

MORRIS. Can I burn it now, Zach?

ZACHARIAH. Burn it! It's an all right letter, man. A little bit of this and a little bit of that.

MORRIS. Like her brother being a policeman.

ZACHARIAH [*ignoring the last remark*]. Hey—supper ready yet,

78

man? Let's talk after supper, man. I'm hungry. What you got for supper, Morrie?

MORRIS. Boiled eggs and chips.

ZACHARIAH. Hey, that's wonderful, Morrie. Hey! We never had that before.

MORRIS [*sulking*]. It was meant to be a surprise.

ZACHARIAH. But that's wonderful.

[*Zachariah is full of vigour and life.*]

No, I mean it, Morrie. Cross my heart, and hope to die. Boiled eggs and chips! Boiled eggs and chips . . . Boiled eggs and chips . . . I never even knew you could do it.

[*Zachariah takes his place at the table, and stands the photograph in front of him. When Morris brings the food to the table, he sees it and hesitates.*]

What's it got here on the back, Morrie?

MORRIS [*examines the back of the photograph*]. 'To Zach, with love, from Ethel.'

[*Another burst of laughter from Zachariah. Morris leaves the table abruptly.*]

ZACHARIAH [*calmly continuing with his meal*]. Hey—what's the matter?

MORRIS. I'm not hungry tonight.

ZACHARIAH. Oh, you mean, you don't like to hear me laugh?

MORRIS. It's not that . . . Zach.

ZACHARIAH. But it is. It's funny, man. She and me. Of course, it wouldn't be so funny if it was you who was pally with her.

MORRIS. What does that mean?

ZACHARIAH. Don't you know?

MORRIS. No. So will you please tell me?

ZACHARIAH. You never seen yourself, Morrie?

MORRIS [*trembling with emotion*]. I'm warning you Zach. Just be careful of where your words are taking you!

ZACHARIAH. Okay. Okay. Okay—

[*Eats in silence.*]

You was telling me about Oudtshoorn the other day. How far you say it was?

MORRIS [*viciously*]. Hundreds of miles.

ZACHARIAH. So far, hey?

MORRIS. Don't fool yourself, Zach. It's not far enough for safety's sake. Cornelius has got a motorbike, remember.

ZACHARIAH. *Ja.* But we don't write to him, man.

MORRIS. Listen. Zach, if you think for one moment that I'm going to write . . .

ZACHARIAH. Think? Think? Who says? I been eating my supper. It was good, Morrie. Boiled eggs and chips, tasty.

MORRIS. Don't try to change the subject-matter!

ZACHARIAH. Who? Me?

MORRIS. *Ja*—you.

ZACHARIAH. I like that. You mean, what's the matter with you? You was the one that spoke about pen-pals first. Not me.

MORRIS. So here it comes at last. I've been waiting for it. I'm to blame, am I? All right. I'll take the blame. I always did, didn't I? But this is where it ends. I'm telling you now, Zach, burn that letter, because when they come around here and ask me, I'll say I got nothing to do with it.

ZACHARIAH. Burn this letter! What's wrong with this letter?

MORRIS. Ethel Lange is a white woman!

ZACHARIAH. Wait . . . wait . . . not so fast, Morrie. I'm a sort of a slow man. We were talking about this letter, not her. Now tell me, what's wrong with what you did read? Does she call me names? No. Does she laugh at me? No. Does she swear at me? No. Just a simple letter with a little bit of this and a little bit of that. Here comes the clue. What sort of chap is it that throws away a few kind words? Hey, Morrie? Aren't they, as you say, precious things these days? And this pretty picture of a lovely girl? I burn it! What sort of doing is that? Bad. Think, man, think of Ethel, man. Think! Sitting up there in Oudtshoorn with Lucy, waiting . . . and waiting . . . and waiting . . . for what? For nothing. For why? Because bad Zach Pietersen burnt it. No, Morrie. Good is good, and fair is fair. I may be a shade of black, but I go gently as a man.

MORRIS [*pause*]. Are you finished now, Zach? Good, because I want to remind you, Zach, that when I was writing to her you weren't even interested in a single thing I said. But now, suddenly, now you are! Why? Why, I ask myself . . . and a suspicious little voice answers: is it maybe because she's white?

ZACHARIAH. You want to hear me say it?

[*Morris says nothing.*]

It's because she's white! I like this little white girl! I like the thought of this little white girl. I'm telling you I like the thought of this little white Ethel better than our plans, or future, or foot salts or any other damned thing in here. It's the best thought I ever had and I'm keeping it, and don't try no tricks like trying to get it away from me. Who knows? You might get to liking it too, Morrie.

[*Morris says nothing. Zachariah comes closer.*]

Ja. There's a thought there. What about you, Morrie? You never had it before—that thought? A man like you, specially you, always thinking so many things! A man like you who's been places! You're always telling me about the places you been. Wasn't there ever no white woman thereabouts? I mean . . . you must have smelt them someplace. That sweet, white smell, they leave it behind, you know. [*Nudging Morris.*] Come on, confess. Of course, you did. Hey? I bet you had that thought all the time. I bet you been having it in here. Hey? You should have shared it, Morrie. I'm a man with a taste for thoughts these days. It hurts to think you didn't share a good one like that with your brother. Giving me all the other shit about future and plans, and then keeping the real goosie for yourself. You weren't scared, were you? That I'd tell? Come on. Confess. You were. A little bit poopy. I've noticed that. But you needn't worry now. I'm a man for keeping a secret, and anyway, we'll play this very careful . . . very, very careful. Ethel won't never know about us, and I know how to handle that brother. Mustn't let a policeman bugger you about, man. So write. Write! We'll go gently with this one. There'll be others. Later.

[*Morris is defeated. He sits at the table. Zachariah fetches paper and pencil.*]

So we'll take her on friendly terms again. [*Pause.*] 'Dear Ethel,'

[*Morris writes.*] 'I think you'd like to know I got your letter, and the picture. I'd say Oudtshoorn seems okay. You were quite okay too. I would like to send you a picture of me, but it's this way. It's winter down here. The light is bad, the lake is black, the birds have gone. Wait for spring, when things improve. Okay? Good. I heard you ask about my car. Yes. I have it. We pumped the tyres today. And tomorrow I think I'll put in some petrol. I'd like to take you for a drive, Ethel, and Lucy too. In fact, I'd like to drive both of you. They say over here I'm fast. Ethel, I'll tell you this. If I could drive you, Ethel, and Lucy too, I'd do it so fast, fast, fast, fast, fast—'

MORRIS. Okay, Zach!

ZACHARIAH [*pulling himself together*]. '*Ja*! But don't worry. I got brakes.' [*Pause.*] 'I notice your brother got boots. All policemen got boots. Good luck to him, anyway, and Lucy too. Write soon. Zachariah Pietersen.' [*Pause.*] Okay, Morrie. There, you see! Just a simple letter with a little bit of this and a little bit of that and nothing about some things. When Ethel gets it she'll say: 'He's okay. This Zachariah Pietersen is okay, Lucy!' Oh, say something, Morrie.

MORRIS. Zach, please listen to me. [*Pause.*] Let me burn it.

ZACHARIAH. My letter?

MORRIS. Yes.

ZACHARIAH. The one we just done?

MORRIS. Yes.

ZACHARIAH. Ethel's letter, now my letter!

[*He gets up and takes the letter in question away from Morris.*]
You're in a burning mood tonight, Morrie.

MORRIS. Please, Zach. You're going to get hurt.

ZACHARIAH [*aggression*]. Such as by who?

MORRIS. Ethel. Then yourself.

[*Zachariah laughs.*]
Oh yes. That. There in your hand. To Miss Ethel Lange. Oudtshoorn. You think that's a letter? I'm telling you it's a dream, and the most dangerous one. And now you have it on paper as well. That's what they call evidence, you know. [*Pause.*] Shit, Zach, I have a feeling about this business, man!

ZACHARIAH. Oh come on, cheer up, Morrie. It's not so bad.

MORRIS. But you're playing with fire, Zach.

ZACHARIAH. Maybe. But then I never had much to play with.

MORRIS. Didn't you?

ZACHARIAH. Don't you remember? You got the toys.

MORRIS. Did I?

ZACHARIAH. *Ja.* Like that top, Morrie. I have always remembered that brown stinkwood top. She gave me her old cottonreels to play with, but it wasn't the same. I wanted a top.

MORRIS. Who? Who gave me the top?

ZACHARIAH. Mother.

MORRIS. Mother!

ZACHARIAH. *Ja.* She said she only had one. There was always only one.

MORRIS. Zach, you're telling me a thing now!

ZACHARIAH. What? Did you forget her?

MORRIS. No, Zach. I meant the top. I can't remember that top. And what about her, Zach? There's a memory for you. I tried it out the other night. 'Mother', I said, 'Mother'! A sadness, I thought.

ZACHARIAH. *Ja.*

MORRIS. Just a touch of sadness.

ZACHARIAH. A soft touch with sadness.

MORRIS. And soapsuds on brown hands.

ZACHARIAH. And sore feet.

[*Pause. Morris looks at Zachariah.*]

MORRIS. What do you mean?

ZACHARIAH. There was her feet, man.

MORRIS. Who had feet?

ZACHARIAH. Mother, man.

MORRIS. I don't remember her feet, Zach.

ZACHARIAH [*serenely confident*]. There was her feet, man. The toes were crooked, the nails skew, and there was pain. They didn't fit the shoes.

MORRIS [*growing agitation*]. Zach, are you sure that wasn't somebody else?

ZACHARIAH. It was mother's feet. She let me feel the hardness and then pruned them down with a razor blade.

MORRIS. No, Zach. You got me worried now! A grey dress?

ZACHARIAH. Maybe.

MORRIS [*persistent*]. Going to church, remember? She wore it going to—

ZACHARIAH. The butcher shop! That's it! That's where she went.

MORRIS. What for?

ZACHARIAH. For tripe.

MORRIS. Tripe? Stop, Zach. Stop! This is beginning to sound like some other mother.

ZACHARIAH [*gently*]. How can that be?

MORRIS. Listen, Zach. Do you remember the songs she sang?

ZACHARIAH. Do I! [*He laughs and then sings:*]

'My skin is black
The soap is blue,
But the washing comes out white.

I took a man
On a Friday night;
Now I'm washing a baby too.

Just a little bit black,
And a little bit white,
He's a Capie through and through.'

[*Morris is staring at him in horror.*]

MORRIS. That wasn't what she sang to me. 'Lullabye baby', it was, 'You'll get to the top.' [*Anguish.*] This is some sort of terrible error. Wait . . . wait! I've got it . . . Oh, God, please let it be that I've got it! [*To Zachariah.*] How about the games we played? Think, Zach. Think carefully! There was one special one. Just me and you. I'll give you a clue. Toot-toot. Toot-toot.

ZACHARIAH [*thinking*]. Wasn't there an old car?

MORRIS. Where would it be?

ZACHARIAH. Rusting by the side of the road.

MORRIS. Could it be the ruins of an old Chevy, Zach?

ZACHARIAH. Yes, it could.

MORRIS. And can we say without tyres and wires and things?

ZACHARIAH. We may.

MORRIS. . . . and all the glass blown away by the wind?

ZACHARIAH. Dusty.

MORRIS. Deserted.

ZACHARIAH. Sting bees on the bonnet.

MORRIS. Webs in the windscreen.

ZACHARIAH. Nothing in the boot.

MORRIS. And us?

ZACHARIAH. In it.

MORRIS. We are? How?

ZACHARIAH. Side by side.

MORRIS. Like this?

[*He sits beside Zachariah.*]

ZACHARIAH. Uh-huh.

MORRIS. Doing what?

ZACHARIAH. Staring.

MORRIS. Not both of us!

ZACHARIAH. Me at the wheel, you at the window.

MORRIS. Okay. Now what?

ZACHARIAH. Now, I got this gear here and I'm going to go.

MORRIS. Where?

ZACHARIAH. To hell and gone, and we aren't coming back.

MORRIS. What will I do while you drive?

ZACHARIAH. You must tell me what we pass. Are you ready? Here we go!

[*Zachariah goes through the motion of driving a car. Morris looks eagerly out of the window.*]

MORRIS. We're slipping through the streets, passing houses and people on the pavements who are quite friendly and wave as we drive by. It's a fine, sunny sort of a day. What are we doing?

ZACHARIAH. Twenty-four.

MORRIS. Do you see that bus ahead of us?

85

[*They lean over to one side as Zachariah swings the wheel. Morris looks back.*]

Chock-a-block with early morning workers. Shame. And what about those children over there, going to school? Shame again. On such a nice day. What are we doing?

ZACHARIAH. Thirty-four.

MORRIS. That means we're coming to open country. The houses have given way to patches of green and animals and not so many people anymore. But they still wave . . . with their spades.

ZACHARIAH. Fifty.

MORRIS. You're going quite fast. You've killed a cat, flattened a frog, frightened a dog . . . who jumped!

ZACHARIAH. Sixty.

MORRIS. Passing trees, and haystacks, and sunshine, and the smoke from little houses drifting up . . . shooting by!

ZACHARIAH. Eighty!

MORRIS. Birds flying abreast, and bulls, billygoats, black sheep . . .

ZACHARIAH. One hundred!

MORRIS. . . . . cross a river, up a hill, to the top, coming down, down, down . . . stop! Stop!

ZACHARIAH [*slamming on the brakes*]. Eeeeeoooooooaah! [*Pause.*] Why?

MORRIS. Look! There's a butterfly.

ZACHARIAH. On your side?

MORRIS. Yours as well. Just look.

ZACHARIAH. All around us, hey!

MORRIS. This is rare, Zach! We've driven into a flock of butterflies.

ZACHARIAH. Butterflies! [*Smiles and then laughs.*]

MORRIS. We've found it, Zach. We've found it! This is our youth!

ZACHARIAH. And driving to hell and gone was our game.

MORRIS. Our best one! Hell, Zach, the things a man can forget!

ZACHARIAH. *Ja*, those were the days.

MORRIS. God knows.

ZACHARIAH. Goodness, hey!

MORRIS. They were that.

ZACHARIAH. And gladness too.

MORRIS. Making hay, man, come and play, man, while the sun is shining . . . which it did.

ZACHARIAH. Hey—what's that . . . that *nice* thing you say, Morrie?

MORRIS 'So sweet—

ZACHARIAH. Uh-huh.

MORRIS. '—did pass that summertime
Of youth and fruit upon the tree
When laughing boys and pretty girls
Did hop and skip and all were free.'

ZACHARIAH. Did *skop* and skip the pretty girls.

MORRIS. Hopscotch.

ZACHARIAH. That was it.

MORRIS We played our games, Zach.

ZACHARIAH. And now?

MORRIS. See for yourself, Zach. Here we are, later, and now there is Ethel as well and that makes me frightened.

ZACHARIAH. Sounds like another game.

MORRIS. Yes . . . but not ours this time. Hell, man, I often wonder.

ZACHARIAH. Same here.

MORRIS. I mean, where do they go, the good times, in a man's life?

ZACHARIAH. And the bad ones?

MORRIS. That's a thought. Where do *they* come from?

ZACHARIAH. Oudtshoorn.

SCENE FOUR

An evening later.

Zachariah is seated at the table, eating. He is obviously in good spirits, radiating inward satisfaction and secrecy. Morris moves about nervously behind his back.

MORRIS. So, it has come to this. Who would have thought it, hey! That one day, one of us would come in here with a secret and keep it to himself! If someone had told me that, I would have thrown up my hands in horror. To Morrie and Zach! . . . I would have cried. No! Emphatically not! [*Pause.*] It just goes to show you. Because I was wrong, wasn't I? There is a secret in this room, at this very moment. This is how brotherhood gets wrecked, you know, Zach, in secrecy. It's the hidden things that hurt and do the harm. [*Pause. Morris watches Zachariah's back.*] So, do you want to tell me?

ZACHARIAH. What are you talking about, Morrie?

MORRIS. You got a letter today, didn't you?

ZACHARIAH. Who?

MORRIS. You.

ZACHARIAH. What?

MORRIS. A letter. From Ethel. And you're not telling me about it. [*Zachariah continues eating, unaffected by Morris's words.*] Okay. Same sort as usual? [*Zachariah looks at Morris.*] The letter. [*Zachariah puts down his bread and thinks. Morris seizes his opportunity.*] Didn't you notice? Hell, Zach! You surprise me.

ZACHARIAH. No, what do you mean: the same sort?

MORRIS. Zach?

ZACHARIAH. So I'm asking you—what do you mean?

MORRIS. To begin with, there's the . . . envelope. Is it the same colour, or isn't it? I can see somebody didn't take a good look, did he?

[*Reluctantly, Zachariah takes the letter out of his inside pocket.*]

She's changed her colours! They used to be blue, remember? What about inside?

ZACHARIAH. I'm not ready for that yet.,

MORRIS. Okay. All I'm saying is . . . I don't care.

ZACHARIAH [*studying the envelope*]. I see they got animals on stamps nowadays. Donkeys with stripes.

MORRIS. Zebras.

ZACHARIAH. *Ja* . . . with stripes.

MORRIS. That's not the point about a letter, Zach.

ZACHARIAH. What?

MORRIS. The stamps. You're wasting your time with the stamps, man. It's what's inside that you got to read.

ZACHARIAH. You're in a hurry, Morrie.

MORRIS. Who?

ZACHARIAH. You.

MORRIS. Look, I told you before, all I'm saying is . . . I don't care and those stamps don't count.

ZACHARIAH. And my name on the envelope. How do you like that, hey?

MORRIS. Your name?

ZACHARIAH. *Ja*. My name.

MORRIS. Oh.

ZACHARIAH. Now what do you mean, with an 'Oh' like that?

MORRIS. What makes you so sure that that is your name? [*Zachariah is trapped.*] How do you spell your name, Zach? Come on, let's hear.

ZACHARIAH [*after a long struggle*]. Zach . . . ar . . . ri . . . yah.

MORRIS. Oh, no, you don't! That's no spelling. That's a pronounciation. A b c d and e . . . that's the alphabet.

[*After a moment's hesitation, Zachariah holds up the letter so that Morris can see the address.*]

ZACHARIAH. Is it for me, Morrie?

MORRIS. I'm not sure.

ZACHARIAH. Zachariah Pietersen.

MORRIS. I know your name. It's for one Z. Pietersen.

ZACHARIAH. Well, that's okay then.

MORRIS. Is it?

ZACHARIAH. Isn't it?

MORRIS. Since when are you the only thing around here that

begins with a Z? And how many Pietersens didn't we know as boys right here in this very selfsame Korsten?

ZACHARIAH [*keeps the letter for a few more seconds, then hands it to Morris*]. You win. Read it.

MORRIS I win! Good old Zach. [*Laughs happily, nudging Zachariah.*] It pays to have a brother who can read, hey? [*Opens the letter.*] Okay, Zach. 'Dear Zach, How's things? I'm okay, today, again. I got your letter . . . Lucy had a laugh at you . . .'

ZACHARIAH. What's funny?

MORRIS. I don't think she means that sort of laugh, Zach. I'm sure she means the friendly sort. [*Continues reading.*] 'Lucy had a laugh at you, but my brother is not so sure.' [*Pause.*] That, I feel, means something, Zach. What does it do to you?

ZACHARIAH. Nothing.

MORRIS. Remember his boots.

ZACHARIAH. No, nothing.

MORRIS [*reads on*]. 'I'm looking forward to a ride in your car . . .' Zach, they believed it. [*Zachariah smiles.*] They believed our cock-and-bull about the car.

ZACHARIAH. [*Laughing.*] I told you.

MORRIS. 'I'm looking forward to a ride in your car . . . and what about Lucy? Can she come?'

[*Their amusement knows no bounds.*]

ZACHARIAH. You must come too, Morrie. You and Lucy! Hey! We'll take them at ninety.

MORRIS. To hell and gone! [*Reads on through his laughter.*] Okay, Zach. 'We're coming down for a holiday in June, so where . . . can we . . . meet you?' [*Long pause. He reads again.*] 'We're coming down for a holiday in June, so where can we meet you?'

ZACHARIAH. Ethel . . . ?

MORRIS. Is coming here.

ZACHARIAH. Coming here?

MORRIS [*puts down the letter and stands up*]. I warned you, didn't I? I said: I have a feeling about this business. I remember my words. And wise ones they turned out to be. I told you to leave it alone. Hands off! I said. Don't touch! Not for you! But oh no, Mr Z. Pietersen was clever. He knew how to handle it. Well, handle this, will you please?

ZACHARIAH [*dumbly*]. What else does she say?

MORRIS [*brutally*]. I'm not going to read it. You want to know why? Because it doesn't matter. The game's up, man. Nothing matters except: 'I'm coming down in June, so where can I meet you?' That is what Mr Z. Pietersen had better start thinking about . . . and quick, boy, quick!

ZACHARIAH. When's June?

MORRIS. Soon.

ZACHARIAH. How soon?

MORRIS [*ticking them off on his fingers*]. June, July, August, September, October, November, December, January, February, March, April, May, June. Satisfied?

[*Another long pause.*]

ZACHARIAH. So?

MORRIS [*to the table, where he reads further into the letter*]. I'll be staying with my uncle at Kensington.' [*Little laugh.*] Kensington! Near enough for you, Zach? About five minutes walking from here, hey?

ZACHARIAH [*frightened*]. Morrie, I know. I'll tell her I can't see her.

MORRIS. She'll want to know why.

ZACHARIAH. Because I'm sick, with my heart.

MORRIS. And if she feels sorry and comes to comfort you?

ZACHARIAH [*growing desperation*]. No, but I'm going away.

MORRIS. When?

ZACHARIAH. Soon, soon. June. June! Morrie, June!

MORRIS. And what about where, and why and what, if she says she'll wait until you come back?

ZACHARIAH. Then I'll tell her . . .

[*Pause. He can think of nothing else to say.*]

MORRIS. What? You can't even tell her you're dead. You see, I happen to know. There is no white-washing away a man's facts. They'll speak for themselves at first sight, if you don't say it.

ZACHARIAH. Say what?

MORRIS. The truth. You know it.

ZACHARIAH. I don't. I know nothing.

MORRIS. Then listen, Zach, because I know it. 'Dear Ethel, forgive me, but I was born a dark sort of boy who wanted to play with whiteness . . .'

ZACHARIAH [*rebelling*]. No!

MORRIS. What else can you say? Come on. Let's hear it. What is there a man can say or pray that will change the colour of his skin or blind them to it?

ZACHARIAH. There must be something.

MORRIS. There's nothing . . . when it's a question of smiles and whispers and thoughts in strange eyes there is only the truth and . . . then . . . [*He pauses.*]

ZACHARIAH. And then what?

MORRIS. And then to make a run for it. They don't like these games with their whiteness, Zach. Ethel's got a policeman brother, remember, and an uncle and your address.

ZACHARIAH. What have I done, hey? I done nothing.

MORRIS. What have you thought, Zach! That's the crime. I seem to remember somebody saying: 'I like the thought of this little white girl.' And what about your dreams, Zach? They've kept me awake these past few nights. I've heard them mumbling and moaning away in the darkness. They'll hear them quick enough. When they get their hands on a dark-born boy playing with a white idea, you think they don't find out what he's been dreaming at night? They've got ways and means, Zach. Mean ways. Like confinement, in a cell, on bread and water, for days without end. They got time. All they need for evidence is a man's dreams. Not so much his hate. They say they can live with that. It's his dreams that they drag off to judgement. [*Pause. Goes back to the window. Turns to Zachariah.*] What are you going to do, Zach?

ZACHARIAH. I'm thinking about it, Morrie.

MORRIS. What are you thinking about it?

ZACHARIAH. What am I going to do?

MORRIS. You'd better be quick, man.

ZACHARIAH. Help me, Morrie.

MORRIS. Are you serious?

ZACHARIAH. I'm not smiling.

MORRIS. Okay, let's begin at the beginning, Zach. Give me the first fact.

ZACHARIAH [*severe and bitter*]. Ethel is white, and I am black.

MORRIS. That's a very good beginning, Zach.

ZACHARIAH. If she sees me . . .

MORRIS. Keep it up.

ZACHARIAH. . . . she'll be surprised.

MORRIS. Harder, Zach.

ZACHARIAH. She'll laugh.

MORRIS. Let it hurt, man!

ZACHARIAH. She'll scream!

MORRIS. Good! Now for yourself. She's surprised, remember?

ZACHARIAH. I'm not strange.

MORRIS. She swears?

ZACHARIAH. I'm no dog.

MORRIS. She screams!

ZACHARIAH. I just wanted to smell you, lady!

MORRIS. Good, Zach. Very good. You're seeing this clearly, man. But, remember there is still the others.

ZACHARIAH. What others?

MORRIS. The uncles with fists and brothers in boots who come running when a lady screams. What about them?

ZACHARIAH. What about them?

MORRIS. They've come to ransack you.

ZACHARIAH. I'll say it wasn't me.

MORRIS. They won't believe you.

ZACHARIAH. Leave me alone!

MORRIS. They'll hit you for that.

ZACHARIAH. I'll fight.

MORRIS. Too many for you.

ZACHARIAH. I'll call a policeman.

MORRIS. He's on their side.

ZACHARIAH. I'll run away!

MORRIS. That's better. Go back to the beginning. Give me that first fact, again. [*Pause.*] It started with Ethel, remember Ethel . . . is

ZACHARIAH. . . . is white.

MORRIS. That's it. And . . .

ZACHARIAH. . . . and I am black.

MORRIS. Let's hear it.

ZACHARIAH. Ethel is so . . . so . . . snow white.

MORRIS. And . . . come on . . .

ZACHARIAH. And I am too . . . truly . . . too black.

MORRIS. Now, this is the hard part, Zach. So let it hurt, man. It has to hurt a man to do him good. I know, just this one cry and then never again . . . Come one, Zach . . . let's hear it.

ZACHARIAH. I can never have her.

MORRIS. Never ever.

ZACHARIAH. She wouldn't want me anyway.

MORRIS. It's as simple as that.

ZACHARIAH. She's too white to want me anyway.

MORRIS. For better or for worse.

ZACHARIAH. So I won't want her anymore.

MORRIS. Not in this life, or that next one if death us do part, God help us! For ever and ever no more, thank you!

ZACHARIAH. The whole, rotten, stinking lot is all because I'm black! Black days, black ways, black things. They're me. I'm happy. Ha Ha Ha! Can you hear my black happiness? What is there is black as me?

MORRIS [*quietly, and with absolute sincerity*]. Oh, Zach! When I hear that certainty about whys and wherefores, about how to live and what not to love, I wish, believe me, man, I wish that old washerwoman had bruised me too at birth. I wish I was as—[*The alarm goes off.*] Bedtime.

[*Morris looks up to find Zachariah staring strangely at him. Morris goes to the window to avoid Zachariah's eyes. He turns from the window to find Zachariah still staring at him. Morris goes to the table to turn off the lamp.*]

ZACHARIAH. Morris!

MORRIS. Zach?

ZACHARIAH. Keep on the light.

MORRIS. Why?

ZACHARIAH. I saw something.

MORRIS. What?

ZACHARIAH. Your skin. How can I put it? It's . . . [*Pause.*]

MORRIS [*easily*]. On the light side.

ZACHARIAH. *Ja.*

MORRIS [*very easily*]. One of those things. [*Another move to the lamp.*]

ZACHARIAH. No, wait, wait, Morrie! I want to have a good look at you, man.

MORRIS. It's a bit late in the day to be seeing your brother for the first time. I been here a whole year, now, you know.

ZACHARIAH. *Ja.* But after a whole life I only seen myself properly tonight. You helped me. I'm grateful.

MORRIS. It was nothing,—Zach.

ZACHARIAH. No! I'm not a man that forgets a favour. I want to help you now.

MORRIS. I don't need any assistance, thank you, Zach.

ZACHARIAH. But you do. [*Morris sits.*] You're on the lighter side of life all right. You like that . . . all over? Your legs and things?

MORRIS. It's evenly spread.

ZACHARIAH. Not even a foot in the darker side, hey! I'd say you must be quite a bright boy with nothing on.

MORRIS. Please, Zach!

ZACHARIAH. You're shy! You always get undressed in the dark. Always well closed up. Like a woman. Like Ethel. I bet she shines. You know something? I bet if it was you she saw and not me she wouldn't say nothing.

[*Morris closes his eyes and gives a light, nervous laugh. Zachariah also laughs, but hollowly.*]

I'm sure she wouldn't be surprised, or laugh, or swear or scream. No one would come running. I bet all she would do is say: 'How do you do, Mr Pietersen?' [*Pause.*] There's a thought there, Morrie. You ever think of it?

MORRIS. No.

ZACHARIAH. Not even a little bit of it? Like there, where you say: 'Hello, Ethel—' and shake hands. Ah, yes, I see this now. You would manage all right, Morrie. One thing is for certain: you would look all right, with her, and that's the main thing.

MORRIS. You're dreaming again, Zach.

ZACHARIAH. This is not my sort of dream. My dream was different. [*He laughs.*] I didn't shake her hands, Morrie. You're the man for shaking hands, Morrie.

MORRIS. Are you finished now, Zach?

ZACHARIAH. No. We're still coming to the big thought. Why don't you meet her? [*Pause.*]

MORRIS. You want to know why?

ZACHARIAH. *Ja.*

MORRIS. You really want to know?

ZACHARIAH. *Ja.*

MORRIS. She's not my pen-pal.

[*Morris moves to get away. Zachariah stops him.*]

ZACHARIAH. Okay, okay. Let's try it this way. Would you like to meet her?

MORRIS. Listen, Zach. I've told you before. Ethel is your—

ZACHARIAH [*pained*]. Please, Morrie! Would—you—like—to—meet—her?

MORRIS. That's no sort of question.

ZACHARIAH. Why not?

MORRIS. Because all my life I've been interested in meeting people. Not just Ethel—anybody!

ZACHARIAH. Okay, let's try it another way. Would you like to see her, or hear her, or maybe touch her?

MORRIS. That still doesn't give the question any meaning! You know me, Zach. Don't I like to hear church bells? Don't I like to touch horses? And anyway, I've told you before, Zach, Ethel is your pen-pal.

ZACHARIAH. You can have her.

MORRIS. What's this now?

ZACHARIAH. I'm giving her to you.

MORRIS [angry]. This is no bloody game, Zach!

ZACHARIAH. But I mean it. Look. I can't use her. We seen that. She'll see it too. But why throw away a good pen-pal if somebody else can do it? You can. Morrie, I'm telling you now, as your brother, that when Ethel sees you all she will do is say: 'How do you do, Mr Pietersen?' She'll never know otherwise.

MORRIS. You think so?

ZACHARIAH. You could fool me, if I didn't know who you were, Morrie.

MORRIS. You mean that, Zach?

ZACHARIAH. Cross my heart and hope to die. And the way you can talk! She'd be impressed, man.

MORRIS. That's true. I like to talk.

ZACHARIAH. No harm in it, is there? A couple of words, a little walk, and a packet of monkey-nuts.

MORRIS. Monkey-nuts?

ZACHARIAH. Ja. Something to chew.

MORRIS. Good God, Zach! You take a lady friend to tea, man!

ZACHARIAH. To tea, hey!

MORRIS. Ja, with buns, if she's hungry. Hot-cross buns.

ZACHARIAH. Now, you see! I would have just bought monkey-nuts. She's definitely not for me.

MORRIS. To tea. A pot of afternoon tea. When she wants to sit down, you pull out her chair . . . like this. [He demonstrates.]

ZACHARIAH. Hey—I think I seen that.

MORRIS. The woman pours the tea but the man butters the bun.

ZACHARIAH. Well, well, well.

MORRIS. Only two spoons of sugar, and don't drink out of the saucer.

ZACHARIAH. That's very good.

MORRIS. If she wants to blow her nose, offer your hanky, which you keep in your breast pocket.

97

ZACHARIAH. Go on.

MORRIS [*waking up to reality*]. You're wasting my time, Zach. I'm going to bed.

ZACHARIAH. But what's the matter, man? You been telling me everything so damn nice. Come on. Tell me. [*Coaxing.*] Tell your brother what's the matter.

MORRIS. I haven't got a hanky.

ZACHARIAH. I think we can buy one.

MORRIS. And the breast pocket?

ZACHARIAH. What's the problem there? Let's also—

MORRIS. Don't be a bloody fool! You got to buy a whole suit to get a breast pocket. And that's still not all. What about socks, decent shoes, a spotty tie, and a clean white shirt? How do you think a man steps out to meet a waiting lady. On his bare feet, wearing rags, and stinking because he hasn't had a bath? She'd even laugh and scream at me if I went like this. So I'm giving Ethel back to you. There is nothing I can do with her, thank you very much.

[*Morris crosses to his bed. Zachariah thinks.*]

ZACHARIAH. Haven't we got that sort of money?

MORRIS. All I got left until you get paid tomorrow is twenty cents. What the hell am I talking about! You know what a right sort of for-a-meeting-with-the-lady type of suit costs? Rands and rands and rands. Shoes? Rands and rands. Shirt? Rands. Then there's still two socks and a tie.

ZACHARIAH [*patiently*]. We got that sort of money.

MORRIS. Here you are. Twenty cents. Go buy me a suit.

ZACHARIAH. Thank you, Morrie. Where's the tin?

MORRIS. Tin?

ZACHARIAH. Square sort of tin.

MORRIS [*horror*]. You mean—our tin?

ZACHARIAH. There was sweets in it at Christmas.

MORRIS. Our future?

ZACHARIAH. That's the one. The future tin.

MORRIS. Our two-man farm?

ZACHARIAH. Yeah, where is it?

MORRIS. I won't tell you.

[*He runs and stands spread-eagled in front of the cupboard where the tin is hidden.*]

ZACHARIAH. Ah-ha!

MORRIS. No, Zach!

ZACHARIAH. Give it to me! Morrie!

MORRIS. No, Zach!—Zach, no . . .

[*Grabs the tin and runs away. Zachariah lurches after him. Morris is quick and elusive.*]

Zach, please! Just stop! Please! Just stand still and listen to me. Everything . . . everything we got, the most precious thing a man can have, a future, is in here. You've worked hard, I've done the saving.

ZACHARIAH. We'll start again.

MORRIS. It will take too long.

ZACHARIAH. I'll work overtime.

MORRIS. It won't be the same.

[*Zachariah lunges suddenly, but Morris escapes.*]

ZACHARIAH. Wait, Morrie! Wait! Fair is fair. Now this time you stand still . . . and listen.

MORRIS. I won't. I won't—no.

ZACHARIAH. Yes, you will, because Ethel is coming and you want to meet her. But like you say, not like any old *hotnot* in the street, but smartly. Now this is it. You're wearing a pretty-smart-for-a-meeting-with-the-lady type of suit.

[*Morris, clutching the tin to his chest, closes his eyes. Zachariah creeps closer.*]

Shiny shoes, white socks, a good shirt, and a spotty tie. And the people watch you go by and say: 'Hey! Who's you? There goes something!' And Ethel says: 'Who's this coming? Could it be my friend, Mr Pietersen?' And you say: 'Good day, Miss Ethel. Can I shake your white hands with my white hands?' 'Of course, Mr Pietersen.'

[*Zachariah has reached Morris. He takes the tin.*]

Thank you, Morrie.

[*Morris doesn't move. Zachariah opens the tin, takes out the money,*] *and then callously throws the tin away. He takes the money to the table where he counts it.*]

MORRIS. Why are you doing this to me?

ZACHARIAH. Aren't we brothers? [*Pause.*] What sort of suit? And what about the shoes?

MORRIS. Go to a good shop. Ask for the outfit, for a gentleman.

SCENE FIVE

The next day.

   Morris is lying on his bed, staring up at the ceiling. There is a knock at the door. Morris rises slowly on his bed.

MORRIS. Who's there? [*The knock is heard again.*] Speak up! I can't hear. [*Knocking.*] Who are you? [*Silence. Morris's fear is now apparent. He waits until the knock is heard a third time.*] Ethel . . . I mean, Madam . . . No! . . . I mean to say, Miss Ethel Lange, could that be you? [*In reply there is a raucous burst of laughter, unmistakably Zachariah's.*] What's this? [*Silence.*] What's the meaning of this? [*Morris rushes to his bed and looks at the alarm clock.*] It's still only the middle of the day.

ZACHARIAH. I know!

MORRIS. Go back to work! At once!

ZACHARIAH. I can't.

MORRIS. Why not?

ZACHARIAH. I took some leave, and left. Let me in, Morrie.

MORRIS. What's the matter with you? The door's not locked.

ZACHARIAH. My hands are full. [*Pause.*] I been shopping, Morrie.

   [*Morris rushes to the door, but collects himself before opening it. Zachariah comes in, his arms piled with parcels. He smiles slyly at Morris, who has assumed a pose of indifference.*]

Oh no you don't. I heard you run. So you thought it was our little Miss Ethel. And a little bit poopy at that thought. Well, don't worry, Morrie, 'cause you know what this is? Your outfit! Number one, and what do we have? A wonderful hat . . . sir.

   [*Takes it out and holds it up for approval. His manner is exaggerated, a caricature of the shopkeeper who sold him the clothing.*]

Which is guaranteed to protect the head on Sundays and rainy days. And next we have a good shirt and a grey tie, which is much better taste, because spots are too loud for a gentleman. Next we have—two grey socks, left and right, and a hanky to blow her nose. [*Next parcel.*] Aha! Now we've come to the suit. But before I show you the suit, my friend, I want to ask you, what does a man really look for in a good suit? A good cloth. Isn't that so?

MORRIS. What are you talking about?

ZACHARIAH. That's what he said. The fashion might be a season too old, but will you please feel the difference. It's lasted for years already. All what I can say is, take it or leave it. But only a fool would leave it at that price. So I took it. [*Next parcel.*] And next we have a real ostrich wallet.

MORRIS. What for?

ZACHARIAH. Your inside pocket. *Ja!* You forgot about the inside pocket. A gentleman always got a wallet for the inside pocket. [*Next parcel.*] And a cigarette case, and a cigarette lighter, for the outside pocket. Chramonium!

MORRIS. Since when do I smoke?

ZACHARIAH. I know, but Ethel might, he said.

MORRIS [*fear*]. You told him? Zach, are you out of your mind?

ZACHARIAH. Don't worry. I just said there was a lady who someone was going to meet. He winked at me and said it was a good thing, now and then, and reminded me that ladies like presents. [*Holds up a scarf.*] A pretty *doek* in case the wind blows her hair away. Ah-ha. And next we have an umbrella in case it's sopping wet. And over here . . . [*Last parcel.*] Guess what's in this box. I'll shake it. Listen.

MORRIS. Shoes.

ZACHARIAH [*triumphantly*]. No! It's boots! Ha, ha! *Ja.* [*Watching Morris's reaction.*] They frighten an *ou*, don't they? [*Happy.*] Satisfied, Morrie?

MORRIS [*looking at the pile of clothing*]. It seems all right

ZACHARIAH. It wasn't easy. At the first shop, when I asked for the outfit for a gentleman, they said I was an agitator, *ja*, and was going to call the police. I had to get out, man . . . quick! Even this fellow . . . Mr Moses . . . 'You're drunk,' he said. But when I showed him our future he sobered up. You know what he said? He said, 'Are you the gentleman?' So I said, 'Do I look like a gentleman, Mr Moses?' He said: 'My friend, it takes all sorts of different sorts to make this world.' 'I'm the black sort,' I said. So he said: 'You don't say.' He also said to mention his name to any other gentlemen wanting reasonable outfits. Go ahead, Morrie. [*The clothing.*] Let's see the gentle sort of man.

MORRIS. Okay. Okay. Don't rush me.

[*Moves cautiously to the pile of clothing. Flicks an imaginary speck of dust off the hat. Zachariah is waiting.*]

ZACHARIAH. Well?

MORRIS. Give me time.

ZACHARIAH. What for? You got the clothes, man.

MORRIS. For God's sake, Zach! This is deep water. I'm not just going to jump right in. You must paddle around first.

ZACHARIAH. Paddle around?

MORRIS. Try it out!

ZACHARIAH [*offering him the hat*]. No, try it on.

MORRIS. The idea, man. I got to try it out. There's more to wearing a white skin than just putting on a hat. You've seen white men before without hats, but they're still white men, aren't they?

ZACHARIAH. *Ja.*

MORRIS. And without suits or socks, or shoes . . .

ZACHARIAH. No, Morrie. Never without socks and shoes. Never a barefoot white man.

MORRIS. Well, the suit then. Look, Zach, what I'm trying to say is this. The clothes will help, but only help. They don't maketh the white man. It's that white something inside you, that special meaning and manner of whiteness. I know what I'm talking about because . . . I'll be honest with you now, Zach . . . I've thought about it for a long time. And the first fruit of my thought, Zach, is that this whiteness of theirs is not just in the skin, otherwise . . . well, I mean . . . I'd be one of them, wouldn't I? Because, let me tell you, Zach, I seen them that's darker than me.

ZACHARIAH. *Ja?*

MORRIS. Yes. Really dark, man. Only they had that something I'm telling you about . . . that's what I got to pin down in here.

ZACHARIAH. What?

MORRIS. White living, man! Like . . . like . . . like looking at things. Haven't you noticed it, Zach? They look at things

103

differently. Haven't you seen their eyes when they look at you?
It's even in their way of walking.

ZACHARIAH. Ah—so you must learn to walk properly then.

MORRIS. Yes.

ZACHARIAH. And to look right at things.

MORRIS. *Ja.*

ZACHARIAH. And to sound right.

MORRIS. Yes! There's that, as well. The sound of it.

ZACHARIAH. So go on. [*Again offering the hat.*] Try it. For size.
Just for the sake of the size.

[*Morris takes the hat, plays with it for a few seconds, then impulsively
puts it on.*]

MORRIS. Just for size, okay.

ZACHARIAH. Ha!

MORRIS. Yes?

ZACHARIAH. Aha!

MORRIS [*whipping off the hat in embarrassment*]. No.

ZACHARIAH. Yes.

MORRIS [*shaking his head*]. Uhuh!

ZACHARIAH. Come.

MORRIS. No, man.

ZACHARIAH. Man. I like the look of that on your head.

MORRIS. It looked right?

ZACHARIAH. I'm telling you.

MORRIS. It seemed to fit.

ZACHARIAH. It did, I know.

MORRIS [*using this as an excuse to get it back on his head*]. The brim
was just right on the brow . . . and with plenty of room for the
brain! I'll try it again, shall I?

ZACHARIAH. Just for the sake of the size. A good fit.

MORRIS [*lifting the hat*]. Good morning!

ZACHARIAH. That's very good.

MORRIS [*again*]. Good morning . . . Miss Ethel Lange!

[*Looks quickly to see Zachariah's reaction. He betrays nothing.*]

ZACHARIAH. Maybe a little higher.

MORRIS. Higher? [*Again.*]

ZACHARIAH. *Ja.*

MORRIS. Good morning . . . [*A flourish.*] . . . and how do you do today, Miss Ethel Lange! [*Laughing with delight.*]

ZACHARIAH. How about the jacket?

MORRIS. Okay.

[*Zachariah hands him the jacket. He puts it on.*]

[*Preening.*] Zach—how did you do it?

ZACHARIAH. I said: 'The gentleman is smaller than me, Mr Moses.'

MORRIS [*once again lifting his hat*]. Good morning, Miss Ethel Lange . . . [*pleading, servile*]. I beg your pardon, but I do hope you wouldn't mind to take a little walk with . . .

ZACHARIAH. Stop!

MORRIS. What's wrong?

ZACHARIAH. Your voice.

MORRIS. What's wrong with it?

ZACHARIAH. Too soft. They don't ever sound like that.

MORRIS. To a lady they do! I admit, if it wasn't Ethel I was addressing it would be different.

ZACHARIAH. Okay. Try me.

MORRIS. You?

ZACHARIAH. You're walking with Ethel. I'm selling monkey-nuts.

MORRIS. So?

ZACHARIAH. So you want some monkey-nuts. Something to chew.

MORRIS. Ah! . . . [*His voice trails off.*]

ZACHARIAH. Go on. I'm selling monkey-nuts. Peanuts! Peanuts!

MORRIS [*after hesitation*]. I can't.

ZACHARIAH [*simulated shock*]. What!

MORRIS [*frightened*]. What I mean is . . . I don't want any monkey-nuts. I'm not hungry.

ZACHARIAH. Ethel wants some.

MORRIS. Ethel?

ZACHARIAH. *Ja*, and I'm selling them.

MORRIS. This is hard for me, Zach.

ZACHARIAH. You got to learn your lesson, Morrie. You want to pass, don't you? Peanuts! Peanuts!

MORRIS [*steeling himself*]. Excuse me!

ZACHARIAH. I'll never hear that. Peanuts!

MORRIS. Hey!

ZACHARIAH. Or that. Peanuts!

MORRIS. Boy!

ZACHARIAH. I'm ignoring you, man. I'm a cheeky one. Peanuts!

MORRIS. You're asking for it, Zach!

ZACHARIAH. I am.

MORRIS. I'm warning you. I will.

ZACHARIAH. Go on.

MORRIS [*with brutality and coarseness*]. Hey, *swartgat!*

[*An immediate reaction from Zachariah. His head whips round. He stares at Morris in disbelief. Morris replies with a weak little laugh, which soon dies on his lips.*]

Just a joke! [*Softly.*] I didn't mean it, Zach. Don't look at me like that! [*A step to Zachariah, who backs away.*] Say something. For God's sake, say anything! I'm your brother.

ZACHARIAH [*disbelief*]. My brother?

MORRIS. It's me, Zach, Morris!

ZACHARIAH. Morris?

MORRIS [*at last realizes what has happened. He tears off the jacket and hat in a frenzy.*] Now do you see?

ZACHARIAH. That's funny. I thought . . . I was looking at a different sort of man.

MORRIS. But don't you see, Zach? It was me! That different sort of man you saw was me. It's happened, man. And I swear, I no longer wanted it. That's why I came back. Because . . . because . . . I'll tell you the whole truth now . . . because I did try it! It didn't seem a sin. If a man was born with a chance at changing why not take it? I thought . . . thinking of worms lying warm in their silk, to come out one day with wings and things! Why not a man? If his dreams are soft and keep him warm at night, why not stand up the next morning? Different . . . Beautiful! So what was stopping me? You. There was always you. What sort of thing was that to do to your own flesh and blood brother? Anywhere, any place or road, there was always you, Zach. So I came back. I'm no Judas. Gentle Jesus, I'm no Judas.

[*Pause. The alarm rings. Neither responds.*]

SCENE SIX

Night.

The two men are asleep. Silence. Suddenly Zachariah sits up in bed. Without looking at Morris he gets up, goes to the corner where the new suit of clothes is hanging, and puts on the suit and hat. The final effect is an absurdity bordering on the grotesque. The hat is too small and so is the jacket, which he has buttoned up incorrectly, while the trousers are too short. Zachariah stands barefooted, holding the umbrella, the hat pulled down low over his eyes so that his face is almost hidden.

ZACHARIAH. Ma. Ma. Ma! Mother! Hello. How are you, old woman? What's that? You don't recognize me? Well, well, well. Take a guess. Nope. Try again. Nope. [*Shakes his head.*] What's the matter with you, Ma? Don't you recognize your own son? [*Shakes his head violently.*] No, no, no, no! Not him! It's me, Zach! [*Sweeps off the hat to show his face.*] *Ja.* Zach! You didn't think I could do it, did you? Well, to tell you the truth, the whole truth so help me God, I got sick of myself and made a change. Him? At home, Ma. A lonely boy, as you say. A sad story, as I will tell you. He went on the road, Ma, but strange to say, he came back quite white. No tan at all. I don't recognize him no more. [*He sits.*] I'll ask you again, how are you, old woman? I see some signs of wear and tear. [*Nodding his head.*] That's true . . . such sorrow . . . tomorrow . . . . *Ja* . . . it's cruel . . . your feet as well? Still a bad fit in the shoe? *Ai ai ai!* Me? [*Pause. He struggles.*] There's something I need to know, Ma. You see, I been talking, to him . . . *ja*, I talk to him, he says it helps . . . and now we got to know. Whose mother were you really? At the bottom of your heart, where your blood is red with pain, whom did you really love? No evil feelings, Ma, but, I mean a man has got to know. You see, he's been such a burden as a brother. [*Agitation.*] Don't be dumb. Don't cry! It was just a question! Look! I brought you a present, old soul. [*Holds out a hand with the fingers lightly closed.*] It's a butterfly. A real beauty butterfly. We were travelling fast, Ma. We hit them at ninety . . . a whole flock. But one was still alive, and it made me think of . . . Mother . . . So I caught it, myself, for you, remembering what I caught from you. This, old Ma of

mine, is gratitude, and it proves it, doesn't it? Some things are
only skin deep, because I got it, here in my hands, I got beauty
. . . too . . . haven't I?

SCENE SEVEN

The next evening.

For the first time the room is untidy. The beds are not made, the table is cluttered, the floor littered with the strings and wrappings of the parcels of the previous day. Morris is alone. He sits lifelessly at the table, his head fallen on his chest, his arms hanging limp at his sides. On the table is a small bundle. Then Zachariah comes in. He behaves normally, going straight to the bed and taking off his shoes. Only when this is done does he realize something is wrong. The footbath hasn't been prepared.

ZACHARIAH. What's this? [*Looking around for the basin.*] Foot-salts finished? Hell, man! Couldn't you have seen? What must I do now? My feet are killing me, you know. [*Touching the toes.*] Forget the salts then. Just give me some hot. A soak will do them good.

[*Morris doesn't move.*]

Some hot, Morrie! Please!

[*Nothing happens.*]

Ag, no, man, don't tell me the stove is buggered up!

[*Goes to the stove and feels the kettle.*]

What the hell's happened? A man works all day, he comes home and finds this . . . [*The stove.*] . . . and this. [*The room.*] Floor not swept! Beds not made!

[*Beginning to realize. Morris struggles to find a word, but fails and drops his shoulders in a gesture of defeat and resignation. Disbelief.*]

You say nothing? [*A little laugh, but this quickly dies. Desperate.*] No, it's not funny. What happened?

MORRIS. I've given up.

ZACHARIAH. What?

MORRIS. I mean, I can't carry on.

ZACHARIAH. Oh, so you've just stopped, hey?

MORRIS. Yes.

ZACHARIAH. But that won't do! Emphatically not! A man can't stop just like that, like you. That's definitely no good, because, because . . . because a man must carry on. Most certainly. [*Sees the bundle on the table for the first time.*] What's this bundle, Morrie?

MORRIS. My belongings.

ZACHARIAH. What's that?

MORRIS. My Bible and my alarm clock. I was leaving, Zach.

ZACHARIAH. Leaving?

MORRIS. Going away.

ZACHARIAH. Where?

MORRIS. The road. Wherever it went.

ZACHARIAH. Oh! [*Pause.*] What about me?

MORRIS. I know, I know.

ZACHARIAH. But you don't care, hey?

MORRIS. I do care, Zach!

ZACHARIAH [*ignoring the denial*]. That's a fine thought for a loving brother. I'm surprised at you. In fact I'm shocked, shocked, shocked, shocked.

MORRIS. Stop it, Zach! I'm still here. I know I can't go . . . so I've given up instead. [*Pause.*]

ZACHARIAH. Come on, cheer up. It's not so bad.

MORRIS. I can't, Zach. Honestly I can't anymore.

ZACHARIAH. Hey, I've got a surprise for you.

MORRIS. It will have to be damn good to make any difference.

ZACHARIAH. How good is a letter from Ethel?

MORRIS. No damn good! You've missed the point, Zach. Don't you see, man! She's the blame.

   [*Zachariah takes out the letter.*]
   I don't want it. Take it away.

ZACHARIAH [*putting the letter down on the table so that Morris can see it*]. She's yours. I gave her to you.

MORRIS. Everything was fine until she came along.

ZACHARIAH. No, no, no. She hasn't yet.

MORRIS. What do you mean?

ZACHARIAH. Come along. You've missed the problem. Ethel coming along was the problem. She hasn't yet. But I mean, she might be on her way. I mean . . . it could be June, couldn't it? And one fine day, you know what? Another knock at the door. But it won't be me. So, you see, if I were you, just for safety's sake, of course, I'd have a quick peek at that letter.

[*Zachariah goes to his bed. Morris hesitates for a second, then takes the letter, opens it, and reads in silence. When he has finished he puts it down and looks at Zachariah vacantly. Zachariah is unable to contain himself any longer.*]

She's coming! What does she say? Wait! Let me guess. She's on the train, on her way, and it's June. When do you meet, man? What did she say? Tell me, Morrie?

MORRIS. No, Zach, prepare yourself for . . . good news. Ethel's gone and got engaged to get married, to Luckyman Stoffel.

ZACHARIAH. No.

MORRIS. S'true.

ZACHARIAH. No!

MORRIS. Then listen, Zach. [*Reads.*] 'Dear Pen-pal, it's sad news for you but good news for me. I've decided to get married. Ma says it's okay. The lucky man is Stoffel, who plays in my brother's team, fullback. It's a long story. Lucy thought she had him, but she didn't, so now we're not on talking terms no more. Stoffel works at Boetie's Garage and doesn't like competition so he says pen-pals is out if we're going to get married to each other. He's sitting here now and he says he wants to say this: "Leave my woman alone if you know what's good for you." That was Stoffel. He's a one all right. Well, pal, that's all for now, for ever. Ethel.' [*Pause.*] Down here at the bottom she says: 'You can keep the snapshot for a keepsake.'

[*Morris looks vacantly at Zachariah whose attitude has hardened with bitter disappointment.*]

ZACHARIAH. So?

MORRIS. So I think we can begin again, Zach.

ZACHARIAH. What?

MORRIS. That's a good question. [*Pause.*] Well, let's work it out. Where are we? Here. What is this? Our house. Me and you, Morrie and Zach . . . live here . . . in peace because the problem's gone . . . and got engaged to be married . . . and I'm Morrie . . . and I was going to go, but now I'm going to stay!

[*With something of his old self, Morris goes to work, opens his bundle and packs out his belongings.*]

Hey, Zach! [*Holding up the clock*.] It's stopped. Like me. What time shall we make it? Supper!

ZACHARIAH. I'm not hungry.

MORRIS. Bedtime?

ZACHARIAH. I don't want to sleep.

MORRIS. Just after supper, then. We'll say we've eaten.

ZACHARIAH. You can say what you like!

MORRIS. What's the matter, Zach?

ZACHARIAH [*slowly*]. You aren't going to wear that suit anymore?

MORRIS. I see. Zach, look at me now. Solemnly, on the holy Bible, I promise I won't.

ZACHARIAH. That's it.

MORRIS. What?

ZACHARIAH [*slyly*]. You looked so damn nice in that suit. It made me feel good.

MORRIS. You mean that?

ZACHARIAH. Cross my heart.

MORRIS. You mean you want to see me in it?

ZACHARIAH. *Ja*.

MORRIS. Be honest now, Zach. You are saying that you would like me to put that suit on?

ZACHARIAH [*emphatically*]. Now.

MORRIS. Now!

ZACHARIAH. *Ja!*

MORRIS. This comes as a surprise, Zach. But if as you say it makes you feel better . . . well . . . that just about makes it my duty, doesn't it? [*Moving to the suit.*] It was a damn good buy, Ethel or no Ethel. I really am tempted.

ZACHARIAH. Then get in.

MORRIS. Not so easy now . . . after yesterday. Say something to help me.

ZACHARIAH. Just for size. Just for the sake of the size, Morrie. Just for size. No harm done, Morrie. No harm done. We're only playing.

MORRIS. Only playing. That does it. Close your eyes, Zach!

[*With a laugh, Morris puts on the suit.*]

No peeking, Zach!

[*When he is dressed, he walks around the room in exaggerated style.*]
Zach!

ZACHARIAH [*encourages him*]. *Ek sê!* Just look! *Hoe's dit vir 'n ding! Links draai, regs swaai . . . Aitsa! Ou pellie*, you're stepping high tonight!

MORRIS [*stops, turns suddenly*]. Hey, *swartgat!*

[*A second of silence, and then Zachariah laughs.*]

No harm done now, hey, Zach?

ZACHARIAH. No pain.

MORRIS. That's the way to take a joke. Hey, *swartgat!*

ZACHARIAH [*playing along*]. *Ja, Baas?*

MORRIS. Who are you?

ZACHARIAH. Your boy, Zach, *Baas.*

MORRIS. And who am I?

ZACHARIAH. *Baas* Morrie, *Baas.*

MORRIS. *Baas* Morrie and his boy, Zach! My God, you're comical! Where'd you get that joke from, Zach?

ZACHARIAH. At the gate.

MORRIS. So that's what it's like.

ZACHARIAH. They're all dressed up smart like you, and go walking by. Come on, come. Try it. Walk past—

MORRIS. What?

ZACHARIAH. Walk past.

MORRIS. You want to play it?

ZACHARIAH. Why not?

MORRIS. I haven't seen the gate before, Zach. It's difficult to play something you haven't seen.

ZACHARIAH. I'll show you. Here it is. [*Vague gesture.*] This here is the gate.

MORRIS. What's on the other side?

ZACHARIAH. Does it matter?

MORRIS. It does if we're going to play this thing properly.

ZACHARIAH [*looking back*]. Trees.

MORRIS. Tall trees, with picnics in the shade.

ZACHARIAH. Grass.

MORRIS. Green. We'll make it spring.

ZACHARIAH. Flowers with butterflies.

MORRIS. That's a good touch, Zach.

ZACHARIAH. And benches.

MORRIS. How thoughtful! I'll want to rest.

ZACHARIAH. And I'm squatting here.

MORRIS. Right. So now you'll open the gate for me when I get there?

ZACHARIAH. No. It's open. I'll just watch your boots as you go by.

MORRIS. Then what's your job at the gate?

ZACHARIAH [*pause*]. They put me there to chase the black kids away.

[*Morris hesitates.*]

MORRIS. Are you sure we should play this?

ZACHARIAH. It's only a game. Walk past.

MORRIS. Just a game. No harm done.

[*He flourishes his umbrella and then saunters slowly towards Zachariah.*]

Shame! Look at that poor old boy. John? What are you doing . . . ?

ZACHARIAH [*cutting him*]. No, Morrie.

MORRIS. What's wrong?

ZACHARIAH. They never talk to me, man. Try it again.

[*Morris tries it again. This time he doesn't speak, but pretends to take a coin out of his pocket and tosses it to Zachariah.*]

How much?

MORRIS. Fifty cents.

ZACHARIAH. What!

MORRIS. Twenty cents.

ZACHARIAH. Too much.

MORRIS. Ten cents.

115

[*Zachariah is still doubtful.*]

All right then, a cent.

ZACHARIAH. *Ja*, that's a bit better, but—

MORRIS. But what?

ZACHARIAH. You think you're the soft sort of white man, giving me a cent like that.

MORRIS. What's wrong with being the soft sort? You find them.

ZACHARIAH. I know. But not with boots, Morrie. Never with boots. That sort doesn't even see me. Come on. Try it again.

[*The mime is repeated. This time Morris walks straight past.*]

MORRIS. Now what?

ZACHARIAH. I have a thought. I'm squatting here, and I think.

MORRIS. Okay.

ZACHARIAH. Bastard!

MORRIS [*sharply*]. Who?

ZACHARIAH. Don't spoil it, man! You can't hear me. It's just a thought.

[*Taps his forehead.*]

MORRIS [*looking away, frowning*]. Carry on.

ZACHARIAH. That's all.

MORRIS. Just . . .

ZACHARIAH. Just . . . Bastard!

MORRIS. What happens now?

ZACHARIAH. I'm watching you, remember? And you're looking up at the trees.

MORRIS. Yes, of course. It's a tall tree. I'm wondering if I've ever seen a tree as tall as this tree. There's also a great weight of birdies on its branches and . . . actually I'm finding difficulty keeping my mind up the tree with you behind my back. I feel your presence. So I think, I'll move further on . . . I mean, I'll have to get away if I want to admire the beauty, won't I? So I'll take this road. Yes. It's a good road. It's going places, because ahead of me I see the sky. I see it through the trees . . . so I'm climbing up a hill in this road, putting miles between us; and now, at last, there ahead of me is the sky, big, blue, beautiful; and I hurry on to the top where I turn against it and look back at you . . . far behind me now, in the distance, outside the gate. Can you see me?

ZACHARIAH. A little.

MORRIS. What is it you see here, in the distance, beyond the trees, upon the hill, against the sky?

ZACHARIAH. Can it be a . . . man?

MORRIS. A white man! Don't you see the way I stand? Didn't you see the way I walked? What do you think now?

ZACHARIAH. He's a bastard!

MORRIS [*reckless in his elation*]. Well, I don't care. It's too far away for me now to see your eyes. In fact, I'm almost free . . . So away I go, laughing, over the green spring grass, into the flowers and among the butterflies. And what do I say? What do I shout? Look at me, will you please! At last—I've changed! [*Pause.*] Now I'm tired. After so many years, so much beauty is a burden. I need rest. And here is one of those thoughtful benches. [*Sits.*] Ah, dearie, dearie me.

[*Zachariah comes past, bent low, miming the picking up of litter in the park. One hand trails a sack, the other is stabbing with a stick pieces of paper. Morris watches this with critical interest.*]

What are you doing?

ZACHARIAH. Picking up rubbish. I got a stick with a nail on the end. This is my rubbish bag. Every afternoon, at four o'clock, I go through the trees and around the benches and pick up the papers.

MORRIS. I thought I left you behind.

ZACHARIAH. I know.

MORRIS. The sight of you affects me, John.

ZACHARIAH [*continuing with his mime*]. I can feel it does.

MORRIS It's interesting. Just looking at you does it. I don't need the other senses. Just sight, just the sight of you crawling around like some . . . thing . . . makes me want to throw up.

ZACHARIAH. I know.

MORRIS [*rising*]. In fact I'd like to . . . [*Stops himself.*]

ZACHARIAH. Carry on.

MORRIS [*walking away*]. I can't.

ZACHARIAH. Why?

MORRIS. I'm telling you I can't.

ZACHARIAH. But, why?

MORRIS. Not with that old woman watching us.

[*Zachariah stops and looks questioningly at Morris.*]

Over there. [*Pointing.*]

ZACHARIAH. Old woman?

MORRIS. Horribly old.

ZACHARIAH. Alone?

MORRIS. All by her lonely self.

ZACHARIAH. And she's watching us?

MORRIS All the time. [*Impatience.*] Can't you see, Zach? She's wearing a grey dress on Sunday.

ZACHARIAH [*recognition dawning*]. Ah, soapsuds . . .

MORRIS. . . . on brown hands.

ZACHARIAH. And sore feet, hey! The toes are crooked.

MORRIS. She's been following me all day . . . begging!

ZACHARIAH. Call the police.

MORRIS. No, no. Not that.

ZACHARIAH. Then what will we do?

MORRIS. Let's work it out. We can't carry on with her watching us . . . behind that bush . . . like an old spy.

ZACHARIAH. So she must go.

MORRIS. I think so, too. [*A step in the direction of the old woman.*] Go away.

ZACHARIAH. Is she moving?

MORRIS. No. [*Trying again.*] Go away, old one! Begat and be gone! Go home! [*Sigh.*] It's no use. She won't listen to me.

ZACHARIAH [*trying to scare her off*]. Hey!

MORRIS [*excited*]. Ha, ha, she jumped!

ZACHARIAH. *Voetsek!*

MORRIS. Another jump.

[*Zachariah goes down on his hands and knees.*]

What are you doing?

ZACHARIAH. Stones.

MORRIS. Hooooooo! She heard you. She's trotted off a little distance. But you're not really going to use them, are you?

ZACHARIAH. It's the only way. [*Throws.*]

MORRIS. Almost.

[*Zachariah throws again.*]

She jumped!

ZACHARIAH. *Voetsek!*

MORRIS. Yes. *Voetsek* off! We don't want you!

ZACHARIAH. Bugger off!

MORRIS. You old bitch! You made life unbearable!

ZACHARIAH [*starts throwing with renewed violence*]. *Hamba!*

MORRIS. She's running now.

ZACHARIAH. Get out!

MORRIS. *Kaffermeid!*

ZACHARIAH. *Ou hoer!*

MORRIS. *Luisgat!*

ZACHARIAH. *Swartgat!*

MORRIS. You've hit her! She's down. Look . . . look!

ZACHARIAH. Look at those old legs sticking up!

MORRIS. She's got no pants on! Get the hell out of here, you old bitch!

[*Their derision rises to a climax, Morris shaking his umbrella, Zachariah his fists.*]

That's the last of her I think. By God, she ran!

[*Pause while they get their breath.*]

Where were we?

ZACHARIAH. It was four o'clock. I was collecting the rubbish. You wanted to do . . . something.

MORRIS. That's right. I remember now. I just wanted to . . . just wanted to . . . poke you with my umbrella. He-he-he! [*He attacks Zachariah savagely.*] Just wanted to poke you a little bit. That's all. He-he! What do you think umbrellas are for when it doesn't rain? Hey?

[*Zachariah tries to escape, but Morris catches him with the crook of the umbrella.*]

119

Wait, wait! Not so fast, John. I want to have a good look at you. My God! What sort of mistake is this? A black man? All over, my boy?

ZACHARIAH. Sorry, *Baas*.

MORRIS. Your pits and privates?

ZACHARIAH. *Ja, Baas*.

MORRIS. Nothing white?

ZACHARIAH. Forgive me please, my *Baas*.

MORRIS. You're horrible.

ZACHARIAH. Sorry, *Baas*.

MORRIS. You stink.

ZACHARIAH. Please, my *Baasie* . . .

MORRIS. What did you mean crawling around like that? Spoiling the view, spoiling my chances! What's your game, hey? Trying to be an embarrassment? Is that it? A two-legged, bloody embarrassment? Well, we'll see about that. I hate you, do you hear? Hate! . . . Hate! . . . Hate! . . .

[*He attacks Zachariah savagely with the umbrella. When his fury is spent he turns away and sits down.*]

It was a good day. The sun shone. The sky was blue. I was happy. [*Smiling, released of all tensions.*] Not the sort of day to forget in a hurry. There's a spiny chill sprung up now, though. [*Shivering, Zachariah is moaning softly.*] Something sighing among the trees . . . must be the wind. Yes! There were trees as well today. The tall trees. So much to remember! Still . . . [*Shivering.*] . . . it is getting nippy . . . and I haven't got an overcoat . . . with me.

ZACHARIAH. Ding-dong . . . ong . . . ong . . . ding-dong . . . ong . . . ong.

MORRIS. What is that sound I hear?

ZACHARIAH. Bells. They're closing up now. Ding-dong . . . ong . . . ong.

MORRIS. Then I'd better hurry home. [*Stands.*] Yes, it was a good day . . . while it lasted.

ZACHARIAH. Ding-dong . . . ong . . . ong.

MORRIS. Ah, there's the gate.

ZACHARIAH. What's the matter with you?

MORRIS. What's the matter with me?

ZACHARIAH. Can't you see the gate is locked?

MORRIS. Is it? [*Tries the gate.*] It is.

ZACHARIAH. I locked it before I rang the bell.

MORRIS. Heavens above! Then I'd better climb over.

ZACHARIAH. Over those sharp pieces of glass they got on the top?

MORRIS. Then the fence.

ZACHARIAH. Barbed wire . . . very high . . .

MORRIS. So what do I do?

ZACHARIAH. You might try calling.

MORRIS. Hello! Hello, anybody there?

ZACHARIAH. Seems like nobody hears you, hey!

MORRIS. Now what?

ZACHARIAH. You think you'll try the gate on the other side.

MORRIS [*alarm*]. All the way back?

ZACHARIAH. Uh-huh. [*Moves quietly to the lamp on the table.*]

MORRIS. Through the trees?

ZACHARIAH. Looks like it. [*Turning down the lamp.*]

MORRIS. But it's getting dark.

ZACHARIAH. It happens every day.

MORRIS. And cold . . . and I never did like shadows . . . [*Pause.*] Where are you?

ZACHARIAH. Behind a tree.

MORRIS. But . . . but I thought you were the good sort of boy?

ZACHARIAH. Me?

MORRIS. Weren't you that? The simple, trustworthy type of John-boy. Weren't you that?

ZACHARIAH. I've changed.

MORRIS. Who gave you the right?

ZACHARIAH. I took it!

MORRIS. That's illegal! They weren't yours. That's theft. 'Thou shalt not steal.' I arrest you in the name of God. *Ja.* Please! [*Looking around wildly.*] My prayers . . .

[*Morris goes down on his knees. Zachariah begins to move to him.*]

Our Father, which art our Father in heaven, because we never knew the other one; forgive us this day our trespassing; I couldn't help it. The gate was open, God, so I didn't see the notice prohibiting! And 'beware of the dog' was in Bantu, so how was I to know, Oh, Lord! My sins are not that black. Furthermore, just some bread for the poor, daily, and please let your Kingdom come as quick as it can, for Yours is the power and the glory, ours is the fear and the judgment of eyes behind our back for the sins of our birth and the man behind the tree in the darkness while I wait . . . no, no, no—

[*Zachariah stands above Morris on the point of violence. The alarm clock rings. Morris crawls frantically away, then jumps up, rushes to the table and turns up the lamp. Zachariah goes to his bed and sits. A long silence. They avoid each other's eyes. Morris takes off the jacket. At the window:*]

Wind's coming up. It's the mystery of my life, that lake. I mean . . . It looks dead, doesn't it? If ever there was a piece of water that looks dead and done for, that's what I'm looking at now. Ah, well. Bedtime! [*Leaving the window.*] We'll sleep well tonight, you'll see.

ZACHARIAH. Morris?

MORRIS. Yes, Zach?

ZACHARIAH. What happened?

MORRIS. You mean?

ZACHARIAH. *Ja.*

MORRIS. We were carried away, as they would say, by the game . . . quite far, in fact. Mustn't get worried, though . . . it was only a game. I'm sure it's a good thing we got the game. Because we got a lot of time left, you know! [*Little laugh.*] . . . Stretching ahead . . . in here . . . [*Pause.*] . . . I'm not too worried. I mean, other men get by without a future. In fact, I think there's quite a lot of people getting by without futures these days.

[*Silence. Morris makes the last preparations for bed.*]

ZACHARIAH. Morris?

MORRIS. Yes, Zach?

ZACHARIAH. What is it, Morrie? You know, the two of us . . . in here?

MORRIS. Home.

ZACHARIAH. Is there no other way?

MORRIS. No, Zach. You see, we're tied together. It's what they call the blood knot . . . the bond between brothers.

[*Morris moves to his bed.*]

HELLO AND GOODBYE

A PLAY
IN TWO ACTS

CHARACTERS

JOHNNIE SMIT
HESTER SMIT, *his sister*

HELLO AND GOODBYE was first produced at the Library Theatre, Johannesburg, on 26 October 1965, directed by Barney Simon, with the following cast:

JOHNNIE	Athol Fugard
HESTER	Molly Seftel

The 'definitive' production, directed by the author, was first presented at The Space, Cape Town, on 26 July 1974, subsequently at Riverside Studios, London (February 1978), and on BBC Television (March 1979), with the following cast:

JOHNNIE	Bill Flynn
HESTER	Yvonne Bryceland

The designer was Douglas Heap.

ACT ONE

A kitchen table and four chairs, lit by a solitary electric light hanging above.

On the table is a bottle of fruit squash, a jug of water, and a glass.

Slumped forward in one of the chairs is a man—his head resting face down on his arms on the table. He holds a spoon in one hand and is tapping it against the side of the glass.

About ten taps in silence, then. . . .

JOHNNIE [*counting as he taps*]. . . . fifty-five, fifty-six, fifty-seven, fifty-eight, fifty-nine, sixty!

[*Stops tapping.*]

Three hundred and. . . .

[*Pause.*]

Five minutes—become hours, become days . . . today! . . . Friday somethingth, nineteen . . . what? . . . sixty-three. One thousand nine hundred and sixty-three! Multiplied by twelve, by thirty, by twenty-four, by sixty . . .

[*Pause.*]

by sixty again! . . . gives you every second. Jee-sus! Millions.

[*Pause.*]

Yes, since Jeesus.

[*He starts tapping again but stops after only a few.*]

No! I'm wrong. It's six. Sixty goes six times into three hundred and sixty. It's six minutes!

[*Looks around.*]

Walls. The table. Chairs—three empty, one . . . occupied. Here and now. Mine. No change. Yes there is! Me. I'm a fraction older. More memories. All the others! Same heres mostly. Here. Other nows. Then, and then when this happened and that happened. My milestones, in here mostly. 'And then one day, after a long illness, his. . . .'

[*Pause. Softly.*]

Which art now in heaven.

[*Pause.*]

Nearly. On the tip of my tongue that time. Just don't rush it. The shock to the nervous system has got to wear off!

[*Stands and exits. Returns a few seconds later and goes back to the table but doesn't sit. When he speaks this time it is in a loud, unnaturally matter-of-fact voice.*]

When the sun shines again. . . .

[*Pause.*]

Tomorrow! God willing, if it's a nice day I'll go to the beach. Bottle of beer and a packet of lemon creams. Make it an outing. Break the monotony. Open the door and leave the house. Walk down Upper Valley Road, then along the river to the bridge. There I'll catch the Summerstrand bus. Number six, and upstairs for the view. Sit on the rocks and watch the waves. Drink the beer and eat the biscuits. Breathe in the breeze. Come back in the twilight, refreshed. A day will have passed.

[*Pause. Softly.*]

How many now?

[*Loud again.*]

As I was saying, back in the twilight. Along the river with the frogs croaking. Back home. No place like here. That's a lie. What's the odds? Walk in, put on the light, have a look-see, look the same . . . NO!

[*Pause.*]

A day will have passed. Emptier. It will be . . . emptier. Somehow it's getting empty. But how? And what? And cold! When was it I went and came back and it was emptier and cold and every thing . . . so still!
Here it comes again! Quick. Something else.

[*He grabs the spoon on the table and starts tapping.*]

One two three four. . . .

[*Grabs the bottle.*]

Lemon squash! Ten tablespoons if there's a drop. Shake the bottle well before use! All the goodness sinks to the bottom! For quick relief of all, or eases, some say soothes. Depends on the pain. Change The Subject!

[*Notices there is some squash left in the glass.*]

Quench my thirst!

[*He drinks. Pause.*]

Am I going mad? No. This is not madness. Those who are, don't know they're mad. Whereas I know . . . I'm mad.

[*Pause.*]

Something wrong there. If you think you're mad you're not. That's it! Only when you think you aren't.

[*Exits and returns, but not to the table. He stops just inside the light.*]

It was the weight that shocked me. Suddenly so heavy! Why didn't I notice? All those times. My arms never ached. But they grunted. Sarel. The one called the other Sarel. 'Let's try it this way, Sarel,' he said. 'You go first.' One two three UP! In black suits with him weighing a weight that made them grunt and me . . . hanging around . . . my two helping hands useless and empty; all of me useless and big and getting in the way when they tried to get him through the door . . . excuse me try it again sorry am I in the way OOOOps gently does it don't drop it I beg your pardon your forgiveness your sorrow. . . . Suddenly they were out, going, and everybody on the pavement was staring at me. . . . Isn't there something to sign, I asked. A form to fill? We've got your name and address, he said. The office will contact you. So that was that. One two three UP! Picked up and carried out. Pushed in the back. Carried away. Bumping up and down because the road is bad. Finally just a thing. Horribly heavy. IT. Smothered by a sheet. Shoved in a hole. . . .

[*Desperate move to the table—grabs the spoon and starts tapping.*]

If this isn't madness it's a nervous breakdown. Think! Anything!

[*Tries to pour himself some squash.*]

Quick quench!

[*He can't get the stopper off the bottle fast enough.*]

Too late. HELP!

[*He grabs hold of the edge of the table, closes his eyes, and starts to speak at a very fast tempo—the first part of the speech is almost gabbled.*]

Queen Victoria's statue is on the square and during the day pigeons sit on it and do their business on it so looking up she said thank god cows don't fly but we've heard that one before and between shifts the bus conductors sit under it on benches with little tin boxes waiting for their buses with boxes on benches buses bunches of bosses all routes here we Go. . . .

[*Takes a deep breath.*]

Summerstrand Humewood Cadles Walmer Perridgevale Newton Park Mount Pleasant Kensington Europeans only and all classes double deckers with standing prohibited spitting prosecuted and alighting while in motion is at your own risk. . . .

[*Tempo gradually slowing down.*]

And sooner or later it starts to get dark in the square, the sun sets, the last light goes riding away on the backs of the buses, and then it's twilight with a sky stretching all the way down Main Street and beyond who knows where, the ends of the earth. . . . And all being well I'm in the gloom on Jetty Street corner watching while it gathers, waiting for nothing in particular with the City Hall clock telling the time, some time, ding-dong, start to count forget to finish because it's all the same . . . the cars get fewer, the newspaper boys stop calling and count their pennies on the pavement while darkness is coming it seems from the sea up Jetty Street. . . . Bringing peace, the end of the day, my moment, everybody hurrying away from it, leaving it, for me, just me, there in the shadows and no questions asked, for once enough, ME is enough, need nothing, whisper my name without shame. . . . Until the lights go on. . . . Suddenly like a small fright, ON, which is my sign to think of going. . . . Which I do. . . . I pull up my roots as the saying goes and go. . . . Down Baakens Street past the police station where the bars on the windows and the pick-up vans give me the creeps. . . . To Baakens Bridge. . . . And near the bus-sheds there, one night . . . I saw a bus-conductor off duty pressing a girl against the wall in a dark corner and he was smiling and holding his time-sheet and she looked sly and then he kissed her. . . . Black water was under the bridge running the wrong way because of the sea. . . . While he kissed her and smiled and she was sly. . . . While he held his time-sheet. . . .

[*Speaking now at an even tempo—each image distinct.*]

And not far away from there I will hear the frogs, without fail, the frogs never fail. In the meantime I hear trains shunting and try not to remember something; with the sky getting darker all this time and an old woman sitting with oranges under a lamp-post not selling any. . . . And me, me, walking, pressing on, I'm. . . .

[*Long pause. He opens his eyes.*]

Safe. Yes. Sure enough. Safe and sound. Firm ground. That was close. Like a hole, black and deep, among all the little thoughts. Suddenly there's nothing, and I'm falling! These are dangerous days. Safety first. Arrive in peace not in pieces. Bloody good!

[*Exits and returns.*]

So he kissed her. Just like that. And I thought, there are things to think about, which I did and still do, things to happen which hadn't and don't seem to. Other things happen to me. I am not complaining. I'm happy with my lot.

[*Pause.*]

My little.

So where were we?

[*Vigorous and clear, as if directing a stranger.*]

After the bridge turn sharp right. Carry on along the foot of the cliff until you come to a fork. Take the bottom prong. Then third to your left. It's on the left-hand side about half-way up. Fifty-seven A. You can't miss it. Green windows and a door . . .

. . . a door I never knock. Because it's my door. Open it with . . . some sort of heart and my right hand, close it with my left hand, behind me. Stand and listen. What sort of heart? Beating loud. Listening.

Stop! Just stop. Easy does it. Count the chairs. One two three four chairs. Table. One man. Friday somethingth. Move. Keep moving. Look for light entertainment.

[*Exits left and returns almost immediately with a comic.*]

Seen like that life's amazing!

[*He sits and reads the comic.*]

[*A woman appears up stage and walks slowly into the light. She is wearing a coat and carrying a large and battered suitcase. This is Hester. Johnnie looks up from his comic and watches her.*]

HESTER [*putting down the suitcase*]. Hello.

JOHNNIE. Hello.

HESTER. Didn't you hear me calling?

JOHNNIE. No.

HESTER. Well I did!

JOHNNIE. I'm not arguing.

HESTER. I thought nobody was home.

JOHNNIE. No. I've been sitting here, minding my own business. . . .

HESTER. Well then listen next time, for God's sake. First the taxi hooted. But he was in a hurry so I told him to drop me. I could see the light was on.

JOHNNIE. I've been reading. . . .

HESTER. I even started to wonder if it was the right place.

JOHNNIE. Fifty-seven A Valley Road. Smit's the name.

HESTER. You being funny? Anyway the door wasn't locked. So what you got to say for yourself?

JOHNNIE. Surprised of course. I mean, put yourself in my shoes. I'm sitting here, reading a comic, passing the time, and then you! Suddenly you're here too.

HESTER. Not even a word of welcome.

[*Pause.*]

JOHNNIE. Welcome.

HESTER. Don't kill yourself!

JOHNNIE. Make yourself at home!

HESTER. I will.

JOHNNIE. What else? HospitaliTEA! How about a nice cup of. . . . No. Milk's finished. Can I offer you a refreshing glass of lemon squash? It's preserved with Benzoic Acid.

HESTER. Later.

[*She moves right and stares off in that direction.*]

Sleeping?

JOHNNIE. Who?

HESTER. Who? Him! Is he sleeping? Hell, you just woken up or something?

JOHNNIE. Me? No. I've been sitting here, reading. . . .

HESTER. Okay, okay. How's things otherwise?

JOHNNIE. Just a comic, mind you. Not a book. I've run out of reading-matter.

HESTER. I didn't come a thousand miles to talk about comics.

JOHNNIE. So?

HESTER. So change the subject.

JOHNNIE. There's no law against reading a comic in my own home.

HESTER. All right.

JOHNNIE. I admitted it wasn't a book.

HESTER. All right I said.

JOHNNIE. But I'm not harming anyone.

HESTER. For God's sake, all right. Read your bloody comic. All I wanted was a word of welcome. Is that asking so much? Look, let's start again. Have a cigarette.

[*They light cigarettes.*]

I'm leaving it to you.

JOHNNIE. What?

HESTER. The questions.

JOHNNIE. What questions?

HESTER. Or news.

JOHNNIE. No news, good news.

HESTER. Who cares? Let's hear it.

JOHNNIE. What?

HESTER. Anything. Just talk!

JOHNNIE. Okay.

HESTER. Good.

JOHNNIE. Can I be frank?

HESTER. Go ahead.

JOHNNIE. What do you want?

HESTER. How the hell do you like that!

JOHNNIE. I'm not telling you to go. Stay as long as you like.

I admire your—what's the word?—pluck. I always admire people who pluck up courage and barge in. But still—you and your suitcase, out of the blue, the dark, on my doorstep and before I could blink an eye in my house! You follow? What's all this in aid of?

HESTER. Listen to him!

JOHNNIE. Look, I said you could stay. I'm just interested. . . .

HESTER. Are you mad?

JOHNNIE. See what I mean. Straight to the point. Anyway, me mad? I worked it out. I don't think I am, therefore. . . . No . . . those that think they are . . . to cut a long story short I'm not.

HESTER. Johnnie?

JOHNNIE. You even know my name.

HESTER. Am I hearing you right? Of course I know your name.

[*Pause.*]

I don't believe it.

JOHNNIE. Truth is stranger than fiction.

HESTER. You don't know who I am.

JOHNNIE. You got me guessing.

HESTER. Don't you recognize me at all?

JOHNNIE. I admit I haven't had a really good look yet. I start with the feet and work up.

HESTER. Shut up! So why did you just sit there? Why didn't you ask?

JOHNNIE. But I did. I asked you. . . .

HESTER. All right!

[*Pause.*]

I'm Hester. Your sister, Hester Smit.

[*Pause.*]

Didn't you get my letter?

JOHNNIE. What letter?

HESTER. I wrote. Fifty-seven A Valley Road, Port Elizabeth. Saying I was coming. I waited and waited for a reply. Didn't you get it?

JOHNNIE. No.

HESTER. Well, I'm Hester, and I come back to visit you, Johnnie, my brother. So what you waiting for? Don't you believe me?

JOHNNIE. Give me time.

HESTER. I'm Hester, I tell you!

JOHNNIE. Prove it.

HESTER. You got a sister called Hester, haven't you?

JOHNNIE. Yes.

HESTER. And she's been gone a long time?

JOHNNIE. Yes.

HESTER. Well, that's me.

JOHNNIE. So prove it.

HESTER. You got a birthmark there . . .

[Pointing.]

. . . what looks like the map of Africa upside down; and on your leg, your left leg I think—yes it is!—there's an operation from that time you were playing with the Boer War bullet and it went off. Are you satisfied?

JOHNNIE. But all of that's me. I know I'm Johnnie. It's *you.* You say you're Hester. Prove it.

HESTER. I'll hit you.

JOHNNIE. No you won't.

HESTER. How the hell would I know all about you if I wasn't me? If I wasn't Hester? I came *here*, didn't I? I know the address, your name, about him. . . .

[Pointing off-right. Pointing off-left.]

That was our room; this was a lounge-cum-kitchen but after Mommie died I went on growing which isn't good for little boys to see so you moved in here and then it was kitchen-cum-bedroom, which also didn't matter because mostly there was a row on the go and nobody was talking to anybody else. Right or wrong? And when you got big and Daddy got worse it was you used to look after him because I was working at the Astoria Café, and that's his room and he's lying there with only one leg left because of the explosion; and all our life it was groaning and moaning and what the

Bible says and what God's going to do and I hated it! Right or wrong? Right! And it was hell. I wanted to scream. I got so sick of it I went away. What more do you want? Must I vomit?

[*Pause.*]

Well, don't just stand there. Take a good look and see it's me.

[*Hester moves close to Johnnie—she sees him properly for the first time. When she speaks again it is with the pain of recognition—what is and what was.*]

Johnnie! It's been a long time, *boetie.*

[*A small impulsive gesture of tenderness—hand to his cheek?—which she breaks off abruptly. She moves away.*]
[*Flat, matter-of-fact voice.*]

Well, is it me?

JOHNNIE [*quiet certainty*]. Yes, it's you.

HESTER. You sure?

JOHNNIE. I'm certain.

HESTER. Hester Smit.

JOHNNIE. I remember. . . .

HESTER. My face hasn't changed?

JOHNNIE. . . . your hate! It hasn't changed. The sound of it. Always so sudden, so loud, so late at night. Nobody else could hate it the way you did.

HESTER [*weary scorn*]. This? Four walls that rattled and a roof that leaked! What's there to hate?

JOHNNIE. Us.

HESTER. I've got better things to do with my hate.

JOHNNIE. You hated something. You said so yourself.

HESTER. All right, something. The way it was! All those years, and all of us, in here.

JOHNNIE. Then why have you come back?

HESTER. That was twelve years ago.

JOHNNIE. You don't hate it now?

HESTER. Now. What's now? I've just arrived.

JOHNNIE. Tonight.

HESTER. I'll tell you tomorrow. Let me look at it in the light.

JOHNNIE. How long will you be staying?

HESTER [*ignoring the question*]. *Ja*. Twelve years ago next month. I worked it out in the train. I was twenty-two. Best thing I ever did getting out of here.

JOHNNIE. Then why have you come back?

HESTER. You got lots of questions all of a sudden!

JOHNNIE. You said. . . .

HESTER. To hell with what I said. I'm here.

[*Looking around.*]

Mind you it's easier than I thought.

JOHNNIE. I've noticed that. It's always easier than we think.

HESTER. I thought it would be hard, or hurt—something like that. But here I am and it isn't so bad.

JOHNNIE. It's never as bad as we think.

HESTER. Do you know what I'm talking about?

JOHNNIE. No.

HESTER. Then shut up and listen!

[*Pause.*]

I'm talking about coming back. You see I tried hell of a hard to remember. That was a mistake. I got frightened.

JOHNNIE. Of what?

HESTER. Not like that. Maybe frightened is wrong. Don't get any ideas I'm scared of you lot. Just because I come back doesn't mean I'm hard-up. But at Kommodagga there was a long stop—I started remembering and that made me. . . .

[*Groping for words.*]

. . . I think 'nerves' is better. The whole business was getting on my nerves! The heat, sitting there sweating and waiting! I'm not one for waiting. It was the slow train, you see. All stops. And then also this old bitch in the compartment. I hate them when they're like that—fat and dressed in black like Bibles because somebody's dead, and calling me *Ou* Sister. I had her from Noupoort and it was non-stop all the time about the Kingdom of Heaven was at hand and swimming on Sunday and all that rubbish.

Because I was remembering, you see! It wasn't that I couldn't. I could. It was seeing it again that worried me. The same.

Do you understand? Coming back and seeing it all still the
same. I wasn't frightened of there being changes. I said to
myself, I hope there is changes. Please let it be different,
and strange, even if I get lost and got to ask my way. I won't
mind. But to think of it all still the same, the way it was,
and me coming back to find it like that . . . ! Sick! It made
me sick on the stomach. There was fruit cake with the afternoon tea and I almost vomited.

And every time just when I'm ready to be brave *Ou* Sister
starts again on the Kingdom and Jesus doesn't like lipstick.
By then I had her in a big way. So when she asks me if I
seen the light I said no because I preferred the dark! Just like
that, and I went outside to stand in the gangway. But next
stop I see it's still only Boesmanspoort and ninety miles to
go so it all starts again. Only it's worse now, because I start
remembering like never before.

Those windy days with nothing to do; the dust in the street!
Even the colour of things—so clear, man, it could have been
yesterday. The way the grass went grey around the laundry
drain on the other side, the foam in the river, and inside
those Indian women ironing white shirts. And the smell, that
special ironing smell—warm and damp—with them talking
funny Indian and looking sad. Smells! I could give you smells
a mile long—backyard smells, Sunday smells, and what about
the Chinaman shop on the corner! Is he still there? That
did it. Don't ask me why—something to do with no pennies
for sweets—but that did it. If it's still there I said, if there's
still those sacks of beans and sugar and rice on the floor with
everything smelling that special way when I walk past, I'll
bring up on the spot like a dog, so help me God.

So then I said, No, this isn't wise. Get off at Coega and
catch the next one back to Jo'burg. Send them a telegram,
even if it's a lie—sick of something, which was almost true.
I was ready to do it. 'Strue's God!

But the next stop was Sandflats and there suddenly I see it's
sunset. Somebody in the gangway said we were two hours
late and it will be dark when we get in. That will help me,
won't it, I think to myself. And it did. Because it was—dark
and me feeling like a stranger in the taxi.

All my life I been noticing this, the way night works, the

way it makes you feel home is somewhere else. Even with
the lights on, like now, looking at this . . . I don't know. It is
and it isn't. I'm not certain. It could be true. Tomorrow
will tell. I never have doubts in daylight.

So that was that. Jo'burg to P.E. second class. Over to you.

JOHNNIE. Why have you come back?

[*Hester lights a cigarette, giving no sign of replying to the question.*]

That was a very good description. My journey to P.E. on the
S.A.R. I'd give you eight out of ten.

[*Pause.*]

Why have you come back?

HESTER. It's also my home. I've got a right to come here if
I want to. I'm still his daughter. How is he?

JOHNNIE. How long you staying?

HESTER. What you worried about? I'll buy my own food.

JOHNNIE. Is this a holiday? Back home for old times sake
sort of thing. Two weeks annually.

HESTER. In here? I got better things to do with my holidays.

JOHNNIE. So why have you come?

HESTER. Look, stop worrying! I'm passing through. It's hello
and goodbye. Maybe I'm gone tomorrow.

[*Looking off-right to father's room.*]

And him?

[*Johnnie stares at her.*]

Speak up! I don't care what you say.

[*Pause.*]

So he still hates me. I wasn't expecting miracles. Any case I
also got a memory. Don't think I've forgotten some of the
things that was said in here. It's my life and I'll do what
I like.

JOHNNIE. Yes, he still hates you. He doesn't want to see you.

HESTER. So what? Just remember Mommie didn't hate me
and half of this house was hers so I'm entitled to be here.
You can tell him that from me.

JOHNNIE. He's sleeping.

HESTER. I heard he was in a bad way.

JOHNNIE. He's sleeping in there.

HESTER. I know he's sleeping in there! But I heard he was in a bad way.

[*Pause.*]

Well, is it true?

JOHNNIE. No.

HESTER. I met old Magda Swanepoel and she told me nobody ever sees him any more and that she heard he was in a bad way. Death's door. Those were her words.

JOHNNIE. NO!

HESTER. So then tell me what's happening.

JOHNNIE. He's recovering.

HESTER. Well, it can't last for ever.

JOHNNIE. He's making a splendid recovery! Improving day by day. I've got him on Wilson's Beef and Iron tonic—one tablespoon with water after every meal. It's working wonders. Building up his strength. . . .

HESTER. But he's still cripple.

JOHNNIE. Yes.

HESTER. Still in bed most of the time.

JOHNNIE. Yes.

HESTER. Don't tell him I'm here. I'll be quiet. I'm not scared of him! But I can't stay long. Maybe tomorrow. Like I said it's just hello and goodbye. Anyway, let's see. Yes.

[*To her suitcase, which she opens, taking out a small packet.*]

There's no hard feelings between us so I bought you a present. We got on well together, didn't we?

[*Hands it over to Johnnie.*]

Well, aren't you going to open it? What's the matter with you, man? You never used to be like this. It's a cigar called a cheroot. Put one in your mouth and let's see. Oh well. . . . What else?

[*Back to her suitcase, rummaging through its contents.*]

I had some tea left, and this tin of condensed milk. Jam. It all helps. You want a pot? Here. I'm damned if I was going to leave her anything.

JOHNNIE. Who?

HESTER. Mrs. Humphries. Trocadero Court. The landlady. As it is she gets . . . let's see. I'm paid up till the end of the month. Ten days! By rights she owes me.

[*Back to the suitcase.*]

My own knife and fork. Spoon. Plate. That's all.

[*Rummaging.*]

Just my clothes.

JOHNNIE [*watching her*]. You've come back for something, Hester.

HESTER. Have I?

JOHNNIE. What?

HESTER. I didn't say yes.

JOHNNIE. I say you've come back for something.

HESTER. You can say what you like, my boy.

JOHNNIE. I know you.

HESTER. You know me, do you? Ten minutes ago you were singing another song.

[*Standing.*]

I feel dirty. Still the old zinc bath from the yard and a kettle of hot?

JOHNNIE. Yes.

HESTER. *Ag*, it can wait. I'm too tired. I suppose you're in my room now?

JOHNNIE. You take it.

HESTER. I'll be all right in here.

JOHNNIE. No! You take the bed. He needs me. He calls.

[*Pause.*]

HESTER. Yes. I remember that too. Late . . . *late* at night, when everybody was in bed, groaning or calling softly, on and on. . . .

JOHNNIE. He never called for you!

HESTER. I heard him all the same. Don't you hate it?

JOHNNIE. I don't know . . . NO! I don't hate it. I don't think about it. He's my father.

141

[*Hester breaks off staring at Johnnie and struggles off-left with her suitcase. Johnnie remains motionless at the table. Hester reappears a few seconds later.*]

HESTER. You're going to empty those slops in there sometime, I hope?

[*Exit Johnnie left with Hester following.*]

Christ Almighty, no wonder!

[*Johnnie reappears carrying a white enamel bucket.*]

[*Off.*]

And leave it out. Let it get some fresh air!

[*Exit Johnnie up stage. Returns to the table, empty-handed.*]

[*Off.*]

I can't understand why you never got that letter! I posted it. Fifty-seven A Valley Road. Where the hell is my. . . ?

[*Indistinct mumble of words—occasional phrases are heard.*]

. . . good ironing . . . second class . . . all that dust . . . one thing about a good drip-dry. . . .

[*Again loud and distinct.*]

Hell, man, why don't you get the broom in here? It's inches thick. I'm not fussy but this is the bloody limit. Just look at it!

JOHNNIE. Ssssh!

[*Hester appears in her petticoat.*]

He's sleeping.

HESTER. I wasn't making so much noise.

JOHNNIE. He needs all the sleep he can get.

HESTER. So who's stopping him?

JOHNNIE. You were shouting. The doctor said. . . .

HESTER. I know, I know. Good night.

[*Exit Hester. Johnnie waits a few seconds, listening, then follows her to the edge of light.*]

Close your door. Just in case.

[*As soon as he is satisfied that Hester has closed her door, Johnnie moves quickly to the table and looks wildly around the room. Hurried exit into father's room, returning immediately but stopping just inside the light to stare at Hester's room. Another impulsive move, this time*] *to the table to collect two chairs which he stacks up at the entrance to the father's room, blocking it. But he almost immediately changes his mind and takes them back to the table.*]

JOHNNIE. Hester, back in the land of the living. It's her all right. Large as life. Loud as . . . something. Bold! And not answering questions. The danger signal! Hold your breath and wait. What else? Think. Go back . . . back . . . all the days, right back, further than I've ever been . . . memories. Wind, as she said. Dust, and nothing to do . . . and Hester! I'm crying and she's got her fingers in her ears. Does that help me? Her fingers in her ears, and shouting or singing at the top of her voice to drown my crying. How does that help me? Or those times . . . saying nothing! That way of hers —can't sit still, ants in her pants and saying nothing. Hester with a scheme up her sleeve. There's a word—beer does it in the dark—Brewing! And then trouble. Without fail. She wants something. The letter!

[*Johnnie exits up stage, returning a few seconds later with a bundle of mail—mostly commercial circulars. He goes through them hurriedly and finds a letter, but before he can open it Hester reappears, smoking a cigarette, a small mirror in her hand. Johnnie quickly tucks the letter back into the pile of mail on the table.*]

HESTER. What you up to?

JOHNNIE [*picking up one of the commercial circulars*]. Boswell's Circus. Behind the new Law Courts. Cheap seats five bob.

HESTER. Do you sit up all night?

JOHNNIE. When he's bad.

HESTER. You said he was better.

JOHNNIE. He's getting better.

HESTER. So he was bad.

JOHNNIE. Well on the road to recovery.

HESTER. But he *was*. . . .

JOHNNIE. We mustn't talk loud.

HESTER. I'm not talking loud.

JOHNNIE. I'm just saying.

HESTER. Well say it when I'm talking loud!

JOHNNIE. You're starting.

HESTER. Oh shit!

JOHNNIE. Why don't you get a good night's rest?

HESTER. Are you trying to get rid of me?

JOHNNIE. You look tired.

HESTER. Just now. It's those damn frogs. Were they always so loud?

JOHNNIE. Croak.

HESTER. What?

JOHNNIE. Ducks quack, dogs bark, frogs croak.

HESTER. All right, professor. I still don't remember them being so loud.

JOHNNIE. Some nights they don't croak at all.

[*Back to the mail.*]

Spick! 'Spick for your pots
       Spick for your pans
       Cleans like a shot
       And soft on the hands.'
They're damned clever, you know.

HESTER. There is something I want to ask you.

JOHNNIE. Now in a family pack.

HESTER. Hey! I've got a question.

JOHNNIE. As long as it's not loud.

HESTER. For God's sake! I'm talking at the bottom of my voice.

[*Johnnie goes back to the circular.*]

I haven't asked my question yet! What do *I* look like? When you saw me, and you knew it was me, Hester, did you remember much?

JOHNNIE. Like what?

HESTER. Like I was. I mean, am I changed much?

JOHNNIE [*not looking at her*]. Hard to say. . . .

HESTER. Have you had a good look at me yet?

JOHNNIE. It's the light in here. I feel it when I'm reading. Maybe I need glasses.

HESTER. Rubbish! Look at me. Come close! You're not looking properly! I can see it in your eyes.

JOHNNIE. I'm trying to.

HESTER. What's the matter with you?

JOHNNIE. It's rude to stare.

HESTER. I'm asking you to. Now come on!

JOHNNIE. All right, but don't stare at me. Look the other way.

[*Pause. He looks at Hester.*]

Okay.

HESTER. Well?

JOHNNIE. What do you want me to say?

HESTER. What you saw.

JOHNNIE. You—my sister Hester—a few years older. Satisfied?

HESTER. No! Am I also . . . were you shocked? At the changes? My face?

[*Mirror in her hand.*]

What do I really look like now? I can't see myself. Mirrors don't work. I can't watch . . . Me. When I look, *I* look back.

JOHNNIE [*back to the commercial circular*]. One cap-full is enough for a sink-full of dishes. That's a hell of a lot of dishes. One sink-full! Big families I suppose, and three meals a day. Porridge, stews, puddings. You'd need it then. Anything with gravy or fat, or soft fried eggs with that yellowy yolk. Once it's cold you've had it. As for the pot you've boiled milk in . . . ! Bread's the best. Dust off the plate and use it again. Also cheese, very hard-boiled eggs, biscuits—anything that comes in crumbs. Watch out for jam. It looks easy but once it's on the plate. . . .

HESTER. And you, Johnnie?

JOHNNIE. If I could afford it beer and lemon creams three times a day.

HESTER. Johnnie!

JOHNNIE. I'm all ears.

HESTER. What happened to you?

JOHNNIE. Who said anything happened to me?

HESTER. All these years! Wasn't it learner-stoker once upon a time? At the Kroonstad Railway School? You had the forms to fill in and everything. Then I left. What happened?

[*Johnnie is staring straight ahead.*]

Ever since I can remember you always wanted to be an engine driver. What. . . .

JOHNNIE. Ssssssh!

[*Exit into father's room. Returns a few seconds later but doesn't sit.*]

He's sleeping soundly. I gave him a dose of Wilson's Beef and Iron after supper. Instructions on the label. One tablespoon with water after meals. Here's the bottle if you don't believe me. Satisfied?

[*He sits.*]

HESTER. I'm not interested in him. I was asking what happened to you.

JOHNNIE. And I heard you. That was a long time ago. But I remember now. I changed my mind.

HESTER [*not believing him*]. Just like that!

JOHNNIE. Just like that.

HESTER. After all those years?

JOHNNIE. After all those years one morning I changed my mind just like that and didn't go. I tore up the application forms.

[*Back to the mail on the table.*]

We've had Spick, Boswell's Circus . . . what's left? Providential Assurance. Looks like arithmetic. And this?

[*The letter is uncovered.*]

Is this your handwriting?

HESTER. Give here. Hey, yes. This is it.

JOHNNIE [*taking it back*]. Let's see what you said.

[*He opens it.*]

HESTER. But I posted that weeks ago.

JOHNNIE. Isn't there something called surface mail?

HESTER [*watching him open the envelope*]. You going to read it?

JOHNNIE. You wrote it to me.

HESTER. No, wait. That's not fair.

JOHNNIE. Fair?

HESTER. I'm already here.

146

JOHNNIE. That makes it even fairer. You know . . . in your presence.

HESTER. I said wait! Let me think. NO. Hand over.

JOHNNIE. Strictly speaking it's mine now.

HESTER. Give it!

[*She grabs it out of his hands.*]

I want to read it first.

[*Hester reads the letter. Johnnie waits passively for a few seconds, then starts his next speech while she is reading.*]

JOHNNIE. Yes, it all comes back. Clear as daylight—which it was. Just after breakfast, in fact. I changed my mind! There are bigger things in life than driving an engine, I said. So I tore up the forms in duplicate, and never looked back. It's best, they say, and they're right. I never do. Habit. One of those that help. Good and bad. Onward, always onward. Eyes on the road. Leave the corner and over the bridge, under the cliffs and along the river and no regrets. I never look back. I'll see it all again tomorrow. Always onwards. That's me in a nutshell.

HESTER [*folding up the letter*]. Nothing much. I wouldn't worry about it if I was you.

JOHNNIE [*holding out his hand*]. Who cares?

HESTER [*ignoring the hand*]. Stick to your comics if you want a laugh. It's not worth reading.

JOHNNIE. Let's see what you said.

HESTER. Just that I'm coming by train.

JOHNNIE. Two pages.

HESTER. And how are you and I'm okay. The usual.

JOHNNIE. Two pages on both sides.

HESTER. Mrs. Humphries only had two pages left.

JOHNNIE. So it's really four pages to say you're coming by train and how am I and you're okay.

HESTER. And news.

JOHNNIE. What news?

HESTER. Just news, for God's sake. Don't you know what news is? Anyway you wouldn't be interested.

JOHNNIE. Then why did you write it?

HESTER. You got to write something.

JOHNNIE. I am interested. I've thought about it. I am definitely interested.

HESTER. All right. Don't panic. Remember Pearl Harbour. I said. . . .

JOHNNIE [*holding out his hand*]. Let me read it.

HESTER. I want to have another look.

JOHNNIE. I'll give it back.

HESTER. What you in such a hurry for?

JOHNNIE. I'm not in a hurry.

HESTER. Oh no? Look at your hand.

JOHNNIE [*withdrawing his hand*]. I'll wait.

[*He waits. Hester watches him.*]

HESTER. If you're trying to be funny, Johnnie Smit . . . !

[*Johnnie waits.*]

I'm warning you!

[*Johnnie waits.*]

Right, you asked for it!

[*Tearing up the letter.*]

That . . . and that . . . and that . . . and may God strike me stone dead if I ever write you another one.

[*She lights a cigarette; the letter has brought a tension to her.*]

JOHNNIE. Happy?

HESTER. Why should I be happy?

JOHNNIE. You didn't want me to read it.

HESTER [*vindictive*]. Yes! I didn't want you to read it.

JOHNNIE. That's what I said.

HESTER. And now you *can't* read it.

JOHNNIE. And that's why you're happy.

HESTER. Happy? In here? Don't make me laugh. Nothing in here knows what happy means.

JOHNNIE. 'That way of hers . . . saying nothing!'

HESTER. Who?

JOHNNIE. Hester with a scheme up her sleeve! What was in that letter?

HESTER. My own business.

JOHNNIE. Why didn't you want me to read it?

HESTER. Because it's going to stay my own business.

JOHNNIE. Suppose I found it before you arrived?

HESTER. Suppose, suppose. Suppose I didn't come, what then? Suppose he was dead, what then?

JOHNNIE. You Must Not Say That!

HESTER. I said suppose, for God's sake.

JOHNNIE. He's our father.

HESTER. Here we go again! And I'm his daughter and you're his son and I'm your sister and where's our mother? Well, I'm also ME! Just ME. Hester. And something is going to be mine—just mine—and no sharing with brothers or fathers. . . .

JOHNNIE. Twenty years ago you used to say that.

[*This remark stops her tirade. She moves about restlessly.*]

What are you looking for?

HESTER. I'm not looking for anything.

JOHNNIE. You're looking in all the corners.

HESTER. Twenty years ago. That puts him in his sixties.

JOHNNIE. All the corners—not answering questions.

HESTER. I said that puts him in his sixties.

JOHNNIE. Does it?

HESTER. Work it out.

JOHNNIE. Multiplied by. . . .

HESTER. Add.

JOHNNIE. Multiplication gives you the seconds.

HESTER. Just add. Middle age plus twenty years. Puts him in his old age. He must be getting grey then. Eyesight bad and the shakes. Isn't he grey?

JOHNNIE [*his eyes closed*]. . . . become minutes, become hours, days of the week. . . .

HESTER. Answer me! Is he grey?

JOHNNIE. Sssssssh!

[*Gets up and goes into father's room. Hester waits, lights another cigarette. After a few seconds Johnnie returns.*]

JOHNNIE. I thought I heard a groan. But he's still asleep. That doesn't mean he didn't groan. Sometimes he groans in his sleep. But not from pain in the stump. It's his dreams that make him groan. You know what he's doing in his dreams? He's working again on the railway line to Graaff-Reinet in the olden days. It's the hard work that makes him groan, he says. Other times it's the pain. I can't tell the difference. I've tried to guess. How many nights haven't I listened and said, Is that hard work or is it pain? Then in the morning I go in to him and say: You were dreaming again last night, chum. No, he says, ... the pain in my stump. I never slept a wink. Or when I say: It seemed to hurt last night, Daddy, he looks at me and says, ... Maybe. I didn't feel it. I dreamed we reached Heuningvlei. We're living in tents on the side of the line at Heuningvlei.

[*Pause.*]

You asked if he's grey. I had a good look at him. Yes, he's gone grey, but. . . .

HESTER. That's what I said.

JOHNNIE. BUT ... it suits him. In fact he's looking handsome these days. Don't you believe me?

HESTER. I didn't say that.

JOHNNIE [*watching Hester closely*]. Suppose I were to tell you he's grown a moustache. A smart little Errol Flynn moustache.

HESTER. Good luck to him.

JOHNNIE. And a beard! A voortrekker beard to go with it. And he's getting fat ... plump!

HESTER. So who cares?

JOHNNIE. You believe me?

HESTER. If you say so.

JOHNNIE. No. He still shaves. Tries to. Cuts himself. Misses little patches where the hairs grow longer and longer until I have to fetch the scissors. He's thin. Skin and bone. He won't eat. I try all sorts of delicacies. Sardines on toast. Warm buttered toast with the silver little fishes. . . .

HESTER. Does he ask about me?

JOHNNIE. No.

HESTER. But he remembers me.

JOHNNIE. I don't know.

HESTER. So then how can you say he still hates me?

JOHNNIE. Because he doesn't speak about you.

HESTER. Maybe he's thinking about me.

JOHNNIE. When you left he said, 'We won't speak about her any more.' You weren't a real Afrikaner by nature, he said. Must be some English blood somewhere, on Mommie's side. He hated you then. He doesn't dream about you. Only the railway line in the old days, the bad old days.

HESTER. Well, just remember that in the eyes of the law it doesn't mean a thing. Just because he doesn't remember or isn't thinking about me doesn't mean a damned thing.

JOHNNIE. Who says it does?

HESTER. Exactly? So when the time comes I want you to be a witness to what you just said.

JOHNNIE. What time?

HESTER. Don't panic. Nothing's happened yet.

JOHNNIE. What's going to happen? I don't like the sound of this. You want something, Hester. You're scheming. You've come back because you want something.

HESTER. I'm saying nothing. I'm passing through and my name is Hester Smit.

JOHNNIE. I know you.

HESTER. No you don't. None of you know me.

JOHNNIE. That's what you used to say.

HESTER. I'll say it again: None of you know me!

JOHNNIE. Just like that, and then there was trouble. None of you know me and you took that job in the café that nearly gave him the stroke, and stayed out late and brought those soldiers home. None of you know me, and you was gone for a week. None of you know me and you went for good. What is it this time? Why have you come back?

HESTER. Must I have a reason to visit my own home?

JOHNNIE. Just leave us alone. We're doing all right.

HESTER. I haven't done anything, for Christ's sake.

JOHNNIE. You're here.

HESTER. Because this is also my home. And him forgetting me doesn't count. She was my mother and he's still my father even if he hates me. So half of everything in here is mine when the time comes.

JOHNNIE. What time is going to come?

HESTER. Something is going to happen some day.

JOHNNIE. Such as what?

HESTER. Such as being dead when your time comes. That happens.

JOHNNIE. The second time.

HESTER. Well, you know what I mean.

JOHNNIE. That's the second time you've said it.

HESTER. You forced me.

JOHNNIE. You're wishing it.

HESTER. I'm not.

JOHNNIE. That's wicked.

HESTER. Dry up, for God's sake.

JOHNNIE. That's sin.

HESTER. It's not Sunday, Dominee.

JOHNNIE [loudly]. Wishing for him to die is the wickedest sin in the world!

HESTER. Who's making the noise now?

[Abrupt silence. Johnnie goes into father's room, returning in a few seconds very nervous and agitated.]

JOHNNIE. Now you've done it! He's groaning.

HESTER. I've done it?

JOHNNIE. I warned you.

HESTER. Jesus.

JOHNNIE. If there's a stroke you know who's to blame! It looks bad. Wait for the worst, pray for the best.

HESTER. How the hell do you like that!

[Johnnie now busies himself with the bottle of medicine; a lot of

movement in and out of the light to clean the glass, fetch the spoon,
measure out the medicine, add water, etc., etc.]

Fifteen years gone and one hour back but I done it again!
Home sweet home where who did it means Hester done it.
'I didn't do it. She did it!' If I laughed too loud that did it.
Have a little cry and that will do it. Sit still and mind your
own business but sure as the lavatory stinks that will also do it.
Well one day I will. And then God help the lot of you.

JOHNNIE. Will what?

HESTER. *Really* do it.

JOHNNIE. Your worst.

HESTER. Worse!

JOHNNIE. There's a word . . . catastrophe. Calamity. Ruin
staring us in the face.

HESTER. That's it! In ruins. The lot of you.

JOHNNIE. Smashed to smithereens.

HESTER. And I'll be happy. It's broken and I'm to blame but
I'm happy because this time I'll know I did it. So hello be
damned and goodbye for good and go back home.

JOHNNIE. You're a rotten egg. There's one in every dozen.

[*Shouting to father's room.*]

Hold on I'm coming!

[*To Hester.*]

For your sake I hope this works.

[*Exit with medicine. Exhausted by her outburst Hester sinks into a
chair . . . her elbows on the table, her forehead resting on her palms.
She holds this position in silence for a few seconds.*]

HESTER [*without looking up*]. Home.

[*A few more seconds in silence and without movement and then she
lifts her head once to look around the room and then drops it back
on to her palms. Johnnie returns from his father's room, but stays
some distance away from the table in half light.*]

[*Without looking up.*]

You?

JOHNNIE. Yes.

HESTER. I meant a room.

JOHNNIE. What?

HESTER. When I go back. I said I would go back Home. But this is it, isn't it? I'll go back to a room. I'm not hard up for a home.

JOHNNIE [*still in the shadows*]. Leave me your address. I'll write. Let you know how things. . . .

HESTER [*abruptly*]. There's no address.

JOHNNIE. When you settle down and find a new place.

HESTER. There's no address! No names, no numbers. A room somewhere, in a street somewhere. To Let is always the longest list, and they're all the same. Rent in advance and one week's notice—one week to notice it's walls again and a door with nobody knocking, a table, a bed, a window for your face when there's nothing to do. So many times! Then I started waking in the middle of the night wondering which one it was, which room . . . lie there in the dark not knowing. And later still, who it was. Just like that. Who was it lying there wondering where she was? Who was where? Me. And I'm Hester. But what's that mean? What does Hester Smit mean? So you listen. But men dream about other women. The names they call are not yours. That's all. You don't know the room, you're not in his dream. Where do you belong?

JOHNNIE. So what do you do?

HESTER. Wait. Lie there, let it happen, and wait. For a memory. That's the way it works. A memory comes. Suddenly there's going to be a memory of you, somewhere, some other time. And then you can work it all out again. In the meantime, just wait, listen to the questions and have no answers . . . no danger or pain or anything like that, just something missing, the meaning of your name.

[*Pause.*]

It was always the same memory. I was a little girl and I was lying awake one night. I was in here, the kitchen, sleeping in here because you got the mumps in the other room. Mommie and Daddy are in there . . .

[*Pointing to father's room.*]

. . . the door is open and I can hear them talking.

Compensation, he says. They got to. I've only got one leg and a wife and two children. He was talking about the accident, the explosion and everything is just compensation, compensation . . . hundreds of pounds!

JOHNNIE [*stepping forward into the light*]. The earth opened up! Just like in the Bible. And the mountain fell down on top of him! I know it by heart.

[*Clears his throat and tells the story in a strong vigorous voice.*]

Two miles the other side of Perseverance. They were relaying a section of the line to Uitenhage. It was as hot as hell, which isn't swearing because that's what Bible says. He had slipped away when the others weren't looking to eat prickly pears. There was a bush on the hill, covered with them, fat and ripe. So he was standing there in the shade sucking a juicy one when one of the men from headquarters—those in the white coats—saw him and started to shout. At first Daddy pretended he didn't see him. But then this man got more excited, shouting and swearing and running towards him. The others had all stopped working and were watching. Daddy said he knew then he was in trouble . . . maybe the prickly pear bush was on private property or something. So he picked up his spade and started to go back. But then the man in the white coat went completely mad, screaming and swearing in English like nothing Daddy had ever heard. The others also were jumping up and down—old Dolf, Van Rooyen, Elsie, the lot—jumping up and down and shouting and waving at him. This is it, he thought, I'm fired. The spade was heavy, it was uphill—because he was so frightened he had turned around and was running away for good—and then with a tremendous roar the earth opened! Right in front of his own eyes it just opened and half a mountain was coming down towards him!

[*Pause.*]

He woke up in hospital minus one leg. Dynamite! It's a hell of a word.

HESTER. Does he still talk about it?

JOHNNIE. It's my favourite of all the stories.

HESTER. And the compensation? What does he say about the compensation? Don't look stupid. He was paid hundreds of pounds compensation.

JOHNNIE. He never . . . he doesn't talk about that.

HESTER. Well, he was! I heard him myself, in here. And not just once. There was a lot of talk those days about compensation, and him saying they got to pay. Hundreds of pounds! Because it wasn't his fault. They didn't tell him there was dynamite.

JOHNNIE. So?

HESTER. So I'm just saying.

JOHNNIE. He must have spent it.

HESTER. Him? Hundreds of pounds? Don't make me laugh. Does this look like hundreds of pounds was spent in our lives?

JOHNNIE. What about food? Rent?

HESTER. No you don't! I worked it out. He still gets his disability grant, doesn't he?

JOHNNIE. Yes.

HESTER. And his pension. Well, you work it out and you'll see it covers household and upkeep and all we ever got out of life in here.

JOHNNIE. So then it's in the bank or a post-office book or something.

HESTER. Maybe—only I don't think it is, you see. Because I thought about that one too. When Mommie died and he had to pay the expenses—the coffin and all that—he didn't go to no bank or post-office, he went in there!

[Pointing to father's room.]

I was sitting here with the man from the funeral firm and Daddy went in *there* and came back and paid cash!

JOHNNIE. So?

HESTER. So I'm just saying for Christ's sake.

[*Johnnie moves closer to the table, watching Hester carefully. She is tensed and restless.*]

[*Uncertain of how to put her next question.*]

Tell me . . . is . . . a . . . ?

JOHNNIE [*quickly*]. What?

HESTER. Hold your horses! Hell you're in a hurry. What's it like in there?

JOHNNIE. It was a bad turn, but I think he's pulling around. Wilson's Beef and Iron did the trick. Double dose. Calms the nerves and eases the pain. With water after every. . . .

HESTER. Yes, yes, I know. What I mean is, all that old junk —those boxes, man, and suitcases, all that old junk that was packed away when Mommie died and he wouldn't let us fiddle in.

JOHNNIE. You mean his private possessions.

HESTER. Is it still in there? On the wardrobe and under the bed, you know the way it was.

JOHNNIE. Yes.

[*Johnnie watching Hester carefully. She knows it but works up enough courage to continue.*]

HESTER. You want to know something?

JOHNNIE. NO!

HESTER. It's in one of them. The compensation. I'll take you any bet you like it's hidden in one of those boxes.

JOHNNIE. So that's it.

HESTER [*embarrassed but determined*]. Is it?

JOHNNIE. That's why you've come back! That was in your letter!

HESTER. Since when are you a mind-reader?

JOHNNIE. Tell me I'm wrong.

HESTER. What's that prove? Can you deny it's there? No. Because it is. And I'm entitled to half. What would have happened to my share if he passed away and I hadn't come? You didn't know where I was?

JOHNNIE [*closing his eyes*]. He Is Not. . . .

HESTER. HE IS! Some day. He's got to. Everybody does. Sooner or later. . . .

JOHNNIE. No.

HESTER. Yes.

JOHNNIE. The Wilson's Beef and Iron. . . .

HESTER. Shut up! And wake up. Open your eyes! You said so yourself. Grey, you said. And thin. Your own words. Old age and grey and bad turns. Well, that's knocking at death's door . . . LISTEN! If you don't want a slap in your face just shut up and listen. I'm still alive, you see. Alive. He's passing away but I'm still alive. And I'm his daughter. So half of that compensation is mine. Ask any lawyer you like. It's legal and I'm entitled. What good is it doing in there? He doesn't need it. The disability and pension keep him going. So it's just lying there rotting away. Maybe the mould has got it. It got everything else in this house. Or the cockroaches. And then one day when we find it it's cockrotted and useless. So what then is the use of anything? I want it now. Not next year, or when I'm ready for the rubbish heap like him, but Now! Is that such a sin?

JOHNNIE. Yes! It's his, and he's your father. . . .

HESTER. And you're my brother and I'm his daughter so we must all love each other and live happily ever after! Well I got news for you, brother. I don't. There's no fathers, no brothers, no sisters, or Sunday, or sin. There's nothing. The fairy stories is finished. They died in a hundred Jo'burg rooms. There's man. And I'm a woman. It's as simple as that. You want a sin, well there's one. I *Hoer*. I've *hoer*ed all the brothers and fathers and sons and sweethearts in this world into one thing . . . Man. That's how I live and that's why I don't care. And now I'm here and waiting. Because when he wakes up I'm going in there to tell him I want it. My share.

JOHNNIE. No.

HESTER. You think I'm scared of him?

JOHNNIE. No, I mean yes. You will. But don't. Wait. One minute. Just stay still. . . . Sssssh! Let me think. I'm coming!

[*Hurried exit into father's room. Hester lights a cigarette and waits. After a few seconds Johnnie returns.*]

If you find it, will you go?

HESTER. Only my share. All I'm asking for. . . .

JOHNNIE. If you find it, will you go?

HESTER. Yes.

JOHNNIE. Straight away?

HESTER. Yes.

JOHNNIE. You won't worry him?

HESTER. No.

[*Pause.*]

Anything else?

JOHNNIE. You won't come back.

HESTER. This is also my home, you know.

JOHNNIE. I'll make a bargain. You take the money, all of it. Leave me the home.

HESTER. Fair exchange.

JOHNNIE. Then you won't come back, ever?

HESTER. No. So what do we do?

JOHNNIE. He's sleeping. I'll bring in the boxes. You say it's in the boxes.

HESTER. Or those old suitcases under the bed. I'm prepared to bet you anything. . . .

JOHNNIE. I'll bring them in.

[*Exit Johnnie. Hester clears the table and waits. Johnnie returns with the first box—cardboard and tied up with a piece of flaxen twine —which he puts on the table. Hester stands to one side watching it.*]

Number one.

[*He starts to untie the string.*]

HESTER [*going to the table*]. I'll do that! You just bring in the boxes.

[*Johnnie sits down and watches her.*]

You think I'm low, don't you?

JOHNNIE. I didn't say that.

HESTER. But you think it.

JOHNNIE. No.

HESTER. So then what you staring at?

JOHNNIE. How much did they pay you?

HESTER. Who?

JOHNNIE. The men. The ones you . . . you know. Your boy-friends. What's the tariff of charges?

[*Hester ignores the question. She has untied the twine and is now opening the box. There is a sheet of brown paper on top.*]

It depends on your age, doesn't it? The older you get, and so on.

HESTER. Mind your own business.

JOHNNIE. Just asking. I'm interested. There's a few in P.E., you know. Jetty Street. I watch them.

[*The first thing to come out of the box is a woman's dress. Hester smells it.*]

HESTER. Hey!

[*Another smell.*]

My God, Johnnie! Smell!

JOHNNIE. What?

HESTER. It's her.

JOHNNIE. Who?

HESTER. Mommie. Smell, man. It's Mommie's smell.

JOHNNIE [*smelling the dress*]. I can't remember.

HESTER. I'm telling you, it's her. I remember. How do you like that, hey? All these years. Hell, man, it hurts. Look, I claim this too. You don't need it. I'll put it on one side and pack it in with my things when I go. Remind me.

[*Back to the box.*]

JOHNNIE [*watching her again*]. Were there many? Hester! On an average, how many times a week?

[*Hester ignores him.*]

I've often wondered, when I see them in Jetty Street. It's illegal of course. You know that.

HESTER [*another dress out of the box—this time a young girl's*]. And this! Jesus, Johnnie. Look.

JOHNNIE. Ribbons.

HESTER. Me, man. Don't you remember? On Sundays? NO!

[*She puts the dress back hurriedly into the box and walks away—sudden fear.*]

JOHNNIE. And now?

HESTER. I've got a funny feeling.

JOHNNIE. What about the money?

[*After a silent struggle Hester goes back to the box and resumes her unpacking. Johnnie watches her.*]

HESTER. Bring in the others.

ACT TWO

The same, about an hour later.

Three or four suitcases and the same number of boxes—all opened —clutter the stage, their contents spilling out on to the floor, gathered together in piles, etc., etc.

Hester is sitting on a suitcase, a photo album open on her lap. She is studying a loose photo in her hands. Johnnie stands to one side holding another, as yet unopened box from his father's room.

A pair of crutches are leaning against a chair.

JOHNNIE. What about that Jansen girl? What was it? Gertrude! Gertrude Jansen!

[*Hester, still studying the photo, shakes her head.*]

She married a De Villiers.

HESTER. Give me some other names.

JOHNNIE. Bet you anything you like it's Gertrude.

HESTER. I said no. Now come on. Who were the others?

JOHNNIE. Let me see, sayeth the blind man. I'll give it to you in alphabetic order. A. Abel. The Abel boys. Ronnie and Dennis. No good. B. Blank. C . . . C. D. . . .

HESTER. Her brother worked at G.M.

JOHNNIE. I've got it. Carrol. Jessie Carrol.

HESTER. That's the one!

JOHNNIE. Jessica Carrol.

[*Places the box beside Hester and studies the photo over her shoulder.*]

Yes, that's her.

HESTER. She hated me.

JOHNNIE. Doesn't look like it.

HESTER. She hated my guts.

JOHNNIE. Got her arm through yours. Smiling. You too.

HESTER. Because we were having this picture taken! But she hated me all right. That time when I got the job at the Astoria Café—she also tried for it, but they took me. So she hated me more. And Stevie Jackson. He was supposed to be her boyfriend, but when he came home on leave it was me he was always running after and taking to Happy Valley. That's when she started telling everyone I had a price. So I buggered her up.

JOHNNIE. I remember now. Daddy was going to send you to reformatory for fighting in the streets.

HESTER. She started it. Scandalizing my name.

JOHNNIE. Hell of a thought, isn't it? Girls' reformatory! All the tough ones together.

HESTER. Who else was there? Me, her, the Abels, Stevie, Gertrude. There was about ten of us.

JOHNNIE. Magda Swanepoel.

HESTER. Yes.

JOHNNIE. Legransie.

HESTER. The Valley Road gang!

JOHNNIE. That's only eight. Me! Nine. . . .

HESTER. You weren't.

JOHNNIE. Wasn't I?

HESTER. You were too small.

JOHNNIE. I joined in the games.

HESTER. You mean you got in the way. Games! What could you play? Nothing. You were a nuisance. Always hanging around! We cook up an idea for something to do and off we go; and then somebody says: Your little brother is following us, Hester. I look back and there you are, trying to hide behind a lamp-post.

JOHNNIE. You used to throw stones at me.

HESTER. Not really.

JOHNNIE. You did, you know.

HESTER. I mean I never really aimed at you.

JOHNNIE [*persistent in his memory*]. Once or twice. . . .

HESTER. When you wouldn't go back!

JOHNNIE. . . . they came quite close.

HESTER. 'Where you going, Hester?' 'Can I come with, Hester?'

JOHNNIE. Because you were supposed to look after me.

HESTER. Didn't I?

JOHNNIE. Not always.

162

HESTER. What you complaining about? You're still alive.

JOHNNIE. That's true.

HESTER. You messed up some good times for me, my boy. When I did take you with me, you was always getting tired and crying and then I had to carry you. And when we got back always telling him . . . what we did.

JOHNNIE. He asked me.

HESTER. No, he didn't. You just told him.

JOHNNIE. Only to make him happy!

HESTER. By getting me in trouble.

JOHNNIE. NO! By telling him the truth. I just wanted to make him happy by telling him the truth. There was nothing else to tell the truth about. After you went there was nothing left. So many times he said: You always used to tell me the truth, Johnnie. I tried to explain. Hester's gone. There's nothing else, Daddy.

HESTER. You and him! There's a picture somewhere here, of him holding you . . . in the backyard.

[*She is paging through the album.*]

JOHNNIE [*moving away*]. I don't want to see!

HESTER. What's the matter with you? Here it is.

[*She studies the photo. Johnnie watches her.*]

JOHNNIE. Describe it.

HESTER. You're crying, and he's not smiling.

JOHNNIE. More.

HESTER. The backyard—just next to the door. . . .

[*Examining it closely.*]

If you look hard you can just see. . . .

JOHNNIE. Him! Daddy!

HESTER. His crutches.

JOHNNIE. Yes.

HESTER. The way he used to lean on them—sort of forward, but his head up, looking up. . . .

JOHNNIE. That's right.

HESTER. Not smiling. It looks like Sunday. What's the bet it was Sunday? He's got his suit on.

JOHNNIE [*turning to the crutches*]. I forgot all about these.

HESTER [*paging through the album*]. Look at them. What a mob!

[*Examining another one closely*.]

Frikkie! Frikkie Who? Relatives, I suppose.

JOHNNIE. Can you believe it? I forgot all about these being in there.

HESTER. Is this what we look like? A lot of mistakes? It's enough to make the dog vomit.

[*Closing the album*.]

Which box did it come from? Doesn't matter.

[*Defeated by the disorder around her, she puts the album aside negligently*.]

So what's going on?

JOHNNIE. There's another one next to you.

HESTER [*pointing*]. We been through that one?

JOHNNIE. Yes. Those old curtains.

HESTER [*pointing to the new box*]. Well, it better be in here.

[*This box is also tied with string*.]

Where's that knife?

JOHNNIE [*pointing to the crutches*]. I put them on top of the wardrobe after he had that fall—he said his walking days were over—and then I forgot all about them.

HESTER. What?

JOHNNIE. These. The crutches.

HESTER [*She can't find the knife and is trying to break the string with her hands*]. Doesn't he use them any more?

[*Pause. Johnnie stares at her*.]

I asked doesn't he use them any more!

JOHNNIE. Sssssssh! I thought I heard a groan. No. I carry him. When I sweep the room I carry him in here. He's not heavy.

HESTER. Where's that knife? This looks good, man. It's tied up tight. Maybe it's in here!

JOHNNIE. It wasn't heavy.

HESTER. That doesn't mean a thing. It would be bank-notes. Come on, use your muscles.

JOHNNIE. You promised you would go, remember.

HESTER. Yes, yes. Hurry up.

[*The box is opened. Johnnie looks in past Hester's greedy hands.*]

JOHNNIE. Shoes!

[*Hester burrows through a collection of old shoes—men's, women's, and children's. From the bottom of the box she brings out a paper bag which she tears open. The contents spill on to the floor. Johnnie retrieves one.*]

Crutch-rubbers. Shoes and crutch-rubbers. Do you get it? Footwear! Amazing!

[*After a final scrabble through the box, Hester sits down wearily on the suitcase.*]

HESTER. What's the time? No, don't tell me. It doesn't matter.

JOHNNIE [*holding up a pair of girl's shoes*]. Yours?

HESTER. Turn them around. Yes.

JOHNNIE. Dainty. How old? Seven, eight, nine . . . ?

HESTER. Older. Ten or eleven.

[*Johnnie drops them carelessly on the floor.*]

Don't do that! Give here.

[*He passes her the shoes.*]

Yes, one of my birthdays. Mommie bought them, I think. I wore them all that day and after that they were my specials —Sundays and so on—until they pinched so much I couldn't wear them any more.

JOHNNIE. They're still in good shape.

HESTER. So what good was it saving them up for best? What's the use of them now? I wanted them then, when they fitted, when the other girls were laughing at my old ones and my father's socks. The second-hand Smits of Valley Road. That was us! You in my vests, me in his socks, Mommie in his old shoes because the best went into boxes, the boxes into cupboards, and then the door was locked. 'One day you'll thank me,' she used to say. *Ai*, Mommie! You were wrong. There should have been more.

JOHNNIE. More what?

HESTER. Anything. Everything. There wasn't enough of anything except hard times.

JOHNNIE. Because we were hard up. Breadwinner out of action.

HESTER. Other people are also poor but they don't live like we did. Look at the Abels—with only an *Ouma*!

[*Shoes in her hands.*]

Even the birthdays were buggered up by a present you didn't want, and didn't get anyway because it had to be saved. For the rainy day! I've hated rain all my life. The terrible tomorrow—when we're broke, when we're hungry, when we're cold, when we're sick. Why the hell did we go on living?

JOHNNIE [*leaving the box*]. This is fascinating. Let's test your powers of observation.

[*He puts three men's shoes on the floor in front of Hester.*]

HESTER. So?

JOHNNIE. Notice anything strange?

HESTER. I didn't come here to play games.

JOHNNIE. I spotted it. They're all left shoes. They're Daddy's. That's the leg he lost in the explosion!

[*Hester pushes the shoes away with her foot.*]

That's not a very nice thing to do.

HESTER. Run and tell him I did it. Go on . . . Run! Waste my time with rubbish.

[*Looking around.*]

That's what this is. Second-hand rubbish. What's it good for?

[*Johnnie is back on the crutches, examining them, tentatively trying one and then the other. He takes two crutch-rubbers out of his pocket and starts to put them on.*]

JOHNNIE. Our inheritance.

HESTER. All I'm inheriting tonight is bad memories. Makes me sick just to look at it. Can't we pack some away?

[*Hester scoops up an armful and goes around looking for an empty box, but can't find one.*]

JOHNNIE. I can't say I'm bored. Some interesting things are coming to light.

[*The crutch-rubbers are on.*]

There! Good as new.

HESTER [*pointing to a box*]. You quite sure we been through all this? Carefully? I can't remember these hats.

JOHNNIE. You should know. You said you would search the boxes.

HESTER. But you're supposed to tell me when you bring in a new one.

[*Drops the armful she is carrying for a greedy scrabble through the box—hats come out.*]

JOHNNIE. I can't get over this. These crutches. . . .

HESTER. Leave them alone. They're getting on my nerves.

JOHNNIE. But they're comfortable. I used to think they hurt, it looked so sore.

HESTER. I saw enough of them in the old days.

JOHNNIE. Remember his fear of banana-skins? How he used to stand at the window and watch the traffic in the street?

HESTER. Spying on us!

JOHNNIE. Hours on end. But no wonder. I could. It's like being propped up.

HESTER. Soon as I did something . . . Hester! I'm watching you! And there he was peeping behind the curtains.

[*Looks into another box.*]

JOHNNIE. You been through that one.

HESTER. I'm just making sure.

[*Sits.*]

Five hundred pounds is a lot of money.

JOHNNIE. Be the biggest wad I ever seen. Fat as a roll of lavatory paper. What you going to do with it?

HESTER. Plenty.

JOHNNIE. Such as?

HESTER. Such as anything I like. Once you got money you can do anything you like. Change my name! Stay at a posh hotel! I could. And then let them try and refuse to serve me just because I'm sitting by myself in the lounge.

JOHNNIE. What do you mean?

[*During Hester's next speech he moves behind her back and there*] *tries out the crutches—a few steps, different positions, opening an imaginary door, etc., etc.*]

HESTER. Some of those big-shot places don't serve you if you're a woman by yourself. I wasn't trying for a pick-up. I just wanted a few beers and a little peace and quiet somewhere nice for a change. They're supposed to be open to the public! But when I walked in they all started staring and then this coolie waiter comes to me and says they don't serve 'ladies' by themselves. Well, this time they will. Because I'll be a boarder. I'll pay in advance. And then let one of those bitches smile as though she's not also selling what she's got between her legs. Give them a chance to say Yes and I DO —because who the hell ever says no—put a ring on their finger and they think they're better! That being married gives them a licence to do it! I'm sick of that lot with their husbands and fashions and happy families. They don't fool me. And I'll tell them. Happy families is fat men crawling on to frightened women. And when you've had enough he doesn't stop, 'lady'. I've washed more of your husbands out of me than ever gave you babies.

JOHNNIE. That's known as exposing your dirty linen in a place of public entertainment.

HESTER. Who the hell do they think they are? Laughing at us like we're a dirty joke or something. Let them live in a back-room where the lavatory is blocked again and the drain is crawling with cockroaches and see if they go on smelling like the soap counter in Woolworth's. Money, brother. Money! You can do anything with money. And my turn is coming. Bring in the boxes. I've wasted enough time.

[*Johnnie leans the crutches against a chair and exits into father's room. Hester moves with a new resolution—clearing a space around her for the next boxes. Johnnie returns with one.*]

JOHNNIE. Light as a feather.

HESTER. Get the others! And put them down here. I don't want them mixed up any more. I mean business now. Soon as I find the money I'm on my way.

[*Johnnie is back with the crutches.*]

And leave those crutches alone for Christ sake.

JOHNNIE. Just—what's the word?—practising.

HESTER. That's mockery.

JOHNNIE. Who?

HESTER. You. You're mocking him.

JOHNNIE. 'Oh, no.

HESTER. Yes it is. Mockery of a cripple.

JOHNNIE. No, no, no, no.

HESTER. You wait until he catches you.

JOHNNIE. Sssssssh! Keep it down.

[*Exit Johnnie, returning a few seconds later with another load—two bundles of newspapers wrapped up in brown paper and tied with string.*]

HESTER [*still busy with the last box*]. What's all this?

JOHNNIE [*joins her to examine the contents of the box*]. Looks like seeds. Yes. Look here. . . .

[*Pointing to one of the brown paper packets which have come out.*]

. . . Marigolds, Well, I'll be. . . .

[*Taking out other packets.*]

Watermelons, pumpkins, onions . . . beans!

HESTER [*abandoning the box and turning to the bundles*]. And these?

JOHNNIE. Old Mother Earth!

HESTER. Wake up. What's these?

JOHNNIE. Dunno. In the corner next to the wardrobe.

HESTER. Break the strings.

[*Johnnie breaks the string—newspapers spill out. He returns to the seeds.*]

Liewe God!

JOHNNIE. I think they would grow, you know. They've been kept in a cool dry place. All they need now is direct sunlight and Bob's Your Uncle . . . fresh veg.

HESTER. Leave them.

JOHNNIE. But think of it. Ripe watermelons!

HESTER. Get the other boxes.

[*A last scrabble through the pile of newspapers—she picks up one.*]

1937. Six years old. You weren't even born yet.

JOHNNIE. Let's see. 'Roosevelt refuses. . . .'

HESTER [*tearing the paper out of his hands*]. If you don't get those boxes I'll go in there myself!

JOHNNIE. Don't move. I'm on my way.

[*Exit into father's room.*]

[*Hester tries to push back the second flood of rubbish. Johnnie returns with two boxes, puts them down, and exits again. Hester opens these two boxes to find old clothes. She is still busy with them when Johnnie returns with yet another.*]

JOHNNIE. Here's one. Heavy as lead. And listen!

[*He shakes it—Hester abandons the boxes she is busy with and turns feverishly on the new one. It contains packets of old nails, screws, a few tools, a brass door-handle, old keys, etc., etc.*]

Hardware! They thought of everything.

HESTER. More junk. Ten bob on the sale.

JOHNNIE [*holding up a hammer*]. You couldn't buy a ball-pane like this today for love or money.

HESTER. Ten bob on the sale—if you're lucky!

[*She returns to the two half-empty boxes. Johnnie goes through the papers on the floor.*]

[*Holding up a badly torn but clean white shirt.*]

Look at this!

JOHNNIE. 'Chamberlain refuses German offer!' January 1937.

HESTER. A kaffir wouldn't polish the floor with it.

JOHNNIE [*looking at another headline*]. . . . .

HESTER. Other people would have chucked it away.

JOHNNIE. Thirty-six. December 1936.

[*He starts examining the dates on all the papers.*]

HESTER. But we kept it. The Smits of Valley Road washed it, ironed it, folded it up, and packed it away.

JOHNNIE. November 1936. Nearer!

HESTER. Nearer what?

JOHNNIE. 1931, or '30 or '32. Don't you remember? The Bad Years.* 1931 onwards. When he worked on the line to Graaff-Reinet. You remember, man. Daddy. He was always telling us. Something terrible had happened somewhere and it was

Bad Times . . . no jobs, no money. That's what he dreams about now.

The kaffirs sit and watch them work. The white men are hungry. Everybody is greedy. Specially about work—more greedy even than with food. Because work is food—not just today but tomorrow is work. So men look at another man's work the way they used to look at his wife. And those that got it work until the blisters burst and their backs break. He queued for a week to get the job—laying sleepers. Last week ten of his friends was fired. So you work like devils. *They got to see you work!*

And all the time the kaffirs sit and watch the white man doing kaffir work—hungry for the work. They are dying by the dozen!

And then one day in the kloof the other side of Heuningvlei he thought the end had come. His back was hurting like never before, his blisters were running blood. So he cried in the wilderness. 'Why hast thou forsaken me, Lord?' Like Moses. 'Why hast thou forsaken thy lamb?' But it wasn't the end.

That night the railway doctor came to the tents with embrocation and bandages—and he carried on. One mile a day. Heuningvlei, Boesmanspoort, Tierberg, Potterstop. . . . He knows them all! And when they reached Graaff-Reinet the Lord's purpose in all suffering was revealed. Because there he met Mommie.

'I was there in the wilderness—like Moses. The sleepers bent my back, the Lord bent my spirit. But I was not broken. It took dynamite to do that!' Hey?

HESTER. Don't make me sick.

JOHNNIE [*attempting another quote*]. 'And God said unto Moses. . . .'

HESTER. Dry up! I've heard it all. Moses said this, and Abraham said that, and Jesus says something else. Sunday School is over. I'm not a kid any more. Get the other boxes.

JOHNNIE [*collecting the newspapers together*]. In a jiffy.

HESTER. What you doing with those?

JOHNNIE. You might not know it but this is history.

HESTER. Chuck them out.

JOHNNIE. I'd like to read them. When you're gone and life settles down again. There's enough here for. . . .

HESTER. You're as bad as them. It's rubbish.

JOHNNIE. That doesn't stop it from being interesting.

HESTER. I'll chuck them out.

JOHNNIE. No, you won't.

HESTER. Who's going to stop me?

JOHNNIE. Hester!

HESTER. You and who? Him?

JOHNNIE. Hester, if you start something and he wakes up and has a stroke . . . God help you.

HESTER. Here we go again. God help you. God help us. No chance of that, my boy. He never gave a damn about what happened in this house.

JOHNNIE. That sort of talk is not for my ears. I'll get the boxes.

   [*Exit.*]

HESTER. And I don't blame him! Look at it. Who the hell would have wanted anything to do with us? We weren't just poor. It was something worse. Second-hand! Life in here was second-hand . . . used up and old before we even got it. Nothing ever reached us new. Even the days felt like the whole world had lived them out before they reached us.

   [*Johnnie reappears empty-handed.*]

JOHNNIE. Hester.

HESTER. Where's the box?

   [*Exit Johnnie.*]

   Why the hell did I ever come back?

   [*Johnnie reappears, a box in his hand, but he doesn't hand it over immediately.*]

JOHNNIE. Hester.

HESTER. Wasn't there one thing worth saving from all those years?

JOHNNIE. Hester!

HESTER. I'm not talking loud.

JOHNNIE. What will you do if you don't find it?

HESTER. I don't know. I don't even know what it is yet. Just one thing that's got a good memory. I think and think. I try to remember. There must have been something that made me happy. All those years. Just once. Happy.

JOHNNIE. No, I mean the money. The compensation. What will you do if you don't. . . .

[*Pause.*]

Have you . . . ? Yes, you have, haven't you?

[*Hester looks with bewilderment at the chaos around her.*]

You've forgotten what you're looking for!

HESTER. Shut up!

[*She moves among the boxes with growing desperation.*]

You think I've missed it? How long have I been . . . ? Which one did you bring in last? Are you deaf? When did this one come in?

JOHNNIE. I don't know. I've just been fetching. You . . . you said you would. . . .

[*Hester scratches around on the edge of panic.*]

What will you do if you don't . . . ?

HESTER. Something that will make you regret the day you were born.

JOHNNIE [*closing his eyes*]. Dear God, please let Hester find the money!

[*Opening his eyes.*]

Any luck?

HESTER. Get the other!

[*She takes the box from his hand and when he doesn't move immediately gives him a violent shove.*]

Move!

[*Exit Johnnie. As soon as he is out of the room, Hester collapses into a chair, placing the box on the floor at her feet. She stares at it without seeing it—a few seconds of complete vacancy. Then gradually we feel the box intrude itself into her consciousness, challenging her. Without any of the panic of a few seconds previously she opens it and starts to work methodically through its contents. Near the top she finds a bundle of papers.*
Johnnie returns—he is tensed and watches Hester in silence for a few seconds.]

JOHNNIE. All those in favour of sleep hold up their hands!

[*Hester is busy with the papers and ignores him.*]

Hester!

HESTER. What?

JOHNNIE. Bedtime.

HESTER. No.

JOHNNIE. Nothing's going to run away. Tell you what. . . .

HESTER. I said no! Now shut up! Sleep. In here? I'd rather pay a penny and sit all night in a public lavatory. Bring in the other boxes.

[*Goes back to the papers. Johnnie sees the crutches and goes on to them.*]

Documents.

JOHNNIE. I've got something to tell you.

HESTER [*looking at the papers*]. Somebody was born, somebody was baptized, somebody was something else . . . married. . . .

[*Retrieves the paper just discarded.*]

Them. Mommie and Daddy. 1931. Graaff-Reinet. Johannes Cornelius Smit. Anna Van Rooyen.

JOHNNIE. Happily married, faithfully parted by death.

HESTER. Since when?

JOHNNIE. 1931 onwards. Through the years, the setbacks, the hardships. . . .

HESTER. Since when was it happily married?

JOHNNIE. Daddy. He told me. . . .

HESTER. Then tell him from me he's a liar.

JOHNNIE. I've always believed it.

HESTER. Well, you're wrong. What did you know about her? You wasn't even five years when she died.

JOHNNIE. That's true. I've no memories.

HESTER. And I've got plenty. So don't talk to me about happily married.

JOHNNIE. What was she like?

HESTER. See for yourself. There's a picture in the album— it's here somewhere. Smallish. None of her things fitted me when I was big. Always working—working, working, working. . . .

[*Pause.*]

Frightened. She worked harder than anybody I ever seen in my life, because she was frightened. He frightened her. She said I frightened her. Our fights frightened her. She died frightened of being dead.

[*She sees Johnnie staring at her.*]

I saw her face in the coffin.

JOHNNIE. You what?

HESTER. Saw her, in the coffin.

JOHNNIE. You peeped?

HESTER. They gave you a last look.

[*She is talking with the calculated indifference of someone not sure of their self-control.*]

He was there. Some uncles and aunties.

JOHNNIE. Where was I?

HESTER. Somewhere else. You were too young.

They pushed me forward. 'Say goodbye to your Mommie, Hester.' I said it—but I couldn't cry. I was dry and hot inside. Ashamed! Of us. Of her, Mommie, for being dead and causing all the fuss. Of him, Daddy, his face cracked like one of our old plates, saying things he never said when she was alive.

And all the uncles and aunties kissing him and patting him on the back and saying 'Shame!' every time they saw you. It was those cousins of his from Despatch, who never ever came to visit us. The whole mob of them, all in black, the little girls in pretty dresses, looking at everything in the house, and us looking like poor whites because there wasn't enough cups to give everybody coffee at the same time. I hated it! I hated Mommie for being dead. I couldn't cry. I cried later. I don't know, maybe two days. Everything was over, the relatives gone. He was in bed with shock. The house was quiet like never before.

Then there was a knock at the back door. I opened it and it was that coolie who always sold the vegetables. 'Where's your Mommie?' he asked. I couldn't say anything at first. 'Girlie, where's your Mommie?' Then I told him. 'Dead.' I just said, 'Dead,' and started to cry. He took off his hat and stood there watching me until I shouted, '*Voetsek!*' and chased him away—and sat down and cried and cried. Because suddenly I knew she was dead, and what it meant, being dead. It's goodbye for keeps. She was gone for ever. So I cried. There was something I wanted to do, but it was too late.

JOHNNIE. What did you want to do?

HESTER. Nothing.

[*Looking at the certificate in her hand.*]

Johannes Cornelius Smit—Anna Van Rooyen. Biggest mistake she ever made!

JOHNNIE. You don't know what you're saying.

HESTER. Yes, I do! I'm saying this was the biggest mistake she ever made. Marriage! One man's slave all your life, slog away until you're in your grave. For what? Happiness in Heaven? I seen them—Ma and the others like her, with more kids than they can count, and no money; bruises every pay-day because he comes home drunk or another one in the belly because he was so drunk he didn't know it was his old wife and got into bed!

JOHNNIE. Daddy never beat Mommie. He was never drunk.

HESTER. Because he couldn't. He was a crock. But he did it other ways. She fell into her grave the way they all do—tired, *moeg*. Frightened! I saw her.

JOHNNIE. This is terrible, Hester.

HESTER. You're damned right it is. It's hell. They live in hell, but they're too frightened to do anything about it because there's always somebody around shouting God and Judgement.

Mommie should have taken what she wanted and then kicked him out.

JOHNNIE. And the children.

HESTER. So what! If you get them you get them and if you don't want them there's ways.

JOHNNIE. Hester! Hester!

HESTER. Hester, Hester what? Hester who? Hester Smit! That's me. I've done it. And I don't care a damn. Two months old and I got rid of it.

JOHNNIE. When the time comes to face your maker. . . .

HESTER. THIS is my time. Now! And no man is going to bugger it up for me the way he did for Mommie.

JOHNNIE. You can be grateful Mommie didn't think like you.

HESTER. Look, there's a couple of words I hate and grateful is one of them.

JOHNNIE. Suppose she had done what you did, and it was YOU. You wouldn't be here now.

HESTER. So I'm here because she was a fool. We're all somebody else's mistake. You. Him too. This. The whole damned thing is a mistake. The sooner they blow it up with their atom bombs the better.

JOHNNIE. You'd like that!

HESTER. Yes.

JOHNNIE. The end of the world.

HESTER. Couldn't care less.

JOHNNIE. If it really had to happen. . . .

HESTER. I'd die laughing. At the look on your faces.

JOHNNIE. Nothing . . . nothing matters?

HESTER. Such as what? Find it.

[*Pointing to the chaos around her.*]

One thing. Marriage?

[*She crumples up the certificate in her hand and throws it away.*]

Being born? Being dead? They're mistakes. All we unpacked here tonight is mistakes.

JOHNNIE. Hester.

HESTER. And the sooner somebody rubs it out the better.

JOHNNIE. Hester, wait.

HESTER. What?

JOHNNIE. I dare you . . . I dare you to commit suicide. Now!

[*She stares at him.*]

JOHNNIE. You said nothing matters. Prove it. I dare you!

HESTER [*statement of fact*]. You dare me.

JOHNNIE. Yes.

HESTER. *Ja*, that's right.

JOHNNIE. You will?

HESTER [*ignoring his question*]. You were always daring me. You used to find it—the thing you were too scared to do, and dare me, and watch while I did it and got into trouble. That's what you want, hey? You and him. 'Hester's in trouble again, Pa!'

JOHNNIE. You won't?

HESTER. No.

[*She goes back to the papers.*]

JOHNNIE [*to himself*]. Too much to hope for.

HESTER. You won't get rid of me that easily.

JOHNNIE. But I tried. Whatever happens nobody can say I didn't try. Be brave.

HESTER [*reading from one of the papers*]. 'Johannes Albertus Smit.' That's you.

JOHNNIE. Yes, in full. What's it say?

HESTER [*scanning the letter*]. 'Your application. . . .' The Kroonstad Railway School. From the Principal. Saying they accept your application to be a learner-stoker. And a second-class voucher to get there. November, 1958.

JOHNNIE. Too late now.

HESTER. But you said you tore up your application.

JOHNNIE. That's right.

HESTER. Because you didn't want to go.

JOHNNIE. So?

HESTER. So here he says he *got* your application.

JOHNNIE. These things happen.

[*Pause. Hester thinks about this.*]

HESTER. No. No, they don't. He wouldn't tell you to come if you didn't have asked him if you could come.

JOHNNIE. Where does that get us?

HESTER. You *did* post that application.

JOHNNIE. I see.

HESTER. But you told me you didn't.

JOHNNIE. All right I made a mistake. I forgot. I applied. Satisfied?

HESTER. You didn't forget. You lied to me. You know you posted it.

JOHNNIE. I'm telling you I forgot.

HESTER. You knew they said you must come.

JOHNNIE. Can't I forget things too?

HESTER. And you wanted to go!

JOHNNIE. Maybe . . . it's a long time ago . . . ten years . . . my memory. . . .

HESTER. Don't try to get out of it.

JOHNNIE [*desperate*]. What do you want me to say?

HESTER. What are you trying to hide?

JOHNNIE. Nothing. So leave me alone. Understand? Just leave us alone. Take what you want and go!

[*He is squirming—then a clumsy move and the crutches fall—he stands on his feet.*]

Look, what you've made me do!!

[*Pause.*]

Yes, I wanted to go.

They are the most beautiful things in the world! Black, and hot, hissing, and the red glow of their furnaces, their whistles blowing out like ribbons in the wind! And the engine driver, grade one, and his stoker up there, leaning out of the cab, watching the world like kings!

Yes, I wanted to go.

I could have gone. It was up to me. He didn't say anything to stop me posting the forms in duplicate. And when I got the letter saying I must come he even said he was happy because now his son would also work for the railways. I said I'd come home for all my holidays to be with him and give the house a good sweep out. And when I was packing my suitcase he gave me one of his railway shirts—even made a joke, with tears in his eyes—said it would fit when my muscles were big. So there we stood with tears in our eyes, him on his crutches—me with my suitcase. He came to the door and waved to me all the way down Valley Road.

[*Pause.*]

I got as far as the bridge. Nine o'clock in the morning, sun shining, the world a hustle and a bustle, everybody busy, happy—only him, back there. . . .

So, back there. Simple as that. Here. I told him I missed the train. We agreed it was God's will being done. He helped me unpack. Said I could still keep the shirt.

[*Pause.*]

He's not to blame. He was no problem. What he wants, or God wants, I can do. I fetch, I cook, I sweep, I wash, I wait . . . it was ME. What I wanted.

HESTER. What's the matter, Johnnie? Are you scared of hating him?

JOHNNIE. He was my father.

HESTER. He did that to Mommie.

JOHNNIE. She was his wife.

HESTER. Said God and you all felt like sinners. Hate him!

JOHNNIE. How can I hate . . . ?

HESTER. You're frightened of him.

JOHNNIE. Maybe.

HESTER. Yes!

JOHNNIE. All right, yes!

HESTER. You're frightened of hating him!

JOHNNIE. No.

HESTER. You want to hate him.

JOHNNIE. Definitely, no.

HESTER. I hate him! There, I've said it, and I'm still alive. I hate my father.

JOHNNIE. I don't love, I don't hate. I play it safe. I come when called, I go when chased, I laugh when laughed at. . . .

HESTER. Don't make yourself another piece of junk! Hate him! It's clean and new. Let's find something tonight that isn't worn out and second-hand—something bright and sharp and dangerous.

[*Johnnie reacts with terror to this tirade. He picks up the crutches but Hester tries to stop him from going on to them.*]

Don't, Johnnie!

JOHNNIE. Let go.

HESTER. No.

JOHNNIE. I feel faint.

HESTER. They're not yours.

JOHNNIE. They fit.

HESTER. Don't you understand? They're his. They're him.

JOHNNIE. I'll ask him for them—tomorrow—when you're gone—I'll tell him. . . .

HESTER. Are you mad?

JOHNNIE. He doesn't need them. I carry him. . . .

HESTER. YOU don't need them!

JOHNNIE [*anguish*]. I NEED SOMETHING! LOOK AT ME!

[*Hester lets go of them and Johnnie goes on to them with feverish intensity.*]
Aina! Aina!

HESTER. Then take them. Be cripple!

JOHNNIE. God's will be done. . . .

HESTER. You already look like him. . . .

JOHNNIE. . . . in hell as in heaven. . . .

HESTER. . . . and sound like him. . . .

JOHNNIE. I am his son. He is my father. Flesh of his flesh.

HESTER. That's right. Lick his arse, crawl right up it until your feet hang out. Be HIM.

JOHNNIE. God forgive. . . .

HESTER. That's what you want, isn't it?

JOHNNIE. God forgive you for what you are saying.

HESTER. THERE IS NO GOD! THERE NEVER WAS!
We've unpacked our life, Johannes Cornelius Smit, the years in Valley Road, and there is no God. Nothing but rubbish. In this house there was nothing but useless . . .

[*Amok among the contents of the boxes—picking up and throwing about whatever she can get her hands on.*]

. . . second-hand poor-white junk!

[*Realizes too late that she has just hurled her mother's dress to the floor.*]

No, no! Look what I've done. Why didn't you stop me?

[*She retrieves it.*]

Mommie, not you. I forgot, not you.

[*Smelling it.*]

She's gone. The smell. . . . I can't. . . . It's gone.

Too late again. Just a rag. An empty rag.

That's how it happened. She got lost, among the rubbish. I forgot she was here—in here, alive, to touch, to talk to, to love. She was a chance in here to love something. I wanted to. The hating was hard. Hate! Hate! So much to hate I forgot she was here.

[*Smelling the dress.*]

What was it? Mothballs and blue soap. Mothballs in the wardrobe, sixpence blue soap from the Chinaman on the corner. Washing, always washing. She was clean. I stink, Mommie. I'm dirty and I stink. All the hardships, the hating. I couldn't stop hating and it hurts, it hurts.

JOHNNIE. Pain?

HESTER. It hurts.

JOHNNIE. Home ground!

HESTER. It hurts.

JOHNNIE. An ache or a throb?

HESTER [*intoning non-stop*]. Aina aina aina. . . .

JOHNNIE [*hobbling around on the crutches*]. Wilson's Beef and Iron! Double dose! Kill or cure! Hold your nose! Open your mouth! Down the hatch. . . .

[*He gets a spoonful into Hester's mouth. She spits it out violently and coughs. Johnnie slaps her on the back.*]

Cough it up! Get it off your chest.

HESTER [*pushing him away*]. What's going on?

JOHNNIE. Double dose down the wrong pipe.

HESTER. Shut up!

[*Pause.*]

Here and now!

JOHNNIE. This? This is . . . was . . . will be for ever and ever. -. . . . Let us pray: Oh Lord . . . something . . . our daily bread, brown bread, the broken loaf and Amen. Grace at supper. By the grace of God, you me and him in the light of the lamp with our heads bowed at supper.

This . . . is our home. You've come home. The prodigal daughter has. . . .

HESTER. The Compensation!

[*Pause.*]

JOHNNIE. That's right. But. . . .

HESTER. Five hundred pounds!

JOHNNIE. According to you.

HESTER. I'll be rich.

JOHNNIE. If you ever find it.

HESTER. So what are we waiting for? Bring in the boxes.

JOHNNIE. There's a catch.

HESTER. Bring in the boxes!!

JOHNNIE. There's none left.

[*Pause.*]

You've had the lot.

HESTER. This . . . ?

JOHNNIE. Is all. The lot. There's nothing left.

HESTER. So where's the money?

JOHNNIE. I tried to warn you.

HESTER. Five hundred pounds. Where is it?

JOHNNIE. I suppose he never got it.

[*Pause.*]

Now you must go. You promised. I'll help you pack.

HESTER. NO!

You've found it.

JOHNNIE. Hester. . . .

HESTER. Let me feel your pockets.

JOHNNIE. You promised you would go.

HESTER. Then he's got it.

JOHNNIE. No.

HESTER. He's awake!

JOHNNIE. NO.

HESTER. He knows I'm looking for it and he's hiding it. Go in there and tell him I want it.

JOHNNIE. 'Strue's there's a living God. . . .

HESTER. If you won't I will!

JOHNNIE. That will kill him. He hates the sight of you.

HESTER [*shouting*]. Johannes Cornelius Smit, I want my share!

JOHNNIE. I'm warning you.

[*Exit Hester into father's room.*]

Something's going to happen now. There's dynamite, some-where in this house. In Hester's heart. The heart that hurts. Was it like this? Did he feel like this? He was running—the others were shouting. I'm standing still, nobody's shouting. . . . 'I was standing still, leaning on my. . . .'

[*Hester returns slowly.*]

Five, four, three, two, one. . . .

HESTER. Where is he?

JOHNNIE. Dead.

HESTER. Dead?

JOHNNIE. Dead as a dud. He died.

[*Hester approaches Johnnie.*]

Gave up the ghost—all the words! . . . called by God, with the singing angels . . . laid to rest. . . .

[*Hester is now in front of Johnnie. She hits him once. He closes his eyes and speaks with bitter violence.*]

The Beef and Iron was a flop! Double dose three times a day! But he died!

[*Hester pulls the crutches out from under his arms. He falls to the ground. She kicks him.*]

More! Explode! Swallow me up. Let the mountain fall! This is the end of the world.

[*Hester goes down on her knees to beat Johnnie with clenched fists—stopping eventually from sheer exhaustion. She gets up and staggers to a chair. Johnnie remains on the floor—he will not move until after Hester's final exit.*]

[*A long pause as the violence ebbs.*]

Don't be fooled. This isn't silence. I can hear you breathing.

Silence isn't what you think it is. Silence is waiting—for it to happen, anything—a noise, or a groan or a call.

Sometimes it wasn't any of them—just the sound of his medicine bottles rattling in the dark in the middle of the night. But I was waiting. I'd go in and see if he was all right. 'Have I got enough?' he'd ask me. So I'd look. 'Yes, chum, you've got enough. Six doses if there's a drop.' 'Even so,' he would say, 'get me another bottle tomorrow—the safe side in case of.'

And sometimes when it was like that, the waiting just stopped, the silence went and there were frogs croaking in the river or a cricket in the yard. Little Happy Noises! And we would talk quietly. One night it was all about modern means of transport and he was saying he could still remember the old ox-wagon days and how long it took to go from Despatch to P.E. . . . Suddenly in the middle of it his face went all sort of puffy! His mouth started shivering, he closed his eyes. I thought it was a stroke! Then I saw he was crying.

'Don't let them cut off my other leg,' he said. 'Promise you won't let them.'

'Don't be silly,' I said. 'Of course they won't. Why would they do a stupid thing like that?' 'But promise me you won't let them if they want to all the same.' 'Over my dead body, chum,' I said. 'Over my dead body.'

I went back to bed.

HESTER. Johnnie.

JOHNNIE [*doesn't hear her*]. I missed the end.

HESTER. Johnnie!

JOHNNIE. He died in my sleep.

HESTER. When?

[*Pause.*]

A long time ago? Yesterday?

JOHNNIE. Something like that.

HESTER. Today?

JOHNNIE. No! The other day.

I woke up on the sofa the other day, just lay there waiting for the first cough or call of the new day. Waited and waited. Started to wonder. Got worried. Went in, 'Rise and Shine!' I said. 'Beef and Iron time, Daddy!'

[*Pause.*]

Nothing.

[*Pause.*]

[*Hester leaves the room quietly, wearily.*]

The room was dark, the curtain still closed. I listened . . . I didn't want to look!

[*Loud.*]

'Daddy!' I sat on my chair next to his bed.

'Wake up, Lazybones! You'll miss the early worm!' . . . all our little jokes. I waited and waited . . . it might have been days . . . called and called till I knew he was dead.

I tried to work it out. 'This is it,' I thought. 'The end.' Of what? Of him. Of Waiting. Of pain in the other room.

'You're on your own, Johnnie Smit,' I said to myself. 'From now on it's you—just you and wherever you are—you in the middle of a moment. The other room is empty.'

[*Hester returns, her coat on, carrying her suitcase. She puts it down and sits on it.*]

HESTER. I'm on my way.

JOHNNIE. Where.

HESTER. Back. My room. I'm paid up for the month. There's a week left. She won't even know I'm gone.

JOHNNIE. When's the train leave?

HESTER. Sometime. Ten o'clock.

JOHNNIE. That's right. All stations via Kommodagga.

HESTER. I'll wait at the station. I've had enough of this.

JOHNNIE. There's some bread somewhere . . . butter and jam . . . make yourself sandwiches. It's a long trip.

HESTER. Get up, Johnnie.

JOHNNIE. I'm just resting.

HESTER. I'm sorry about what happened. I didn't mean it. But why did you lie to me? Bluff he was in there?

JOHNNIE. I am. . . . [*Pause.*]

HESTER. What?

JOHNNIE. It's hard to describe. It feels like . . . I'm ashamed. Of me. Of being alone. Just me in my whole life. It was so different with him. He was in there, something else, somewhere else. Even tonight, just pretending it helped. You believed he was in there, didn't you?

HESTER. Yes.

JOHNNIE. If only his ghost would come back and haunt me! Even if I went grey with fright! Do you believe in ghosts, Hester?

HESTER. Hang on, Johnnie. Listen—pack up and come with me.

JOHNNIE. Where?

HESTER. Jo'burg. Where else?

JOHNNIE. A holiday?

HESTER. Or for good.

JOHNNIE. And then?

HESTER. Anything! Anything's better than this, *Boetie*. Get a job, a girl, have some good times. What do you say?

[*Pause. She realizes it is useless.*]

You won't come.

JOHNNIE. Suppose—just suppose there are ghosts, and he did come back to haunt, and I was gone!
I'll stay. Just in case, I'll wait.

HESTER [*gesture to the chaos on the floor, the house*]. Anyway you can have it. Okay? It's all yours. The house and everything. Tell them I said it's yours.

JOHNNIE. Who?

HESTER. The people. There's always people around when somebody dies. Officials. Tell them I gave you my share. It was my will. Read the newspapers, plant the seeds, have a garden. . . .

JOHNNIE. Don't you need dung?

HESTER. That's it! . . . Live happily. Try, Johnnie, try to be happy.

JOHNNIE. Why? What's this?

HESTER. I don't know. I don't know what it is. But there's something else—something we never had.

JOHNNIE. And you? Any plans?

HESTER. Back like I said. There's always jobs. And I got my room. That's me—a woman in a room. I'm used to it now.

[*Stands and moves upstage to the edge of the light.*]

It's strange, you know. I can see it—see it happening. All of this. I'll walk out of that door, through the streets to the station, sit in the waiting-room. Then the train at ten and all the way back. It's hard. Things are too clear. This, there, Jo'burg tomorrow when I get there. The rooms—the dark rooms, the many faces—and one of them me, Hester Smit. I'm too far away from my life.

I want to get back to it, in it, be it, be me again the way it was when I walked in. It will come, I suppose. But at this moment—there she is waiting, here she is going, and somebody's watching all of it. But it isn't God. It's me.

Goodbye, Johnnie.

[*Exit Hester.*]

[*Johnnie makes a move as if to get up, then sees the crutches some distance away from him on the floor. He stares at them for a few seconds then very laboriously drags himself along the floor to them. With equal effort he holds them upright and goes on to them.*

He stands still, on one leg for a few seconds, then realizes he is standing on the wrong leg and changes over.]

JOHNNIE. Why not? It solves problems. Let's face it—a man on his own two legs is a shaky proposition. She said it was mine. All of it—my inheritance. These, seeds . . . and memories. More than enough!

They can look now. Shine their lights in my face, stare as hard as they like. I've got a reason. I'm a man with a story. 'I was eating prickly pears, Mister, leaning on my spade having a rest, minding my own business, when suddenly the earth opened and the mountain fell on me. . . .'

They'll say 'shame', buy me a beer, help me on buses, stop the traffic when I cross the street . . . slowly. . . .

Yes! Everything slower now. Everything changed. The time it takes. Leave at sunset, arrive in the dark, twilight on the bridge. The shadow on the wall different . . . but me . . . a different me!

What's the word? Birth. Death. Both. Jesus did it in the Bible.
  [*Pause.*]
Resurrection.
  [*Pause.*]

BOESMAN AND LENA

A PLAY
IN TWO ACTS

CHARACTERS

BOESMAN, *a Coloured man*
LENA, *a Coloured woman*
OUTA, *an old African*

BOESMAN AND LENA was first performed at the Rhodes University Little Theatre, Grahamstown, on 10 July 1969, directed by the author, with the following cast:

BOESMAN	Athol Fugard
LENA	Yvonne Bryceland
OUTA	Glynn Day

This version was subsequently substantially revised.

BOESMAN AND LENA was performed at the Circle in the Square Theatre, New York, on 22 June 1970, directed by John Berry, with the following cast:

BOESMAN	James Earl Jones
LENA	Ruby Dee
OUTA	Zakes Mokae

And at the Royal Court Theatre Upstairs, London, on 19 July 1971 with the following cast:

BOESMAN	Zakes Mokae
LENA	Yvonne Bryceland
OUTA	Bloke Modisane

The film version, directed by Ross Devenish (Bluewater Productions) and starring the author and Yvonne Bryceland, appeared in 1973.

ACT ONE

An empty stage.

A Coloured man—Boesman—walks on. Heavily burdened. On his back an old mattress and blanket, a blackened paraffin tin, an apple box . . . these contain a few simple cooking utensils, items of clothing etc., etc. With one hand he is dragging a piece of corrugated iron. Barefoot, shapeless grey trousers rolled up to just below the knee, an old shirt, faded and torn sports-club blazer, cap on his head.

He chooses a spot, then drops the corrugated iron, gets down his load, and slumps to the ground beside it. He has obviously walked very far. He waits.

After a few seconds a Coloured woman—Lena—appears. She is similarly burdened—no mattress though—and carries her load on her head. As a result, she walks with characteristic stiff-necked rigidity. There is a bundle of firewood under one arm. Also barefoot. Wearing one of those sad dresses that reduce the body to an angular, gaunt cipher of poverty.

A life of hardship and dissipation obscures their ages, but they are most probably in their fifties.

Boesman looks up slowly as Lena appears. He watches her with a hard, cruel objectivity. He says nothing. She has been reduced to a dumb, animal-like submission by the weight of her burden and the long walk behind them, and in this condition almost misses him sitting to one side, propped up against his bundle. Realizing she has passed him, she stops, but does not turn to face him in case they have to walk still further.

LENA. Here?

[*Boesman clears his throat and spits. She waits a few seconds longer for a word from him, then turns slowly and joins him. The bundle of firewood falls to the ground. Her arms go up and with the last of her strength she gets her bundle down. Her relief as she does so is almost painful. She sits down slowly. For a few seconds she just rests, her head between her knees, breathing deeply. Then she stretches forward and works a finger between the toes of one of her feet. It comes away with a piece of mud. She looks at it, squashing it between her fingers.*]

Mud! Swartkops!

[*She now looks at the world around her for the first time—she knows*

it well—then still higher up, into the sky, searching for something.]
Too late now. [*Pause.*] No. There's one.

[*She is obviously staring up at a bird. Softly . . .*]

Jou moer!

[*She watches it for a few seconds longer, then scrambles to her feet and shakes her fist at it.*]

Jou moer!!

[*Boesman watches her, then the bird, then Lena again. Her eyes follow it as it glides out of sight.*]

So slowly . . . ! Must be a feeling, hey. Even your shadow so heavy you leave it on the ground.

[*She sits down again, even more exhausted now by her outburst. She cleans the mud from between her other toes while she talks.*]

Tomorrow they'll hang up there in the wind and laugh. We'll be in the mud. I hate them.

[*She looks at Boesman.*]

Why did you walk so hard? In a hurry to get here? 'Here', Boesman! What's here? This . . . [*the mud between her fingers*] . . . and tomorrow. And that will be like this! *Vrot!* This piece of world is rotten. Put down your foot and you're in it up to your knee.

That last *skof* was hard. Against the wind. I thought you were never going to stop. Heavier and heavier. Every step. This afternoon heavier than this morning. This time heavier than last time. And there's other times coming. '*Vat jou goed en trek!* Whiteman says *Voetsek!*' *Eina!*

[*Boesman is watching her with undisguised animosity and disgust.*]

Remember the old times? Quick march! Even run . . . [*a little laugh*] . . . when they chased us. Don't make trouble for us here, Boesman. I can't run any more.

Quiet, hey! Let's have a *dop*.

[*Lena registers Boesman's hard stare. She studies him in return.*]

You're the hell-in. Don't look at me, *ou ding*. Blame the whiteman. Bulldozer!

[*Another laugh.*]

Ja! You were happy this morning. 'Push it over, my *baas!*' '*Dankie, baas!*' '*Weg is ons!*'

It was funny, hey, Boesman! All the *pondoks* flat. The poor people running around trying to save their things. You had a good laugh. And now? Here we sit. Just now it's dark, and Boesman's thinking about another *pondok*. The world feels big when you sit like this. Not even a bush to make it your own size. Now's the time to laugh. This is also funny. Look at us! Boesman and Lena with the sky for a roof again.

[*Pause. . . . Boesman stares at her.*]

What you waiting for?

BOESMAN [*shaking his head as he finally breaks his silence*].
Yessus, Lena! I'm telling you, the next time we walk. . . .

LENA. Don't talk about that now, man.

BOESMAN. The Next Time We Walk! . . .

LENA. Where?

BOESMAN. . . . I'll keep on walking. I'll walk and walk. . . .

LENA. *Eina!*

BOESMAN. . . . until you're so bloody *moeg* that when I stop you can't open your mouth!

LENA. It was almost that way today.

BOESMAN. Not a damn! Wasn't long enough. And I knew it. 'When she puts down her bundle, she'll start her rubbish.' You did.

LENA. Rubbish?

BOESMAN. That long *drol* of nonsense that comes out when you open your mouth!

LENA. What have I said? I'm *moeg*! *Eina!* That's true. And you were happy this morning. That's also true.

BOESMAN. I'm still happy.

LENA. You happy now?

BOESMAN [*aggressively*]. I'm always happy.

LENA [*mirthless laughter, clapping her hands*].
Ek sê! His backside in the Swartkops mud, but Boesman's happy. This is a new sort of happy, *ou ding*. The hell-in happy.

BOESMAN. Why shouldn't I be happy?

LENA. *Ja*, that's the way it is. When I want to cry, you want to laugh.

BOESMAN. Cry!

LENA. Something hurt. Wasn't just your fist.

BOESMAN. Snot and tears because the whiteman pushed over a rotten old *pondok*? That will be the day. He did me a favour. I was sick of it. So I laughed.

LENA. And now?

BOESMAN. Yes. You think I can't laugh now?

LENA. Don't be a bastard.

BOESMAN. You want to hear me?

LENA. NO!

BOESMAN. Then shut up, or you will! I'm a happy *Hotnot*. Laughing all the time . . . inside! I haven't stopped since this morning. You were a big joke then, and if you don't watch out you'll be a big joke now.

LENA. Big joke? Because I cried? No, *here*, Boesman! It was too early in the morning to have your life kicked in its *moer* again. Sitting there in the dust with the pieces . . . *Kaalgat!* That's what it felt like! . . . and thinking of somewhere else again. Put your life on your head and walk, sister.
Another day gone. Other people lived it. We tramped it into the ground. I haven't got so many left, Boesman.

BOESMAN. If your legs worked as hard as your tongue then we were here long ago.

LENA. It's not my fault.

BOESMAN. Then whose? Every few steps . . . 'Rest a bit, Boesman.' 'I'm tired, Boesman.'

LENA. *Arme ou* Lena *se maer ou bene.*

BOESMAN. You weren't resting.

LENA. I was.

BOESMAN. You lie.

LENA. What was I doing?

BOESMAN. You were looking for that *brak* of yours.

LENA. *Brak?*

[*She remembers.*] *Hond!*

Haai! Was it this morning?

BOESMAN. You almost twisted your head off, you were looking

behind you so much. You should have walked backwards today.

LENA. He might have followed me. Dogs smell footsteps.

BOESMAN. Follow you! You fancy yourself, hey.

LENA. Anyway you weren't in such a hurry yourself. You didn't even know where we were going.

BOESMAN. I did.

LENA. Swartkops?

BOESMAN [*emphatically*]. Here! Right here where I am.

LENA. No, Boesman. This time you *lieg*.

BOESMAN. Don't say to me I *lieg*! I'm not mix-up like you. I know what I'm doing.

LENA. Why didn't we come the short way then?

BOESMAN. Short way? Korsten to Swartkops? What you talking about?

LENA. It didn't use to feel so long. That walk never came to an end. I'm still out there, walking!

BOESMAN [*a gesture of defeat*].

It's useless to talk to you.

[*He goes through Lena's bundle and finds two bottles of water. He uncorks one and has a drink. He then starts unpacking his bundle.*]

LENA. All you knew was to load up our things and take the empties to the bottle store. After that . . . !

[*She shakes her head.*]

'Where we going, Boesman?' 'Don't ask questions. Walk!' *Ja*, don't ask questions. Because you didn't know the answers. Where to go, what to do. I remember now. Down this street, up the next one, look down that one, then turn around and go the other way. Not lost? What way takes you past Berry's Corner twice, then back to where you started from? I'm not a fool, Boesman. The roads are crooked enough without you also being in a *dwaal*.

First it looked like Redhouse, or Veeplaas. Then it was Bethelsdorp, or maybe Missionvale. *Sukkel* along! The dogs want to bite but you can't look down. Look ahead, sister. To what? Boesman's back. That's the scenery in my world. You don't know what it's like behind you. Look back one day,

Boesman. It's *me*, that thing you *sleep* along the roads. My life. It felt old today. Sitting there on the pavement when you went inside with the empties. Not just *moeg*. It's been that for a long time. Something else. Something that's been used too long. The old pot that leaks, the blanket that can't even keep the fleas warm. Time to throw it away. How do you do that when it's yourself?

I was still sore where you hit me. Two white children came and looked while I counted the bruises. There's a big one here, hey. . . .

[*Touching a tender spot under one eye.*]

You know what I asked them? 'Does your mother want a girl? Go ask your mother if she wants a girl.' I would have gone, Boesman.

BOESMAN. And then?

LENA. Work for the madam.

[*Boesman laughs derisively.*]

They also laughed, and looked some more, *ja*, look at Lena! *Ou Hotnot meid.* Boesman's her man. Gave her a hiding for dropping the empties. Three bottles broken. Ten cents. Ten cents worth of bruises.

BOESMAN [*indifferently*]. You should have gone.

LENA [*she has to think about it*].

They didn't want me.

BOESMAN [*another laugh, then stops himself abruptly*].

You think *I* want you?

LENA [*she also thinks about this before answering*].

You took me. You came out with the wine, put it in your bundle, then you said 'Come!' and walked. I wanted to say something. The word was in my mouth! But the way you did it . . . no questions, didn't even look at me . . . just picked up and walked. So I followed you. Didn't even know where until I felt the mud between my toes. Then I knew. Swartkops again! Digging for bait. Mudprawns and worms in an old jam tin. A few live ones on top, the dead one at the bottom. 'Sixty cents, my *baas*. Just dug them out!' *Lieg* your soul into hell for enough to live.

How we going to dig? We haven't even got a spade.

198

BOESMAN. I'll get one.

LENA. *Oppas* they don't get *you*. *Blourokkie* next time they catch you stealing.
Haai, Boesman! Why here? This place hasn't been good to us. All we've had next to the Modderspruit is hard times. [*A little laugh.*] And wet ones. Remember that night the water came up so high? When we woke up *pap nat* with all our things floating down to the bridge. You got such a *skrik* you ran the wrong way.

[*She laughs at the memory.*]

BOESMAN. I didn't!

LENA. What were you doing in the deep water? Having a wash?

[*Another laugh.*]

It was almost up with you that night. Hey! When was that? Last time?

[*Pause. . . . Lena thinks.*]

Boesman! When was our last time here? I'm talking to you.

[*Boesman deliberately ignores her, and carries on sorting out the contents of his bundle.*]

Boesman!!!

[*Pause. . . . No reaction from him.*]

Don't be like that tonight, man. This is a lonely place. Just us two. Talk to me.

BOESMAN. I've got nothing left to say to you. Talk to yourself.

LENA. I'll go mad.

BOESMAN. What do you mean, 'go' mad? You've been talking to yourself since . . .

[*Pause. . . . Lena waits, he remembers.*]

Ja! . . . since our first walk.

LENA. First walk?

BOESMAN. That night, in the brickfields.

LENA. Coega to Veeplaas!

BOESMAN. First you cried. When you stopped crying, you started talking. I was tired. I wanted to sleep. But you talked. 'Where we going?' 'Let's go back.' Who? What? How?

Yessus! On and on. Then I thought it. 'Boesman, you've made a mistake!'

LENA. Coega to Veeplaas.

BOESMAN. You talked there too. So I thought it again.

LENA. Mistake.

BOESMAN. Mistake. Every time you opened your mouth . . . until I stopped listening.

LENA. I want somebody to listen.

BOESMAN. To what? That *gebabbel* of yours. When you *poep* it makes more sense. You know why? It stinks. Your words are just noise. Nonsense. *Die geraas van 'n vervloekte lewe.* Look at you! Listen to you! You're asking for a lot, Lena. Must I go mad as well?

LENA. I asked you when we came here last. Is that nonsense?

BOESMAN. Yes! What difference does it make? To anything? You're here now!

LENA [*looking around*]. I'm here now.

[*Surge of anger.*] I know I'm here now. Why? Look at it, for God's sake. Is this the best you could do? What was wrong with Veeplaas?

BOESMAN. What's right with it?

LENA. There's other people there! What's the matter with you? Ashamed of yourself?

[*Boesman turns away from her, dragging their one mattress to the spot where he will build the shelter. He then picks up the piece of corrugated iron and examines it, trying it out in various positions . . . as a roof, a wall, etc.*]

LENA. Or Missionvale! Redhouse! There's a chance of a job there on the saltpans.

Not even a dog to look at us. Everytime we come back here it feels like I've never left. Maybe this is the last time here I'm trying to remember. *Haai!*

[*She shakes her head . . . then pauses.*]

Wasn't it after Redhouse? Out last time here. Remember, that *boer* chased us off his land. Then we came here. Is that right?

[*Boesman ignores her.*]

Then we went to Korsten.

BOESMAN. After here we went to Korsten?

LENA. *Ja.* [*Boesman laughs at her derisively.*] How was it then?
[*Pause.*] You won't tell me.

BOESMAN [*putting down the piece of iron*].
Make the fire.

LENA. Let's have a *dop* first. I'm feeling the cold. Please,
Boesman!

[*Without another look at her he walks off. Lena gets stiffly to her
legs and starts to make the fire. A box is positioned to shield it from
the wind, then the bundle of firewood untied, the wood itself broken
into pieces, a piece of paper to get it started, etc.*]

LENA. Walk our legs off for this! Piece of bread and black tea.
No butter . . . not even for bruises.

[*A thought crosses her mind. She straightens up, thinks hard for a
few seconds, then shakes her head.*]

No. [*She looks around.*] Maybe he's right. What's the difference.
I'm here now.
'Here!' After a long life that's a thin slice. No jam on that
one. Or *kondens melk*! There's *soeterigheid* for you. Maybe if
we get lots of prawns. . . .

[*Another thought. . . . She thinks hard. . . .*]

It was after Redhouse. Collecting prickly pears. Then they
found our place there in the bush. *Loop, Hotnot!* So *Hotnot
loops* . . . to Swartkops. Here. The last time here. I was right!

[*Pause.*]

No, we ran! The *boer* had a gun. When he showed us the
bullets Boesman dropped his tin and went down that road
like a rabbit. . . .

[*Laughing . . . her hands to her backside in an imitation of the scene.*]
. . . *Moenie skiet, baas!*

Me too, but the other way. Where did I find him? . . . looking
at the mud, the hell-in because we had lost all our things
again. Just our clothes, and each other. Never lose that. Run
your legs off the other way but at the end of it Boesman
is waiting. How the hell does that happen?
Redhouse—Swartkops! I was right. He must laugh at himself.

[*Back to her chores.*]

And then? Somewhere else! *Ja*, of course. One of them. Veeplaas. Or Missionvale. Maybe Bethelsdorp. Lena knows them all.

[*Pause.*]

But which one . . . that time?

[*She straightens up and looks around.*]

Which way . . . ?

[*Moving around, trying to orientate herself physically.*]

Let me see now. We came. . . . No. Those lights! What's that? Where is . . . it's round all right . . . where the hell is . . . *Yessus!* I'm right in the middle. No wonder I get drunk when I try to work it out. . . .

[*Sudden desperation.*]

Think, man! It happened to you.

[*Closes her eyes in an effort to remember.*]

We were here. Then we left. Off we go. . . . We're walking . . . and walking . . . where we walking? Boesman never tells me. Wait and see. Walking. . . .

Somewhere, his shadow. In front of me. Small man with a long *maer* shadow. It's stretching back to me over the veld because we're walking to the sun and it's going down. . . .

Veeplaas! That's where the sun goes. Behind it there into the bush. So Veeplaas is. . . .

[*Looking now for the sun.*]

Waar die donner is . . . ?

[*Pause.*]

Finished. So what. I got it in here [*pointing to her head*]. Redhouse—Swartkops—Veeplaas!

[*She is very pleased with herself.*]

Get a move on now. I'm nearly here. Redhouse—Swartkops —Veeplaas. . . .

[*She carries on working, laying out mugs, filling a little pot with water, etc. . . . all the time muttering to herself the sequence of places she has established.*]

It's coming! Korsten! Empties, and the dog. *Hond!* How was it now? Redhouse—Swartkops—Veeplaas—Korsten. Then this morning the bulldozers . . . and then. . . .

[*Pause.*] Here! I've got there!

[*She is very happy.*] 'Here', sister. You ran that last bit. Bundle and all.

[*She is humming away happily to herself when Boesman returns with a few odds and ends—an old sack, few pieces of wood, another piece of corrugated iron, an old motor-car door, etc.—out of which he will fashion their shelter for the night. He registers Lena's good humour and watches her suspiciously as he starts to work. Lena realizes this and laughs.*]

Why you looking at me so *skeef*?

[*He says nothing. Lena hums a little song.*]

Remember the times I used to sing for us?
'Da . . . da . . . da. . . .'

BOESMAN. What's the matter with you?

LENA. Feeling fine, darling. I'm warm. You know why? I've been running. You should have seen me! I'm not as old as I thought. All the way from Redhouse. . . .

[*The rest of her sentence is lost in laughter at the expression on his face.*]

. . . and now I'm here. With you.
Da . . . da . . . da. . . .

BOESMAN [*after watching her for a few more seconds*].
Show me the wine!

LENA. Look for yourself.

[*Boesman leaves his work on the shelter. He goes through his bundle and examines two bottles of wine. They are both intact. Lena laughs at him.*]

How's it for a *dop*?

[*He puts away the bottles and goes back to work.*]

Hey, you know what I was thinking just now. *Blikkie kondens melk*. What do you say? If we get lots of prawns. Sugar's not enough, man. I want some real sweetness. Then you can be as *bedonnerd* as you like.

[*She starts singing, shuffling out a few dance steps at the same time.*]

> *Ou blikkie kondens melk*
> *Maak die lewe soet;*
> *Boesman is 'n Boesman*
> *Maar hy dra 'n Hotnot hoed.*

Look at this! Lena's still got a *vastrap* in her old legs. You
want to dance, Boesman? Not too late to learn. I'll teach you.

BOESMAN. Just now you get a bloody good *klap*!

LENA. *Ja!* See what I mean. This time I'm laughing, and
you . . . ! *Vies!* You don't like it when somebody else laughs.
Well, you laughed at me for nothing. Because I was right!
Last time here *was* after Redhouse. You won't mix me up
this time. I remember. The *boer* pointed his gun and you
were gone, non-stop to Swartkops. Then Veeplaas.
Then Korsten. And now here. How's that!

[*She laughs triumphantly. Boesman lets her enjoy herself. He waits
for his moment.*]

And I'm not finished. Wait and see. I'm going to think some
more. I'll work it out, back and back until I reach Coega
Kop. Then I'll have it. Coega Kop to here. So what you
got to say?

BOESMAN. Nothing.

LENA [*another laugh*]. Now you're really the hell-in. Nothing to
laugh at.

BOESMAN. Nothing to laugh at?

[*He disproves this with a small laugh.*]

LENA. You can't laugh at me.

[*Another laugh from Boesman.*]

I'm right, Boesman!

BOESMAN. How was it? Swartkops after Redhouse?

LENA. Yes!

BOESMAN. And from here we went to . . .

LENA. Korsten!

[*Boesman shakes his head with another laugh.*]

It's no good, Boesman. I know what you're trying. You're
not going to do it this time. Go laugh at yourself.

[*She goes back to her work, but there is an edge of something new
in her voice as she repeats the sequence with exaggerated emphasis.*]

Redhouse—Swartkops—Veeplaas—Korsten . . . Here!
Where I am.

[*She looks up at Boesman, but he pretends total indifference. This
adds to her growing uncertainty. She looks around. We see her trying*]

hard to remember, to work it out yet again. Boesman waits. He knows.
Eventually . . .]

Is it wrong?

BOESMAN [*strolling up to the fire to fetch something*].
Why do you stop singing?

LENA. Is it wrong, Boesman?

BOESMAN [*he takes his time, finding whatever he is looking for first
before answering*].
What about . . . Swartkops—Veeplaas—Redhouse?

LENA [*vacantly*]. Swartkops . . . Veeplaas. . . .

BOESMAN. Or this. Veeplaas.

LENA. Veeplaas.

BOESMAN. Redhouse . . .

LENA. Redhouse . . .

BOESMAN. Korsten!

LENA. Veeplaas—Redhouse—Korsten? [*Pause.*] Where's
Swartkops?

[*The sight of her vacant confusion is too much for Boesman. He has
a good laugh, now thoroughly enjoying himself.*]

To hell with it! I'm not listening to you. I'm here!

BOESMAN. Where? Veeplaas?

LENA [*closing her eyes*]. I'm here. I know how I got here.
Redhouse, then Swartkops. . . .

[*Pause—she has forgotten.*]

Wait . . . ! Redhouse—Swartkops. . . .

BOESMAN. Go on! But don't forget Bethelsdorp this time.
You've been there too. And Missionvale. And Kleinskool.

LENA. Don't mix me up, Boesman!

[*Trying desperately to remember her sequence.*]

Redhouse—Swartkops . . . then Veeplaas . . . then. . . .

BOESMAN. It's wrong!

[*Pause . . . she looks at him desperately. He leaves his work on the
shelter and goes to her.*]

Yes! It's wrong! Now what you going to do?

LENA [*she moves around helplessly, trying to orientate herself
physically*].

It's mixed up again. I had it!

BOESMAN. Look at you! *Babalas!* . . . from yesterday's wine. Yesterday you were drunk. One or the other. Your whole life.

LENA [*staring off in a direction*].
Over there. . . . Where did the sun go?

BOESMAN [*joining her*]. What you looking for?

LENA. Veeplaas.

BOESMAN. That way?

[*Lena studies Boesman's face for a second, then decides she is wrong.*]

LENA. No.

[*Moving in a different direction.*]

That way!

BOESMAN. Wrong!

[*Lena tries yet another direction.*]

Wrong!
Yessus, Lena! You're lost.

LENA. Do you really know, Boesman? Where and how?

BOESMAN. Yes!

LENA. Tell me.

[*He laughs.*]

Help me, Boesman!

BOESMAN. What? Find yourself?

[*Boesman launches into a grotesque pantomime of a search. Lena watches him with hatred.*]

[*Calling.*] Lena! Lena!

[*He rejoins her.*]

Sorry, Auntie. Better go to Veeplaas. Maybe you're there.

LENA [*directly at Boesman, her anger overwhelming her*].
Jou lae donner! Vark. Yes, you. You're a pig. *Voetsek*, you bastard. It's a sin, Boesman.

[*He enjoys her tirade immensely.*]

Wait a bit! One day . . . !

BOESMAN. One day what?

LENA. Something's going to happen.

BOESMAN. That's right.

LENA. What?

BOESMAN. Something's going to happen.

LENA. *Ja!*

[*Pause.*]

What's going to happen?

BOESMAN. I thought you knew. One day you'll ask me who you are.

[*He laughs.*]

LENA. *Ja*, another good laugh for you that day.

BOESMAN. The best one!

'*Ek sê, ou pellie . . .* who am I?' [*More laughter.*]

LENA [*trying her name*]. Lena . . . Lena. . . .

BOESMAN. What about Rosie? Nice name Rose. Maria. Anna. Or Sannie! Sannie who? *Sommer* Sannie Somebody.

LENA. NO!

BOESMAN [*ready to laugh*]. Who are you?

LENA. Mary. I want to be Mary. Who are you?

[*The laugh dies on Boesman's lips.*]

That's what I ask next. *Ja*, you! *Wie's die man?* And then I'm gone. Goodbye, darling. I've had enough. 'Struesgod, that day I'm gone.

BOESMAN. You mean that day you get a bloody *good* hiding.

LENA. *Aikona!* I'll go to the police.

BOESMAN. You tried that before and what happened? 'She's my woman, *baas*. *Net 'n bietjie warm gemaak.*' 'Take her' . . . finish *en klaar*. They know the way it is with our sort.

LENA. Not this time! My name is Mary, remember. 'Don't know this man, *baas*.' So where's your proof?

BOESMAN [*holding up a clenched fist*]. Here!

LENA. *Oppas!* You'll go too far one day. Death penalty.

BOESMAN. For you? [*Derisive laughter.*] Not guilty and discharge.

LENA. Don't talk big. You're frightened of the rope. When you stop hitting it's not because you're *moeg* or had enough. You're frightened! *Ja*.

[*Pause.*]

Ja. That's when I feel it most. When you do it carefully. The last few . . . when you aim. I count them. One . . . another one . . . wait for the next one! He's only resting.

[*Pause.*]

You're right, Boesman. That's proof. When I feel it I'll know. I'm Lena.

BOESMAN [*emphatically*]. And I'm Boesman.

LENA. Boesman and Lena.

BOESMAN. Yes! That's who. That's what. When . . . where . . . why! All your bloody nonsense questions. That's the answer.

LENA. Boesman and Lena.

BOESMAN. So stop asking them!

[*Pause . . . he goes back to work on the shelter. He tries the 'answer' for himself.*]

Boesman and Lena. *Ja!* It explains. So it's another *vrot ou huisie vir die vrot mens.* Look at it! Useless, hey. If it rains tonight you'll get wet. If it blows hard you'll be counting stars.

LENA. I know what it's like in there!

BOESMAN. It's all you'll ever know.

LENA. I'm sick of it.

BOESMAN. Sick of it! You want to live in a house? What do you think you are? A white madam?

LENA. It wasn't always like this. There were better times.

BOESMAN. In your dreams maybe.

LENA. What about Veeplaas? Chopping wood for the China-man? That room in his backyard. Real room, with a door and all that.

BOESMAN. Forget it. *Now* is the only time in your life.

LENA. No! 'Now.' What's that? I wasn't born today. I want my life. Where's it?

BOESMAN. In the mud, where you are, *Now.* Tomorrow it will be there too, and the next day. And if you're still alive when I've had enough of this, you'll load up and walk, somewhere else.

LENA. Roll up in my blanket and crawl into that! [*Pointing to the shelter.*]
Never enough wine to make us sleep the whole night. Wake up in the dark. The fire cold. What time is that in my life? Another 'now'! Black 'now' and empty as hell. Even when you're also awake. You make it worse. When I call you, and I know you hear me, but you say nothing. Sometimes loneliness is two . . . you and the other person who doesn't want to know you're there. I'm sick of you too, Boesman!

BOESMAN. So go.

LENA. Don't joke. I'll walk tonight. *So waar.*

BOESMAN. Go! Goodbye, darling.

[*Lena takes a few steps away from the fire then stops. Boesman watches her.*]

You still lost? Okay. Boesman will help you tonight. That way is Veeplaas. Through Swartkops, over the railway line, past that big thing with chimneys. Then you come to the veld. There's a path. Walk it until you see little lights. That's Veeplaas. Redhouse is that way. Korsten is over there. What else you want? Bethelsdorp? Coega Kop? There! There! I know my way. I know my world.

[*Lena is standing still.*]

So what you waiting for? Walk!

LENA [*her back to him, staring into the darkness*].
There's somebody out there.

[*Pause. Boesman leaves his work on the* pondok *and joins her. They stare in silence for a few seconds.*]

BOESMAN. Drunk.

LENA. No.

BOESMAN. Look at him!

LENA [*shaking her head*]. Nobody comes to the mudflats to get drunk.

BOESMAN. What do you know?

LENA. He's stopped. Maybe he's going to dig.

BOESMAN. Dark before the water's low.

LENA. Or a whiteman.

BOESMAN. When did you see a whiteman sitting like that!

LENA. Maybe he sees us.

[*She waves.*]

BOESMAN [*stopping her*]. What's the matter with you?

LENA. Go see what he wants.

BOESMAN. And then?

LENA. Do something. Help him.

BOESMAN. We got no help.

LENA. I'm not thinking of him.

[*Boesman stares at her.*]

It's another person, Boesman.

BOESMAN. I'm warning you! Don't start any nonsense.

[*He moves back to the shelter. Lena watches him for a few seconds, then decides.*]

LENA [*calling to the other person*].

Hey, I say.

BOESMAN. Lena!

LENA [*ignoring Boesman*]. We got a fire!

BOESMAN. Lena!

LENA. Come over!

BOESMAN. *Jou verdomde. . . .*

LENA [*sees the violence coming and moves away quickly*].

To hell with you! I want him.

[*Calling.*] Hey, darling! *Kom die kant!*

[*To Boesman.*] Sit in the dark and talk to myself because you don't hear me any more? No, Boesman! I want him! Hey! He's coming.

[*A moment of mutual uncertainty at the approach of the stranger. Lena falls back to Boesman's side. He picks up a stick in readiness for trouble. They stand together, waiting.*

An old African appears slowly.

Hat on his head, the rest of him lost in the folds of a shabby old overcoat. He is an image of age and decrepitude.]

BOESMAN. *Kaffer!*

LENA. *Ou kaffer.*

[*Lena almost turns away with disappointment. Boesman sees this and has a good laugh.*]

BOESMAN. Lena calls out in the dark, and what does she get? Look at it.

LENA [*after a few more seconds of hesitation*]. Better than nothing.

BOESMAN. So? Go on. You wanted somebody. There's a black one.

[*Lena takes a few steps towards the old man. He has remained at a distance. As Lena approaches him he murmurs a greeting in Xhosa.**]

LENA. *Molo, Outa.*

[*Boesman watches this, and Lena's other attempts to communicate with the old man, with cruel amusement. She gets another murmur from the old man.*]

BOESMAN. What you waiting for?

LENA. I am Lena. This is my man, Boesman.

BOESMAN. Shake his hand! Fancy *Hotnot* like you. Give him some smart stuff. 'How do you do, darling.'

[*The old man murmurs something in Xhosa.**]

LENA. What's that? You know his language.

[*Boesman laughs.*]

Does the *Outa* want something?

[*Another murmur.*]

Don't you speak English or Afrikaans? '*Môre, baas!*'

BOESMAN. Give him some help.

LENA. He doesn't look so good.

[*A few steps closer to the old man.*]

Come sit, *Outa*. Sit and rest.

[*Nothing happens. She turns to Boesman.*]

How do you say that in the kaffir *taal*?

BOESMAN. *Hamba!*

LENA. All right, Boesman!

[*Back to the old man . . . she pushes forward a box.*]

It's warm by the fire.

[*Nothing happens . . . a spark of anger in her voice.*]

You deaf? Sit!

[*The old man does so.*]

211

Ja, rest your legs. They work hard for us poor people.

[*Boesman looks up in time to see her uncorking one of their bottles of water. They stare at each other in silence for a few seconds.*]

Maybe he's thirsty.

BOESMAN. And us?

LENA. Only water.

BOESMAN. It's scarce here.

LENA. I'll fetch from Swartkops tomorrow.

BOESMAN. To hell! He doesn't belong to us.

[*Grabs the bottle away from her and together with the other one puts it inside the* pondok.]

LENA. There was plenty of times his sort gave us water on the road.

BOESMAN. It's different now.

LENA. How?

BOESMAN. Because I say so.

LENA. Because this time you got the water, hey!

[*Back to the old man.*]

Does *Outa* come far?

[*She stands and waits. . . . Nothing.*]

We're from Korsten. They kicked us out there this morning.

[*Nothing.*]

It's a hard life for us brown people, hey.

BOESMAN. He's not brown people, he's black people.

LENA. They got feelings too. Not so, *Outa*?

BOESMAN. You'll get some feelings if you don't watch that fire.

[*Lena is waiting for a word from the old man with growing desperation and irritation.*]

LENA. What's the matter? You sick? Where's it hurt?

[*Nothing.*]

Hey! I'm speaking to you.

[*The old man murmurs in Xhosa.*]

Stop that baboon language! *Waar kry jy seer?*

[*Another unintelligible response.*]

[*Lena turns away in violent disgust.*] *Ag*, go to hell! *Onnooslike kaffer. My bleddy bek af praat vir niks!*

[*Boesman explodes into laughter at this ending to Lena's encounter with the old man.*]

BOESMAN. Finished with him already? *Ag nee, wat!* You must try something there. He's *mos* better than nothing. Or was nothing better?

Too bad you're both so useless. Could have worked a point. Some sports. You and him. They like *Hotnot meide*. Black bastards!

[*Lena is wandering around helplessly.*]

Going to call again? You'll end up with a tribe of old *kaffers* sitting here. That's all you'll get out of that darkness. They go there to die. I'm warning you, Lena! Pull another one in here and you'll do the rest of your talking tonight with a thick mouth. Turn my place into a *kaffer nes*!

LENA [*coming back dejectedly to the fire*].
Give me a *dop*.

BOESMAN. That's better. Now you're talking like a *Hotnot*. *Weg wêreld, kom brandewyn.*

LENA. A *dop*, please, man!

BOESMAN. You look like one too now. A real one. *Gat op die grond en trane vir 'n bottel.*

LENA [*really desperate*]. Then open one.

BOESMAN. All that fancy talk is thirsty work, hey.

LENA. Open a bottle, Boesman!

BOESMAN. When I'm ready.

LENA [*she stands*]. One of them is mine!

[*She waits for a reaction from Boesman, but gets none.*]

I want it now!

[*Pause.*]

I'm going to take it, Boesman.

[*She moves forward impulsively to where the bottles are hidden. Boesman lets her take a few steps then goes into action.*]

BOESMAN [*grabbing a stick*].
Okay!

LENA [*seeing it coming*].
Eina!

[*Running quickly to the old man.*]

Watch now, *Outa*. You be witness for me. Watch! He's going to kill me.

BOESMAN [*stopping*]. You asking for it tonight, Lena.

LENA. You see how it is, *Outa*?

BOESMAN. He'll see you get it if you don't watch out.

LENA. I got it this morning!

BOESMAN. Just touch those bottles and you'll get it again.

[*He throws down the stick and goes off.*]

LENA [*shouting after him*]. Go on! Why don't you hit me? There's no white *baases* here to laugh. Does this old thing worry you?

[*Turning back to the old man.*]

Look, *Outa*. I want you to look.

[*Showing him the bruises on her arms and face.*]

No, not that one. That's a old one. This one. And here. Just because I dropped the sack with the empties. I would have been dead if they hadn't laughed. When other people laugh he gets ashamed. Now too. I would have got it hard from him if you. . . .

[*Pause.*]

Why didn't you laugh? They laughed this morning. They laugh every time.

[*Growing violence.*]

What's the matter with you? *Kaffers* laugh at it too. It's *mos* funny. Me! *Ou meid* being *donnered*!

[*Pause. . . . She moves away to some small chore at the fire. After this she looks up at the old man, and then goes slowly to him.*]

Wasn't it funny?

[*She moves closer.*]

Hey, look at me?

[*He looks at her.*]

My name is Lena.

[*She pats herself on the chest. Nothing happens. She tries again, but this time she pats him.*]

Outa . . . You . . . [*patting herself*] . . . Lena . . . me.

OLD MAN. Lena.

LENA [*excited*]. *Ewe!* Lena!

OLD MAN. Lena.

LENA [*softly*]. My God!

[*She looks around desperately, then after a quick look in the direction in which Boesman disappeared, she goes to the half-finished shelter and fetches one of the bottles of water. She uncorks it and hurries back to the old man.*]

LENA [*offering the bottle*]. Water. *Water! Manzi!*

[*She helps him get it to his lips. He drinks. In between mouthfuls he murmurs away in Xhosa. Lena picks up the odd phrase and echoes it . . . 'Bhomboloza Outa, Bhomboloza' . . . 'Mlomo, ewe mlomo' . . . 'Yes, Outa, dala' . . . as if she understood him.*
The whole of the monologue follows this pattern: the old man murmuring intermittently—the occasional phrase or even sentence quite clear—and Lena surrendering herself more and more to the illusion of conversation.]

LENA. *Safa . . . safa. . . .*

[*Pause.*]

What's all that mean?

[*He hands her back the bottle.*]

If *Outa's* saying. . . .

[*She stops, takes another quick look to make sure Boesman is out of sight, then returns to the old man's side. She speaks secretively and with intensity.*]

It's true! You're right. [*He is still murmuring.*] Wait now. Listen to mine.

I had a dog. In Korsten. Just a *brak*. Once when we were sitting somewhere counting our bottles and eating he came and looked at us. Must have been a *Kaffer hond*. He didn't bark. I left some bread for him there on the ground when we went. He ate it and followed us all the way back to Korsten.

[*Another look over her shoulder to make sure Boesman isn't near. She continues her story in an even lower tone.*]

215

For two days like that around our place there. When Boesman wasn't looking I threw him things to eat. Boesman knew I was up to something. I'm a bloody fool, *Outa*. Something makes me happy I start singing. So every time Boesman saw the dog, he throws stones. He doesn't like dogs. They don't like him. But when he wasn't looking I threw food.

[*Laughs secretively.*]

I won, *Outa*! One night the dog came in when he was asleep . . . came and sat and looked at me. When Boesman woke up, he moved out. So it was every night after that. We waited for Boesman to sleep, then he came and watched me. All the things I did—making the fire, cooking, counting bottles or bruises, even just sitting, you know, when it's too much . . . he saw it. *Hond!* I called him *Hond*. But any name, he'd wag his tail if you said it nice.

I'll tell you what it is. Eyes, *Outa*. Another pair of eyes. Something to see you.

Then this morning in all the *lawaai* and mix-up—gone!

I wanted to look, but Boesman was in a hurry.

So what! Now I got *Outa*.

[*Nudging him.*] Lena!

OLD MAN. Lena.

LENA [*little laugh*]. You see, I'm not ashamed.

Dè! [*In a fit of generosity she passes the bottle over again.*] Much as you like, darling. Doesn't cost a cent. Drink. Don't worry about him. He's worried about the wine. [*Old man drinks.*]

No heart in that one, *Outa*. Or empty. *Leeggesuip*. Tickey deposit for Boesman's heart. Brandy bottle.

[*She gets the bottle back and takes it to the* pondok, *talking all the time.*]

Outa know the empties. Brandy bottles, beer bottles, wine bottles. Any kind. Medicine. Tomato sauce. Sell them at the Bottle Exchange. We were doing good with the empties there in Korsten. Whiteman's drinking himself to death. Take your sack, knock on some back doors and it's full by no time. It was going easy for us, man. Eating meat. Proper chops! Then this morning: *Loop, Hotnot!* Just had time to grab our things. That's when I dropped the sack. Three bottles broken. I didn't even have on a *broek* or a petticoat when we started walking.

ACT ONE

[*Straightens up at the shelter and registers the old man sitting quietly.*]

You're a nice *Ou* . . . [*correcting herself*] . . . you're one of the good *Bantoes*, hey. I can see it. Sit so nice and listen to Lena.

[*Back to the fire where she puts on a few more pieces of wood.*]

That's why we called. I could see it. I said to Boesman: He's one of the good ones. *Arme ou drommel!* Sorry feelings—for you. 'Let's call him over!'

[*The old man starts murmuring again. This time it is accompanied by much head-shaking. Lena interprets this as a rejection of what she has just said.*]

No, *Outa*, I did! *Haai*, it's true! Why should I lie?

[*Her tone and manner becoming progressively more angry.*]

It's true! What do you know? Don't argue! Bloody old. . . .

[*The old man makes a move to stand up. Lena, changing tone and attitude, forces him to stay seated.*]

Okay! Okay! Okay, *Outa*!! I'll tell you the truth. But mustn't say I *lieg*. Sit still.

[*Pause.*]

It's my eyes. They're not so good any more, specially when the thing is far away. But in the old days . . . ! You know those mountains out there, when you walk Kleinskool way. . . . In the old days so clear, *Outa*. When we were resting I used to put my finger on a point, and then up and down, just the way it is.

[*Demonstrates tracing the outline of a mountain range.*]

I haven't seen them for a long time. Boesman's back gets in the way these days.

[*Breaking the mood.*]

It's not so bad, when the thing is near to me. Like Korsten, this morning. That's quite clear. Tomorrow as well.

I can see that too, we'll be digging.

I say! *Ou* Lena's talking her head off tonight. And you sit so nicely and listen to her. Boesman wouldn't. Tell me to shut up.

[*Secretively.*] We must be careful. He'll try and chase you away just now. Mustn't go, you see.

[*The old man starts murmuring again. For a few seconds Lena*

217

interprets it as small talk as she goes on preparing for their supper.]
That's right. Of course, *ja*, it's going to be cold tonight. You never said a truer thing, darling. I know, I know. Don't you worry. We'll eat just now. Won't take long to boil.

[*Pause. . . . The old man mumbles away, Lena studies him in silence for a few seconds.*]

LENA [*interrupting him*]. It's about Boesman, isn't it?

[*She laughs.*]

I *mos* know. Why shouldn't you and me talk? Well. . . . Too small for a real *Hotnot, Outa*. There's something else there. Bushman blood. And wild! That tickey deposit heart of his is tight, like his *poephol* and his fist.

[*Holds up a clenched fist in an imitation of Boesman.*]

That's how he talks to the world.

[*Much laughter from Lena at her joke, with a lot of nudging and back-slapping as if the old man was also laughing. He isn't.*]

Ja, so it goes. He walks in front. I walk behind. It used to be side by side, with jokes. At night he let me sing, and listened. Never learnt any songs himself.

[*The old man murmurs.*]

I don't know.

[*The old man continues to murmur, Lena gets desperate.*]

Don't start again, *Outa*. I don't know! Behind us. Isn't that enough? Too heavy to carry. The last time we joked, the last time I sang. Behind us somewhere. Our rubbish. We'll leave something here too if there's any last times left.

Yessus! It's so heavy now, *Outa*. Am I crooked? It feels that way when we stop and the bundles come down. What's so heavy? I walk and I think . . . a blanket, a few things in a bucket. . . .

Look! [*Pointing to their possessions.*]

And even when they're down, when you've made your place and the fire is burning and you rest your legs, something stays heavy. Hey! Once you've put your life on your head and walked you never get light again.

We've been walking a long time, *Outa*. Look at my feet.

Those little paths on the veld . . . Boesman and Lena helped write them.

I meet the memory of myself on the old roads. Sometimes young. Sometimes old. Is she coming or going? From where to where? All mixed up. The right time on the wrong road, the right road leading to the wrong place.

[*A murmur from the old man.*]

He won't tell me. That's a sin, isn't it? He'll be punished. But he says there's no God for us. Do you know? Up there!

[*A vague gesture to the sky. No intelligible response from the old man.*]

Doesn't matter.

[*The old man murmurs loudly, urgently.*]

What's that now? Maybe. . . .

[*Straightening up at the fire.*]

Yessus, Outa! You're asking things tonight. [*Sharply.*] Why do you want to know?

[*Pause.*]

It's a long story.

[*She moves over to him, sits down beside him.*]

One, *Outa*, that lived. For six months. The others were born dead.

[*Pause.*]

That all? *Ja.* Only a few words I know, but a long story if you lived it.

[*Murmuring from the old man.*]

That's all. That's all.

Nee, God, Outa! What more must I say? What you asking me about? Pain? Yes! Don't *kaffers* know what that means? One night it was longer than a small piece of candle and then as big as darkness. Somewhere else a donkey looked at it. I crawled under the cart and they looked. Boesman was too far away to call. Just the sound of his axe as he chopped wood. I didn't even have rags!

You asked me and now I've told you. Pain is a candle *entjie* and a donkey's face. What's that mean to you? You weren't there. Nobody was. Why do you ask *now?* You're too late for that. *This* is what I feel now [*the fire, the shelter, her 'here and now'*]. . . . This!

My life is here tonight. Tomorrow or the next day that one

out there will drag it somewhere else. But tonight I sit *here*. You interested in that?

[*The old man gets slowly to his feet and starts to move away. Lena throws herself at him violently.*]

LENA. Not a damn! I'm not finished! You can't just go, walk away like you didn't hear. You asked me, and I've told you. This is what I'm left with. You've got two eyes. Sit and look!

[*She has forced the old man back on his box. Lena calms down.*]

Lena!

OLD MAN. Lena.

LENA [*trying to mollify him*]. I'll ask Boesman to give you a *dop*. Okay? Won't be too bad. Where could you go now? Dark out there, *Outa*. *Skelms* will grab you.

[*She hears a noise . . . moves away a few steps and peers into the darkness.*]

He's coming. Listen, we must be clever now. Don't look happy. And don't say anything. Just sit still. Pretend we're still *kwaai-vriende*.

[*She goes back to her fire. Another idea sends her back hurriedly to the old man.*]

No. I know what you do. When he comes back you must say you'll buy wine for us all tomorrow. Say you got a job in Swartkops and when you get your pay you'll buy wine. You hear me? [*Violently.*] Hey . . . !

[*Before she can say anything more, Boesman appears. He has a few more pieces of firewood, and something else for the shelter. Lena scuttles back to the fire, and makes herself busy. Boesman stops and stares at the two of them.*]

BOESMAN. What you been doing?

LENA [*innocently*]. Nothing. Look at the wine if you don't believe me.

BOESMAN. Then why's he still here?

LENA. I been looking after the fire. Water's nearly boiling.

BOESMAN. *You* called him . . . *you* tell him to go.

LENA [*looking furtively at the old man, waiting for him to speak*]. This wood doesn't mean much. Won't last the night.

BOESMAN. Don't pretend you didn't hear.

LENA. Okay.

[*Tries to lose herself in fussing with the pot.*]

[*Boesman waits.*]

BOESMAN. So when you going to tell him to go?

LENA. Who?

BOESMAN. Don't play stupid with me, Lena!

LENA. Him? Slowly there?

[*Leaves the fire and talks to him with an exaggerated show of secrecy.*]
He's okay.

BOESMAN. What's that mean?

LENA. Good *kaffer*.

BOESMAN. How do you know?

LENA [*to the old man*]. Tell him what you said to me, *Outa*.

BOESMAN. Since when can you speak his language?

LENA. He's got a few words of Afrikaans. *Outa!!*

BOESMAN. What did he say?

LENA. He said he's going to buy wine tomorrow.
[*To the old man.*] Not so?
He's got some jobs there in Swartkops. Some garden jobs.
Ask him.

BOESMAN. Who's going to give *that* a job?

LENA. Somebody with a soft heart.

BOESMAN. You mean a soft head.

LENA [*forcing a laugh*]. Soft head! Bloody good, Boesman.

BOESMAN. Garden job! He hasn't got enough left in him to
dig his own grave.

LENA. Soft heart and a soft head! *Haai!*

[*Lena is laughing too much. Boesman stares at her. She stops.*]

LENA [*weakly*]. Funny *ou grappie*.

[*Boesman's suspicions are aroused. He goes back to work on the shelter,
but watches the other two very carefully. Lena, thinking she has won,
starts to lay out their supper.*]

LENA [*pointing to a loaf of brown bread*]. Can I break it in three
pieces?

BOESMAN. Two pieces!

[*Lena wants to rebuke him, but stops herself in time.*]

LENA [*softly to the old man*]. We'll share mine.

[*Looks up to see Boesman watching her.*]

Pondokkie's looking okay. *Oulike ou nessie.* He's good with his hands, *Outa.*

[*Without realizing what she is doing, Lena starts humming a little song as she works away at the fire. She realizes her mistake too late. Boesman is staring hard at her when she looks up.*]

[*Desperately.*] I'm not happy!

BOESMAN. You're up to something.

LENA. 'Struesgod I'm not happy.

BOESMAN. He must go.

LENA. Please, Boesman!

BOESMAN. He's had his rest. Hey!

LENA. It's dark now.

BOESMAN. That's his troubles. Hey! *Hamba wena!*

LENA. He's not doing any harm.

BOESMAN. He'll bring the others. It's not far to their location from here.

LENA. Boesman! Just for once a favour. Let him stay.

BOESMAN. What's he to me?

LENA. For me, man. [*Pause.*] I want him.

BOESMAN. What for? What you up to, Lena?

[*Pause. . . . Lena can't answer his questions.*]

LENA [*impulsively*]. You can have the wine. All of it. Next time as well.

[*She dives to the shelter, produces the two bottles of wine.*]

There!

BOESMAN [*unbelievingly*]. For that!

LENA. I want him.

BOESMAN. This is wine, Lena. That's a *kaffer*. He won't help you forget. You want to sit sober in this world? You know what it looks like then?

LENA. I want him.

BOESMAN [*shaking his head*]. You off your mind tonight.

[*To the old man.*] You're an expensive *ou drol*. Two bottles of wine! *Ek sê.* Boesman has party tonight.

[*He tantalizes Lena by opening a bottle and passing it under her nose.*]

Smell! *Hotnot's* forget-me-not.

[*First mouthful.*]

Weg wêreld, kom brandewyn.

LENA [*restraining the old man*].

No, *Outa*. I've paid. You can stay the night with us. If we all
lie together it will be warm in there.

BOESMAN [*overhearing*]. What do you mean?

LENA [*after a pause*]. You can have the mattress.

BOESMAN. To hell! He's not coming inside. Bring your *kaffer*
and his fleas into my *pondok*. Not a damn.

LENA. He won't sit there by himself.

BOESMAN. Then sit with him!

[*He sees Lena's dilemma . . . enjoys it.*]

Ja! You can choose. Inside here or take your fleas and keep
him company.

[*Pause. . . . Boesman works away, tries to whistle.*]

I said you can sleep inside with me or. . . .

LENA. I heard you, Boesman.

BOESMAN. So?

[*Lena doesn't answer. Boesman rubs it in.*]

It's going to be cold tonight. When it starts pushing and the
water comes back. Boesman's all right. Two bottles and a
pondokkie. Bakgat!

[*He watches Lena. She moves slowly to their things. For the first
time he is unsure of himself.*]

What you going to do?

[*Lena doesn't answer. She finds one of their blankets and takes it
to the old man.*]

LENA. Here, *Outa*. We'll need it.

BOESMAN [*suddenly on his feet*]. I've changed my mind. He
must go.

LENA [*turning on him with unexpected ferocity*].

Be careful, Boesman!

BOESMAN. Of what?

LENA [*eyes closed, fists clenched*]. Be careful.

[*Her tone stops him. He sits down again, now even more unsure of himself.*]

BOESMAN. You think I care what you do? You want to sit outside and die of cold with a *kaffer*, go ahead!

LENA. I'd sit out there with a dog tonight!

[*Turns back to the old man.*]

We'll need more wood. And something in case it rains. I'm not so handy at making shelter, *Outa*.

[*To Boesman.*] Where did you find that stuff? Anything left out there?

[*This time Boesman doesn't answer. He stares at her with hard disbelief.*]

I'll see what I can find, *Outa*.

[*She wanders off. Boesman, in front of his shelter with the two bottles of wine, watches her go. When she has disappeared he studies the old man. Takes a few more swallows, then gets up and moves a few steps in the direction that Lena left. Certain that she is not about he turns and goes back to the old man.*]

BOESMAN [*standing over him.*] Hond!

[*The old man looks up at him. Boesman pulls the blanket away from him.*]

I want two blankets tonight.

[*Still not satisfied, he sends the old man sprawling with a shove. The old man crawls back laboriously to his seat. Boesman watches him, then hears Lena returning. He throws back the blanket.*]

If you tell her, I'll kill you.
Bulala wena!

[*He returns to his shelter, sits down, and continues drinking. He will remain in this position, watching Lena and the old man, until the end of the Act.*]

LENA [*a few small pieces of wood are all she has found*].
It's too dark now.

[*She goes to the fire. Their tea is now ready. She pours it into two mugs, taking one of them and half the bread to Boesman. Then she joins the old man with her share. She sits beside him.*]

As long as it doesn't rain it won't be so bad. The blanket

will help. Nights are long, but they don't last for ever. This
wind will also get tired.

[*Her mug of tea and bread are placed before them.*]

It's a long time since we had somebody else with us. Sit
close to the fire. That's it!

[*She throws on another piece of wood.*]

It won't last long, but it's big enough. Not much to see.
This is all. This is mine.

Look at this mug, *Outa* . . . old mug, hey. Bitter tea, a piece
of bread. Bitter and brown. The bread should have bruises.
It's my life.

[*Passing him the mug.*]

There, don't waste time. It's still warm.

[*They drink and eat. Boesman is watching them from the shelter,
his bread and tea untouched before him.*]

ACT TWO

An hour later.

Lena and the old man are still sitting together on the box, huddled together under the blanket. Boesman is on his legs in front of them, the second bottle of wine in his hands. Under the influence of the wine his characteristic violence is now heightened by a wild excitability.

His bread and tea are still untouched on the ground.

BOESMAN. Again.

LENA. No.

BOESMAN. Yes!

LENA. You said that was the last time.

BOESMAN. You didn't do it right.

LENA. Have a heart, Boesman. Leave us alone now, man!

BOESMAN. Come on! 'Please, *my baasie!*'
[*Pause.*] Lena!

LENA [*giving in*]. ' Please, *my baasie.*'

BOESMAN. Properly. The way you did it this morning.

LENA. 'Please, *my baasie.*'

BOESMAN [*pointing to the old man*]. Him too. Hey!

LENA. Say it, *Outa.*

[*The old man mumbles something.*]

BOESMAN. '*Ag siestog, my baas.*'

LENA. '*Ag siestog, my baas.*'

BOESMAN. No bloody good.

LENA [*reaching breaking-point, she jumps up*].
Enough, Boesman!

BOESMAN. Not enough. Whiteman won't feel sorry for you.

LENA. Then you try!

BOESMAN. You must make the words crawl to him, with your tongue between their back legs. Then when the *baas* looks at you, wag it just a little . . . '*Siestoggies, my baas! Siestoggies, my groot* little *baasie!*'

LENA. Whiteman! Whiteman! Whiteman's dog. *Voetsek!*

[*Boesman laughs.*]

I'll pick up a stone, Boesman.

226

[*Boesman growls at her.*]

[*Sitting down beside the old man again.*] That's what he is, *Outa*. Make life hell for anything that smells poor. He's worse. They stop barking when you've walked past. This one's following me to my grave.

BOESMAN [*launching into a vulgar parody of Lena, with the appropriate servile postures and gestures*].
'*Sommer* a *ou Hotnot, baas.* Lena, *baas. Van ou* Coega, *baas. Ja, my baas.*'

[*He turns on her.*]
You!

[*He extends the pantomime to a crude imitation of the scene that morning when the Korsten shacks were demolished.*]

[*Peering at something.*] '*En dit? Nee, moer!* Boesman. Hey, Boesman! *Daar kom 'n ding díe kant.* Save our things! [*In and out of the shelter.*] Give us time, *my baas. Al weer sukke tyd.* Poor old Lena. Just one more load, *baas. Arme ou Lena!*'

[*Abandoning the act and turning on Lena again.*]

This morning! That's how you said it. That's what you looked like.

LENA. And did somebody feel sorry for us?

BOESMAN. The lot of you! Crawling out of your holes. Like worms. *Babalas* as the day you were born. That piece of ground was rotten with *dronkies.* Trying to save their rubbish, falling over each other . . . !

'Run you bastards! Whiteman's bulldozer is chasing you!'

[*Big laugh.*]

LENA. And then he hit me for dropping the empties.

BOESMAN [*the bulldozer*]. Slowly it comes . . . slowly . . . big yellow *donner* with its jawbone on the ground. One bite and there's a hole in the earth! Whiteman on top. I watched him. He had to work, *ou boeta.* Wasn't easy to tell that thing where to go. He had to work with those knobs!
In reverse . . . take aim! . . . *maak sy bek oop!* . . . then horsepower in top gear and smashed to hell. One push and it was flat. All of them. Slum clearance! And what did we do? Stand and look.

[*Another imitation*].

'*Haai! Kyk net. Witman is 'n snaakse ding.*'

[*Boesman laughs.*]

But the dogs knew. They had their tails between their legs. They were ready to run.

LENA. He laughed then too, *Outa*. Like a madman. Running around shouting and laughing at our own people.

BOESMAN. So would you if you'd seen them.

LENA. I did.

BOESMAN. You didn't. You were sitting there with our things crying.

LENA. I saw myself.

BOESMAN. And what did that look like?

LENA. Me.

BOESMAN. Only one.

LENA. One's enough.

BOESMAN. Enough! Leave that word alone. You don't know what it means.

LENA. It was the same story for all of us. Once is enough if it's a sad one.

BOESMAN. Sad story? Those two that had the fight because somebody grabbed the wrong *broek*? The *ou* trying to catch his donkey? Or that other one running around with his porridge looking for a fire to finish cooking it? It was bioscope, man! And I watched it. Beginning to end, the way it happened. *I* saw it. *Me.*

The women and children sitting there with their snot and tears. The *pondoks* falling. The men standing, looking, as the yellow *donner* pushed them over and then staring at the pieces when they were the only things left standing. I saw all that! The whiteman stopped the bulldozer and smoked a cigarette. I saw that too.

[*Another act.*]

'*Ek sê, my baas . . . !*' He threw me the *stompie*. '*Dankie, baas.*'

LENA. They made a big pile and burnt everything.

BOESMAN. Bonfire!

LENA. He helped drag what was left of the *pondoks*. . . .

BOESMAN. Of course. Full of disease. That one in the uniform told me. '*Dankie, baas!*'

LENA. Just like that.

BOESMAN [*violently*]. Yes! *Dankie, baas.*
You should have said it too, sitting there with your sad story. Whiteman was doing us a favour. You should have helped him. He wasn't just burning *pondoks*. They alone can't stink like that. Or burn like that.
There was something else in that fire, something rotten. Us! Our sad stories, our smells, our world! And it burnt, *boeta*. It burnt. I watched that too.
The end was a pile of ashes. And quiet.
Then . . . 'Here!' . . . then I went back to the place where our *pondok* had been. It was gone! You understand that? Gone! I wanted to call you and show you. There where we crawled in and out like baboons, where we used to sit like them and eat, our head between our knees, our fingers in the pot, hiding away so that the others wouldn't see our food. . . . I could stand there! There was room for me to stand straight. You know what that is? Listen now. I'm going to use a word. Freedom! *Ja*, I've heard them talk it. Freedom! That's what the whiteman gave us. I've got my feelings too, sister. It was a big one I had when I stood there. That's why I laughed, why I was happy. When we picked up our things and started to walk I wanted to sing. It was Freedom!

LENA. You still got it, *ou ding*?

[*Boesman stares at her dumbly. He wanders around aimlessly, looking at the fire, the other two, the shelter, as if he were itemizing every detail in his present situation. Lena watches him.*]
You lost it?

[*Boesman doesn't answer.*]
Your big word? That made you so happy?

BOESMAN. When I turned off the road, when I said Swartkops. I didn't want to! Say it, or think it. Any of the old places. I didn't want to. I tried!
The world was open this morning. It was big! All the roads . . . new ways, new places. *Yessus!* It made me drunk.

Which one? When the robot said 'Go' there at Berry's Corner I was nearly *bang in my broek*.

LENA. So that's what we were looking for, that *dwaal* there in the back streets. Should have seen us, *Outa*! Down one, up the other, back to where we started from . . . looking for Boesman's Freedom.

BOESMAN. I had it!

It was you with your big mouth and stupid questions. 'Where we going?' Every corner! 'Hey, Boesman, where we going?' 'Let's try Veeplaas.' 'How about Coega?' All you could think of was those old rubbish dumps. 'Bethelsdorp . . . Missionvale. . . .'

Don't listen to her, Boesman! Walk!

'Redhouse . . . Kleinskool. . . .'

They were like fleas on my life. I scratched until I was raw.

LENA. We had to go somewhere. Couldn't walk around Korsten carrying your Freedom for ever.

BOESMAN. Every time you opened your mouth it got worse.

LENA. Bad day for Lena. Three empties and Boesman's Freedom in pieces.

BOESMAN. By the time you shut up we just a *vlenterbroek* and his *meid* in the backyard of the world.

I saw that piece of *sinkplaat* on the side of the road, I should have passed it. Gone on! Freedom's a long walk.

But the sun was low. Our days are too short.

[*Pause.*]

Too late, Boesman. Too late for it today.

So I picked it up. Finish and *klaar*. Another *pondok*.

[*Shouting violently.*]

It's no use, *baas*. Boesman's done it again. Bring your bulldozer tomorrow and push it over!

[*To the old man.*] Then you must run. It will chase you too. *Sa! Sa vir die kaffer!*

LENA. Don't listen to him, *Outa*. There's no hurry. When it's over they let you walk away. Nobody had to run. One by one we went, a few things on the head, different ways, one by one.

BOESMAN. Whiteman's wasting his time trying to help us.

Pushed it over this morning and here it is again. Push this
one over and I'll do it somewhere else. Make another hole
in the ground, crawl into it, and live my life crooked.

One push. That's all we need. Into gaol, out of your job . . .
one push and it's pieces.

Must I tell you why? Listen! I'm thinking deep tonight.
We're whiteman's rubbish. That's why he's so *beneukt* with us.
He can't get rid of his rubbish. He throws it away, we pick
it up. Wear it. Sleep in it. Eat it. We're made of it now.
His rubbish is people.

LENA. Throw yourself away and leave us alone.

BOESMAN. It's been done. Why do you think we sit here like
this? We've been thrown away. Rubbishes. Him too. [*Pointing
to the old man.*] They don't want him any more. Useless. But
there! You see what happens. Lena picks him up. Wraps
him in a blanket. Gives him food.

LENA. You picked up yours. I picked up mine.

BOESMAN. I got mine for nothing. It made a *pondok*. What
you going to do with him?

[*Pause.*]

Hey! I'm speaking to you. You paid a lot for that *ou drol*.
Bottle of wine. You happy now?

LENA. I didn't buy *Outa* for happiness.

BOESMAN. So then what's the use of him? Is he hot stuff?
Keeping you warm there?

LENA. No.

BOESMAN. You two up to something under that blanket?

[*Lena doesn't answer.*]

Lena and *ou* better-than-nothing. Waiting for me to go to
sleep, hey. *Vuilgoed!*

LENA. No, Boesman.

BOESMAN. You're cold, you're hungry, you're not making
Happiness but still you want him.

LENA. Yes.

BOESMAN [*turning away with a forced laugh*].

Nee, God! She's gone mad. Lena's gone mad on the mudflats.
Sit there with a *kaffer*. . . .

[*His laughter spirals up into violent bewilderment. He faces her savagely.*]

Why?! Why?!!!

[*Pause.*]

LENA [*she takes her time*].

What we doing to you, Boesman? Why can't you leave us alone? You've had the wine, you've got the shelter. What else is there? Me?! *Haai*, Boesman, is that why he worries you? You jealous . . . because Lena's turned you down, your *pondok*, and your bottle?

Must I tell you why?

That's not a *pondok*, Boesman. [*Pointing to the shelter.*] It's a coffin. All of them. You bury my life in your *pondoks*. Not tonight. Crawl into darkness and silence before I'm dead.

No! I'm on this earth, not in it.

Look now. [*She nudges the old man.*] Lena!

OLD MAN. Lena.

LENA. *Ewe,* Lena.

[*To Boesman.*] That's me.

You're right, Boesman. It's here and now. This is the time and place. To hell with the others. They're finished, and mixed up anyway. I don't know why I'm here, how I got here. And you won't tell me. Doesn't matter. They've ended *now*. The walks led *here*. Tonight. And he sees it.

BOESMAN. What's there to see? Boesman and Lena on the mudflats at Swartkops. Like any other night.

LENA. That's right.

BOESMAN. And tomorrow night will be the same. What you going to do then? Maybe I'll kick you out again.

LENA. You didn't kick me out.

BOESMAN. Tomorrow night I will. And you'll sit alone. Because he won't be here. That I tell you. Or anybody else.

LENA. He's here now.

[*Boesman leaves her and sits down in front of his shelter, drinking, in a withdrawn and violent silence.*]

[*To the old man.*] Not yet, *Outa*. [*Shaking him.*] It's not finished. Open your eyes.

[*To Boesman.*]

If you don't want your bread and tea pass it this way, man.

[*Boesman studies Lena in silence for a few seconds then stretches out a leg and pushes over the mug of tea. He watches Lena for a reaction. There is none. In a sudden fury he picks up the bread and hurls it into the darkness.*]

BOESMAN. I've told you, we've got no help.

[*Disappears into the shelter with his bottle of wine, reappears, on his knees, almost immediately.*]

I'm kicking you out *now*. Even if you change your mind you can't come in.

LENA. I won't, Boesman.

[*Boesman disappears into the shelter.*]

Maybe he'll sleep now.

[*The old man leans forward.*]

No, *Outa*, not us. [*Shaking him.*]
Listen to me. You'll never sleep long enough.
Sit close. *Ja! Hotnot* and a *Kaffer* got no time for apartheid on a night like this. We must keep that bit of wood for later. After that there's nothing left. Don't think about what you're feeling. Something else. Warm times. Let's talk about warm times. Good walk on a nice day! Not too long, not too hot. Otherwise you're back in hell again . . . as hot as this one's cold. In and out, hey, *Outa*, we poor people. But when it's just right! It's a feeling. And a taste, when you lick your lips. Dust and sweat.
Hard work too. Watch tomorrow. You start to dig for prawns, your hands are stiff, the mud and water is cold, but after a little while you start to sweat and it's okay.
Outa must help us dig tomorrow. Get nice and warm. And a good dance! *Yessus, Outa.* There's a warm feeling. If we had a *dop* inside now we could have tried. Hard to make party without a *dop*.
[*Humming.*] Da . . . da . . . da.
Outa know that one? *Ou Hotnot* dance. Clap your hands. So.

[*She starts clapping and singing softly.*]

'*Die trane die rol vir jou, bokkie!*'
Coegakop days! Lena danced the moon down and the sun up. The parties, *Outa*! Happy Christmas, Happy New Year,

Happy Birthday . . . all the Happies. We danced them. The sad ones too. Somebody born, somebody buried. We danced them in, we danced them out. It helps us forget. Few *dops* and a guitar and it's *voetsek* yesterday and to hell with tomorrow. [*Singing*.] Da . . . da . . . da . . . da. . . .
Outa's not clapping. So.
[*Clapping and singing*.] Da . . . da . . . da . . . da. . . .

> *Ou blikkie kondens melk*
> *Maak die lewe soet;*
> *Boesman is 'n Boesman*
> *Maar hy dra 'n Hotnot hoed.*

Not like your dances. No war-dances for us. They say we were slaves in the old days. Just your feet on the earth and then stamp. Hit it hard!
[*Still seated, she demonstrates.*]
Da . . . da . . . da . . . da. . . .
Nothing fancy. We don't tickle it like the white people. Maybe it laughs for them. It's a hard mother to us. So we dance hard. Let it feel us. Clap with me.
[*Lena is now on her legs. Still clapping she starts to dance. In the course of it Boesman's head appears in the opening to the shelter. He watches her.*]
[*Speaking as she makes the first heavy steps.*]
So for Korsten. *So* for the walk. *So* for Swartkops. *This* time. *Next* time. *Last* time.
[*Singing.*]

> Korsten had its empties
> Swartkops got its bait
> Lena's got her bruises
> Cause Lena's a *Hotnot meid.*
>
> Kleinskool got prickly pears
> Missionvale's got salt
> Lena's got a Boesman
> So it's always Lena's fault.
>
> Coegakop is far away
> Redhouse up the river
> Lena's in the mud again
> *Outa's* sitting with her.

234

[*She stops, breathing heavily, then wipes her forehead with her hand and licks one of the fingers.*]

Sweat! You see, *Outa*, Sweat. Sit close now, I'm warm. You feel me? And we've still got that wood!

[*They huddle together again under the blanket. Boesman is watching from the shelter. He lets them settle down before speaking.*]

BOESMAN. I dropped the empties.

[*Lena looks at him, she doesn't understand.*]

This morning. When we had to clear out of the *pondok*. I carried the sack.

[*It takes Lena a long time.*]

I dropped it.

LENA. [*She understands now. She speaks quietly.*]
You said I did.

BOESMAN. Yes.

LENA. You blamed me. You hit me.

BOESMAN. Yes.

LENA [*to the old man*]. He wanted to count the bottles before we left. Three were broken. He stopped hitting when the whiteman laughed. Took off his hat and smiled at them. 'Jus' a *ou meid, baas.*' They laughed louder. [*Pointing to her bruises.*] Too dark to see them now. He's hit me everywhere.

[*Her arms open . . . looking down at her body. She has a sense of her frail anatomy. She feels herself.*]

Haai, Yessus! Look at it. *Pap ou borste, ribbetjies.*

[*She looks up at Boesman. He is still watching her from the shelter.*]

For nothing then. Why do you tell me now?

[*Pause. . . . He stares at her.*]

You want to hurt me again. Why, Boesman? I've come through a day that God can take back. Even if it was my last one. Isn't that enough for you?

[*Pause.*]

No.

Why must you hurt me so much? What have I really done? Why didn't you hit yourself this morning? You broke the bottles. Or the whiteman that kicked us out? Why did you hit me?

BOESMAN [*now out of the shelter*].

Why do I hit you?

[*He tries to work it out. He looks at his hands, clenches one, and smashes it into the palm of the other.*]

Why?

LENA. To keep your life warm? Learn to dance, Boesman. Leave your bruises on the earth.

BOESMAN [*another blow*]. Why?

LENA [*still quietly*]. Maybe you just want to touch me, to know I'm here. Try it the other way. Open your fist, put your hand on me. I'm here. I'm Lena.

BOESMAN. Lena!

[*Another blow, the hardest. He looks at her and nods.*]

Lena . . . and I'm Boesman.

LENA. Hit yourself!

BOESMAN [*holding up his palm*]. It doesn't hurt.

LENA [*the first note of outrage*].

And when it's me? Does that hurt you?

What have I done, Boesman? It's my life. Hit your own.

BOESMAN [*equally desperate, looking around dumbly*].

Show it to me! Where is it? This thing that happens to me. Where? Is it the *pondok*? Whiteman pushed it over this morning. Wind will do it to this one. The road I walked today? Behind us! Swartkops? Next week it's somewhere else. The wine? Bottles are empty. Where is it?!!

[*Pause.*]

I look, and I see you. I listen, I hear you.

LENA. And when you hit . . . ?

BOESMAN. You. You cry.

LENA. You hear that too?

BOESMAN. Yes.

LENA [*now almost inarticulate with outrage*].

Moer! Moer!

Outa hear all that? Hey! [*She shakes him violently.*] You can't sleep now! [*Changing her tone, pleading.*] Please, *Outa*. Just a little bit longer. I'll put the wood on the fire.

[*She does so.*]

Wake up. This is the truth now. Listen.

BOESMAN [*watching her*]. You have gone mad tonight.

LENA. He's got to listen!

BOESMAN. He doesn't know what you're saying. *You* must wake up!
You've wasted your time with him. You've been talking to yourself tonight the way you've been talking to yourself your whole life. You're dumb. When you make a hole in your face the noise that comes out is as good as nothing, because nobody hears it.

LENA. Say it in the *kaffertaal*. 'You hit me for nothing.' Say it!

BOESMAN. No.

LENA. Then let him see it.

[*She crawls to Boesman in an attitude of abject beggary.*]

Hit me. Please, Boesman. For a favour. My last one, 'strue's-god. Hit me now.

[*To the old man.*] I've shown you the bruises. Now watch.

[*Pause. . . . Boesman is staring at her with disgust.*]

What you waiting for? You don't need reasons. Let him see it. Hit me!

BOESMAN [*withering disgust*]. Sies.

LENA. Who?

BOESMAN. *SIES!*

LENA. Me?

[*This is too much for Lena. She wanders around vacantly, almost as if she were drunk.*]

Nee, God! Nee nee nee nee, God!
I've got the bruises . . . he did it, he broke the bottles, but I've got the bruises and it's '*Sies*' to me?
What have I done?

BOESMAN. He doesn't know what you're saying!

LENA. Look at me, *Outa* . . . Lena! Me.

BOESMAN. There's only me. All you've got is me and I'm saying '*Sies!*'

LENA [*beside the old man on the box . . . softly . . .*]. Outa?

BOESMAN. You think I haven't got secrets in my heart too?

That's mine. *Sies!* Small little word, hey. *Sies.*
But it fits.

[*Parodying himself.*] '*Ja, baas! Dankie, baas!*'

Sies, Boesman!

And you? Don't ask me what you've done. Just look. You
say you can see yourself. Take a good look tonight! Crying
for a bottle, begging for bruises.

Sies, Lena! Boesman and Lena, *sies!*

We're not people any more. Freedom's not for us.

We stood there under the sky . . . two crooked *Hotnots.*

So they laughed.

Sies wêreld!

All there is to say. That's our word. After that our life is
dumb. Like your *moer.* All that came out of it was silence.
There should have been noise. You pushed out silence. And
Boesman buried it. Took the spade the next morning and
pushed our hope back into the dirt. Deep holes! When I
filled them up I said it again: *Sies.*

One day your turn. One day mine. Two more holes somewhere. The earth will get *naar* when they push us in. And
then it's finished. The end of Boesman and Lena.

That's all it is, tonight or any other night. Two dead *Hotnots*
living together.

And you want him to look? To see? He must close his eyes.
That's what I'll say for you in the *kaffertaal.*

Musa khangela! Don't look! That's what you must tell him.
Musa khangela!

LENA. He can't hear you, Boesman.

BOESMAN. *Musa khangela!*

LENA. Don't shout. I'm alone.

BOESMAN. What do you mean?

LENA. He can't hear you.

BOESMAN. Then wake him up.

LENA. Does it look like sleep? *Outa's* closed his eyes. The old
thing must have been tired. I tried to keep them open, make
him look. When he closed them his darkness was mine.

[*Pause. . . . Boesman now realizes. Lena looks up at him.*]

Ja! He's dead.

BOESMAN. How do you know?

LENA. He let go. He was holding my hand. He grabbed it, held it tight, then he let go.

BOESMAN. Feel his heart.

LENA. He's dead, Boesman. His hand is empty.

BOESMAN [*unbelievingly*]. He didn't cry, or something. . . .

LENA. Maybe it wasn't worth it.

BOESMAN. *He* wasn't worth it. Bottle of wine! And now . . . ? Didn't last you long.
[*The bottle in his hand.*] Mine too. Finished.
[*Throws the bottle aside.*] There goes mine.
[*Pause. . . . He looks at Lena and the old man again.*]
Morsdood?

LENA. *Ja.*

BOESMAN [*walking away*]. All yours.

LENA. Help me put him down.

BOESMAN [*quickly*]. He's got nothing to do with me.
[*Sits down in front of his shelter, nervous and uncertain.*]
You wanted him. You called him to the fire.

LENA [*gently easing the body down*].
Hey, heavy! No wonder we get *moeg*. It's not just the things on your head. There's also yourself.
[*She moves away.*]

BOESMAN [*after a pause*]. And now? What's going to happen now?

LENA. Is something going to happen now?

BOESMAN. Dead man.

LENA. Only a *kaffer. Outa.* Didn't even learn his real name. He said mine so nicely. Sorry, *ou ding.* Sorry.

BOESMAN [*false indifference*]. *Ja*, well . . . *môre is nog 'n dag.* I'm tired. Low water early. We'll have to *woel* if we want prawns. I'm going to sleep.
[*Pause.*]
I said I'm going to sleep.

LENA. I heard you.

BOESMAN [*before disappearing into the shelter*]. He's got nothing to do with me.

LENA. '*Môre is nog 'n dag.*' Maybe, hey, *Outa*. Maybe. So that's all. Hold on for as long as you can, and then let go.

BOESMAN [*shouting from inside the shelter*].
What are you doing?

LENA. Put your hands on the things in your life. Yours were full. Mug of tea, piece of bread. . . . Me.
Somebody else. Touch them, hold them. . . .

BOESMAN [*his head appearing in the opening of the shelter*].
What you doing?

LENA [*looking at him*].
. . . or make a fist and hit them.

BOESMAN. You can't just sit there. You better do something.
[*Pause.*]
Listen to me, Lena!

LENA. Why must I listen to you?

BOESMAN [*coming out*].
This is no time for more bloody nonsense! It's serious.

LENA. When *you* want somebody to listen, it's serious.

BOESMAN. That! [*Pointing to the body.*]

LENA. *Outa* still worry you? *Haai*, Boesman. He's dead.

BOESMAN. Dead men are dangerous. You better get rid of it.

LENA. Real piece of rubbish now, hey. What must I do?

BOESMAN. I don't give a damn. Just do it.

LENA. How do you throw away a dead *kaffer*?

BOESMAN. Your problems. He's got nothing . . .

LENA. . . . to do with you. Go back to sleep, Boesman.

BOESMAN. I am! Why must I worry? I did nothing. Clear conscience! Come and do his nonsense here! This is my place. I was here first. He should have stayed with his own sort. Then when I wanted to get rid of him, *you* stopped me.

[*There is no response from Lena to Boesman's growing agitation. This provokes him even more.*]

Are you a bloody fool?

LENA. You say so.

BOESMAN. That's big trouble lying there.

LENA. His troubles are over.

BOESMAN. And ours? What do you think is going to happen tomorrow?

LENA. I don't care.

BOESMAN. Well, I'm just warning you, you better have answers ready. Dead man! There's going to be questions.

LENA. About him? About rubbish? Hey, hey, hey! *Outa* hear that. '*Môre is sommer* a special *dag*.' They're going to ask questions!
About you! Hot stuff, hey. 'What's his name?' 'Where's he come from?'

BOESMAN. Never saw him before in my life!

LENA. 'Who did it?'

BOESMAN [*sharply*]. Did what? He died by himself.

LENA. Too bad you can't tell them, *Outa*.

BOESMAN. I did nothing.

LENA. Why don't they ask some questions when we're alive?

BOESMAN [*interrupting her*]. Hey! You saw.

LENA. What did I see?

BOESMAN. I did nothing to him. You saw that.

LENA. Now you want a witness too.

BOESMAN. I didn't touch him. You tell them.

LENA. What?

BOESMAN. The truth.

LENA. You got some words tonight, Boesman. Freedom. Truth. What's that? *Sies?*

BOESMAN. Stop your jokes, Lena! When they come tomorrow you just tell them. I was minding my own business. I only come here to dig for prawns.

LENA. Teach me again, Boesman. You *mos* know how the whiteman likes to hear it.
'He's just a *Hotnot, baas*. Wasn't doing any harm.' How's that? Will that make him feel sorry for you?

BOESMAN. Then the *kaffer* came. And *you* called him to the fire.

LENA. '*Siestoggies, my baas*.'

BOESMAN. I didn't want him. I didn't touch him.

LENA. 'Boesman didn't want him, *baas*.'

BOESMAN. I hate *kaffers*.

LENA. 'He hates *kaffers, baas*.'

BOESMAN. NO!!

LENA. 'He loves *kaffers, baas*.'

BOESMAN. God, Lena!

[*He grabs a bottle and moves violently towards her. He stops himself in time. Lena has made no move to escape or protect herself.*]

LENA. *Ja*, got to be careful now. There's one already.

[*Boesman is now very frightened. Lena watches him.*]

Whiteman's dog, his tail between his legs because the *baas* is going to be cross. *Yessus!* We crawl, hey. You're right, Boesman. And beg. 'Give us a chance.' *Siesiog.* I'm sorry for you. Hey. Maybe he's not dead.

[*Boesman looks at her.*]

That's a thought, hey! Maybe he's not dead, and everything is still okay.

BOESMAN. You said he was.

LENA. You believe me? You mean you're listening to Lena tonight. Are we talking to each other?

BOESMAN. Is he dead?

[*Lena laughs softly. Boesman moves uncertainly towards the body, unable to ignore the possibility with which she is tormenting him. He looks down at the dead man.*]

LENA. Go on.

BOESMAN. Wake up!

LENA. Doesn't speak our language, remember.

BOESMAN. Hey!

LENA. That's better.

BOESMAN [*nudging the body with his foot*]. *Vuka!*

LENA. Didn't he move there? Imagine he stands up now? Happy days! Dig prawns tomorrow, buy another bottle, give me a hiding.

[*Boesman is hesitating, uncertain of what to do next.*]

Feel his heart.

[*The nudge becomes a kick.*]

Much better. Let him feel your foot.

BOESMAN. Get up!

LENA. Don't let him play stupid with you. Make him get up. Tell him to go.

BOESMAN. *Voetsek!*

LENA. Louder! These *kaffers* are *onnooslik.*

BOESMAN [*his violence building up—another kick*].
Go die in your own world!

LENA. *Nog 'n een!*

[*Pause. . . . Boesman, rigid with anger and hatred, stares down at the inert body.*]

No bloody good. He's dead. And you, *ou boeta*, you're in trouble!

BOESMAN [*his control breaking*].
Bloody fool!

[*He falls to his knees and beats the body violently with his fists. Lena watches in silence. When Boesman is finished he goes back to his place in front of the shelter.*]

LENA. So that's how you do it. I know what it feels like. Now I know what it looks like. What do you think about, in between when you rest? Where to hit next?

[*Boesman is breathing heavily.*]

Hard work to beat the daylights out like that. Too bad there wasn't any left in him. *Outa*'s in darkness. He won't be sore tomorrow, sit and count his bruises in the light. But he'll have them. When you hit me I go blue.

[*Pause.*]

You shouldn't have hit him, Boesman. Those bruises! Finger-prints. Yours. On him. You've made it worse for yourself. Dead *kaffer* and a *Hotnot meid* with bruises . . . and Boesman sitting near by with no skin on his knuckles. What's that look like? The answer to all their questions. They won't even ask them now. They'll just grab you . . . [*carefully*] . . . for something you didn't do!

That's the worst. When you didn't do it. Like the hiding you gave me for dropping the empties. Now you'll know what it feels like. You were clever to tell me. It hurt more

243

than your fists. You know where you feel that one? Inside.
Where your fists can't reach. A bruise there!

Now it's your turn!

[*Boesman, barely controlling his growing panic, gets stiffly to his legs.
He looks around . . . the dead man, Lena, the darkness . . . then
makes up his mind and starts to collect their things together.*]

BOESMAN. Come!

[*Lena doesn't respond.*]

On your legs! We're going.

LENA. *Haai*, Boesman! This hour! Where?

[*Boesman doesn't answer.*]

You don't know again, do you? Just crawl around looking
for a way out of your life.

Why must I go with you? Because you're Boesman and I'm
Lena?

BOESMAN [*urgently packing up their belongings . . . rolling blanket,
etc.*]

Are you coming? It's the last time I ask you.

LENA. No. The first time I tell you. No.

I've walked with you a long way, *ou ding*! It's finished now.
Here, in the Swartkops mud. I wanted to finish it this morning,
sitting there on the pavement. That was the word in my
mouth. NO! Enough! I wasn't ready for it yet. I am now.

[*Boesman is staring at her.*]

Don't you understand? It's over.

Look at you! Look at your hands! Fists again. When Boesman
doesn't understand something, he hits it.

You didn't understand him [*pointing to the dead man*], did you?
I chose him! A *kaffer*! Then he goes and buggers up everything by dying. So you hit him. And now me.

'No, Boesman! I'm not going with you!'
You want to hit me, don't you?

[*Barely controlling his panic now, Boesman goes on packing.*]

Run! It's trouble. Life's showing you bullets again. So run.
But this time you run alone. When you think you're safe
don't rest and wait for me to find you. I'm not running the
other way that leads me back to you. I'm not running at all.
I'm *moeg*. When you're gone I'll crawl in there and sleep.

[*Boesman stops his packing and looks up at Lena. He realizes her intention.*]

BOESMAN. That's what you think!

[*Boesman starts to smash the shelter with methodical and controlled violence.*]

LENA. *Hotnot* bulldozer! Hey, hey!

[*Jumps to her legs and prances around.*]

Dankie, baas Boesman! Smash it to hell! This is my laugh. Run, you old bastard. Whiteman's chasing you!

BOESMAN [*the shelter is totally demolished. He collects their things together with renewed energy.*]

Don't think I'm leaving you anvthing.

LENA [*pursuing him ruthlessly*].

Take the lot!

[*Helping him collect it all together.*] This . . . this. . . .

Don't forget my blanket.

[*It is still wrapped around the dead man. Boesman hesitates.*]

You frightened? There!

[*She pulls it off and throws it at Boesman.*]

Everything! I want boggerall. It's my life but I don't want to feel it any more. I've held on tight too long. I want to let go. I want nothing!

What's your big word? Freedom! Tonight it's Freedom for Lena. Whiteman gave you yours this morning, but you lost it. Must I tell you how? When you put all that on your back. There wasn't room for it as well.

[*All their belongings are now collected together in a pile.*]

You should have thrown it on the bonfire. And me with it. You should have walked away *kaal*!

That's what I'm going to be now. *Kaal*. The noise I make now is going to be new. Maybe I'll cry!! . . . Or laugh? I want to laugh as well. I feel light. Get ready, Boesman. When you walk I'm going to laugh! At you!

[*Boesman is loading himself up with their belongings . . . blankets, mattress, boxes. It is a difficult operation, the bundles are awkward, things keep falling out. But he finally manages to get it all on his back and under his arms. He stands before Lena, a grotesquely overburdened figure.*]

245

Eina! Look at you. *Here*, Boesman, the roads, going to be
long tomorrow. And hard. You'll sweat.

What way you walking? Veeplaas? Follow the sun, that's
where it goes. Sand between your toes tomorrow night.

[*Violently.*] So what you waiting for? Can't we say goodbye?
We'll have to do it one day. It's not for ever. Come on.
Let's say it now. Goodbye! Okay, now go. Go!! Walk!!

[*Lena turns her back on him violently and walks away. Boesman
stands motionless. She ends up beside the old man.*]

Outa, why the hell you do it so soon? There's things I didn't
tell you, man. And now this as well. It's still happening!
[*Softly.*] . . . *Moer moer moer.* Can't throw yourself away before
your time. Hey, *Outa*. Even you had to wait for it.

[*She gets up slowly and goes to Boesman.*]

Give!

[*He passes over the bucket.*]

Hasn't got a hole in it yet. Might be whiteman's rubbish,
but I can still use it.

[*It goes on to her head.*]

Where we going? Better be far. Coegakop. That's our farthest.
That's where we started.

BOESMAN. Coega to Veeplaas.

LENA [*slowly loading up the rest of her share*].
First walk. I always remember that one. It's the others.

BOESMAN [*as Lena loads*]. Veeplaas to Redhouse. On *baas*
Robbie's place.

LENA. My God! *Ou baas* Robbie.

BOESMAN. Redhouse to Missionvale . . . I worked on the salt-
pans. Missionvale to Bethelsdorp.
Back again to Redhouse . . . that's where the child died.
Then to Kleinskool. Kleinskool to Veeplaas. Veeplaas to here.
First time. After that, Redhouse, *baas* Robbie was dead,
Bethelsdorp, Korsten, Veeplaas, back here the second time.
Then Missionvale again, Veeplaas, Korsten, and then here,
now.

LENA [*pause. . . . she is loaded*].
Is that the way it was? How I got here?

BOESMAN. Yes.

LENA. Truly?

BOESMAN. Yes.

[*Pause.*]

LENA. It doesn't explain anything.

BOESMAN. I know.

LENA. Anyway, somebody saw a little bit. Dog and a dead man.

[*They are ready to go.*]

I'm alive, Boesman. There's daylights left in me. You still got a chance. Don't lose it. Next time you want to kill me, do it. Really do it. When you hit, hit those lights out. Don't be too late. Do it yourself. Don't let the old bruises put the rope around your neck. Okay. But not so fast. It's dark.

[*They look around for the last time, then turn and walk off into the darkness.*]

NOTES

'MASTER HAROLD' ... AND THE BOYS, p.16. '... we freed your ancestors here in South Africa long before the Americans' refers to the abolition of slavery throughout the British Empire in 1833, one result of which was to drive many Afrikaners still further from the Cape Colony in order to retain absolute control over their black and 'Coloured' servants.

HELLO AND GOODBYE, Act Two, p. 170. 'The Bad Years': i.e. the Great Depression, one effect of which upon South Africa was to sharpen the demand for racialist legislation to 'protect white jobs'; it is estimated that by the mid-thirties some 300,000 Afrikaners were 'poor whites' (about a quarter of their total number), living below or on the margins of subsistence. If segregation broke down in the urban slums, where unemployed whites (mostly Afrikaans-speaking) lived beside the blacks in squalor, the growing Afrikaner Nationalist movement sought to 'rescue' their people by means of job-reservation laws. Segregation came to be seen as a necessary condition for Afrikaner survival; and still is.

BOESMAN AND LENA, Act One, p. 211. The elderly black man who arrives at their fire out of the dark, 'Outa', speaks only his own language, which in this edition is Xhosa, local to Port Elizabeth and its surroundings: the audience is not meant to understand him, any more than Lena does, and so the language spoken may be (and has been) varied according to production and performer. In the main, it is a long tale of suffering and despair, of travelling from place to place as an outcast.

GLOSSARY

African and Afrikaans words and phrases are printed in bold, others in bold italic type. I would like here to acknowledge the assistance of Dr Elizabeth Gunner and the Reverend Barney Pityana in the compilation of this Glossary.

Ag: exclamation, roughly equivalent to 'oh', and pronounced like German '*ach*'

Ag nee, wat!: exclamatory, literally 'oh no, what!'

Ag siestog, my baas!: exclamatory, literally 'oh pity, my master' (see also **Sies**)

Ai: exclamation, expressing pain, as in 'ah', or 'ow'

Aikona: see **Haaikona**

Aina!: see **Eina!**

Aitsa! exclamation, 'whoops!'

Al weer sukke tyd: roughly equivalent to 'here we go again'

Arme ou drommel: 'poor old thing'

Arme ou Lena se maer ou bene: 'poor old Lena's skinny old legs'

Baas(es), Baasie: 'boss(es)' or 'master(s)'; familiarly, 'little boss/master' (-*ie* is the diminutive)

Babalas!: slang derived from Zulu *i-babalazi*, 'hung-over'

Bakgat!: slang, 'great!'

Bang in my broek: 'shit-scared', literally 'scared in my pants'

Bantoe(s), Bantu: official terms for black South Africans and their languages, disliked by them

Bedonnerd: see **Donner**

Beneukt: 'unreasonable, crazy; fed up'

Bhomboloza Outa, Bhomboloza: 'cry out, old man, cry out', from the Xhosa *ukubhomboloza*.

Bioscope: South African English, 'cinema'

Blikkie kondens melk: 'tin of condensed milk'

Blourokkie: prison slang for long-term prisoner; literally, 'blue dress', the colour of their uniform

Boer: 'farmer'

Boesman: derogatory term for a person of mixed-race, from Afrikaans for 'Bushman', as the Khokhoi people were formerly referred to

Boet, Boetie: 'brother'; 'little brother'; but also used to address a friend colloquially, as, e.g., 'pal'

Boggerall: South African English slang, 'buggerall'

Bokkie: 'little buck'; term of endearment

Boot: i.e. 'trunk' (US)

Brak: 'mongrel'

Broek: 'pants'; 'trousers'

Bulala wena!: 'I'll kill you!', a corruption of the Xhosa *ngizo-bulala wena*!

Capie: a 'Cape Coloured', i.e. person of mixed race

Chick-a-doem, doem, doem: onomatopoeic for a fast tune

Coolie: derogatory term for an Indian

Daar kom 'n ding díe kant: literally, 'there's a thing coming this way, this side'; 'something's coming'

Dala: see **Outa, dala**

Dankie, baas!: 'thank you, boss/ master!'

Dè!: 'there!', possibly from Zulu *kude*, 'far', if not simply English

Die geraas van 'n vervloekte lewe: 'the noise of a cursed life'

Die trane die rol vir jou, bok-kie!: 'I'm crying for you, baby', literally, 'the tears roll for you, little buck'

Doek: 'head-scarf', as worn by black South Africans

Dominee: a minister of the Dutch Reformed Church; 'reverend' or 'minister'

Donner: (verb) 'beat up'; (noun) 'bastard'; thus also *bedonnerd* as an adjective, 'bloody' (abusive slang); derived from *donder*, 'to thrash'

Dop: 'tot' or drink of (hard) liquor

Drol: 'turd'

Dronkies: 'drunks'

Dwaal: 'to be in a *dwaal*', i.e. 'disoriented', 'confused'

Eina!: exclamation of pain, 'ow!'; similarly *Aina!*

Ek sê!: exclamation, 'hey!', literally 'I say!'

Ek sê, ou pellie: elaboration of above: 'hey, pal'

En dit? Nee, moer!: 'and that? No, fuck!' see also **Moer**

En klaar: as in 'finish *en klaar*'; emphatic expression, 'that's that'; 'finished and done with'

Entjie: 'stub-end' (of a cigarette); 'little piece'

Ewe: 'yes' (Xhosa)

G.M.: General Motors

Gat op die grond en trane vir 'n bottel: 'backside on the ground and crying for a bottel' (drink)

Gebabbel: 'babble'

Goosie: South African English slang term of endearment, 'cutie'

Haai!: exclamation of surprise, 'no!', 'well, I never!', from Xhosa *hayi*

Haaikona: emphatic negative, 'no, never', 'oh, no', etc., sometimes given as *aikona*; from Xhosa (and Zulu) *hayikhona*

Haai! Kyk net. Witman is 'n snaakse ding: 'no! Just look. The white man is a funny thing'

Hamba!: 'go!' from Nguni (Xhosa, Zulu) imperative, *ukuhamba*, often used offensively by non-Africans

Hamba wena!: 'push off!', 'get out, you!'; stronger and more insulting than *hamba*

Here: 'Christ', 'oh Lord', colloquial Afrikaans

Hoe's dit vir 'n ding!: 'how's

that!', 'how do you like
that!'
Hoer: 'whore' (noun and verb)
Hond: 'dog'
Hotnot: corrupt form of 'Hottentot', term formerly used of San
tribespeople, now abusive
Ja: 'yes'
Jou lae donner!: 'you dirty bastard'; see also **Donner**
Jou moer!: very obscene: 'you
cunt!' (from *moer*, 'womb')
Jou verdomde . . . : 'you
damned . . .'
Kaal, Kaalgat: 'naked', literally
'bare-arsed'
Kaffer: 'kaffir', abusive term
for African; 'nigger' (US);
hence also *Kaffermeid!*, 'Kaffir
woman' and *kaffertaal*, 'kaffir
language'
Klaar: 'finished', 'ready'; see **En
klaar**
Klap: 'clout', 'blow'
Kom díe kant!: 'come here!', 'on
this side!'
Kondens melk: 'condensed
milk'
Koppies: 'little hills'
Kwaai-vriende: ' "bad" friends',
'not on speaking terms'
Lawaai: 'noise', 'row'
Leeggesuip: 'empty', literally
'drunk dry'
Lieg: 'lie' (noun and verb)
Liewe God!: exclamation, 'dear
God!'
Links draai, regs swaai: 'turn
left, swing right'
Location: segregated area on
outskirts of town or city set
aside for African or 'Coloured'
occupation, as in, e.g.,

Korsten location, Port
Elizabeth; see also 'township'
Loop, Hotnot!: 'bugger off!',
literally 'run, Hottentot'; see
Hotnot
Luisgat!: 'louse' (*-gat*, or 'arse'
reinforces the abusive mean-
ing)
Maak sy bek oop!: 'open its
mouth!' (*bek* is applied to
animals, or abusively to
humans)
Maer: 'thin'
Manzi!: 'water!' a corruption of
Zulu *amanzi*
Meid: 'girl'; 'servant-woman'
Mlomo, ewe mlomo: 'mouth,
yes, mouth', from the Xhosa
Moeg: 'worn-out', 'exhausted'
Moenie skiet, baas!: 'don't
shoot, master!'
Moer!: obscene exclamation,
'fuck!'; 'womb'; see also **Jou
moer!**
Molo, outa: 'hello, old man'
(Xhosa); see **Outa**
Môre, baas!: 'good-day, master',
from *môre*, meaning 'morning'
or 'morrow', hence—
Môre is nog 'n dag: 'tomorrow
is another day'
Morsdood: 'stone dead'
Mos: 'just'
Musa khangela!: 'don't look!',
from Zulu *ukhangela*
My baasie: 'my master' (famil-
iar)
Naar: 'queasy', 'sick'
Nee, God!: 'no, God!'
Nes: 'haunt' (noun), as in *kaffer
nes*
Net 'n bietjie warm gemaak:
'just warmed up a little'

Nog 'n een: 'another one'

Onnooslik: 'stupid', 'witless'

Onnooslike kaffer. My bleddy bek af praat vir niks!: 'stupid "kaffir". To talk my bloody jaw off for nothing!'

Oppas: 'be careful', 'look out'

Opskud en uitkap: to dance fast, literally 'get up and get moving'

Ou: common mode of address to man or boy; 'chap', 'bloke'; also adjectival, meaning 'old' (see below)

Ou blikkie kondens melk: Old tin of condensed milk

Maak die lewe soet: Makes life sweet;

Boesman is 'n Boesman: Boesman is a Bushman

Maar hy dra 'n Hotnot hoed: But he wears a Hottentot hat.

Ou boeta: mode of address to an elder brother, also to an old (i.e. long-term) friend

Ou ding: 'old thing'

Ou drol: 'old turd'

Ou grappie: 'silly little joke'

Ou hoer!: 'whore'

Ou Hotnot meid: 'Hottentot servant-woman'

Ou kaffer: 'old "kaffir"'

Oulike ou nessie: 'cute little nest'

Ouma: 'grandmother', but also a mode of address to an older woman

Ou meid: elderly servant-woman, presumed 'Coloured'

Ou pellie: 'pal'

Ou *Sister*: term of familiarity towards woman belonging to a 'sisterhood'; literally, 'old' sister

Outa: mode of address to an elderly, usually 'Coloured' or African man, often by children as a mark of respect to an elderly servant; derived from *ou* + *ta* (Xhosa, Zulu), 'old' + 'father'

Outa, dala: 'old man, old man', from 'outa' and Xhosa *mdala*, old man

_P.E._: Port Elizabeth

Pap nat: 'sodden'

Pap ou borste, ribbetjies: 'flabby old breasts, thin little ribs'

Poep: 'fart'

Poephol: 'arse-hole'

Pondok, pondokkies: 'hut', 'shack'; 'little lean-tos'

Poopy: South African English slang, 'terrified'

Robot: South African English, 'traffic lights'

_S.A.R._: South African Railways

Sa! Sa vir die kaffer!: 'Get him! After the "kaffir"'; used when setting a dog on someone or something

Safa: 'suffer' in Africanized pronunciation

Shame!: South African English, colloquial, 'poor thing!'

Sies: exclamation of disgust, 'ugh'

Siestoggies, my baas! Siestoggies, my groot _little_ baasie!: expression of sympathy or dismay, 'ah, no, my master! No, my big little master!'

Sies wêreld!: expression of disgust towards the world

Sinkplaat: corrugated iron

Skeef: 'skew', 'crooked'

Skelms: 'rascals', 'rogues'

Skof: 'stretch' in the sense of the leg of a journey

Skop: 'kick' (noun and verb)

Skop and skip: 'hop and skip'

Skrik: 'fright'

Sleep: 'drag', 'pull along'

Soeterigheid: 'sweetness'

Sommer: 'just', 'simply'

Sommer a ou Hotnot, baas . . . Van ou *Coega*, baas. Ja, my baas: 'Just an old Hottentot, master . . . From old Coega, master. Yes, my master'

So waar: 'truly'

Stompie: 'cigarette-butt'

Stinkwood: wood of an indigenous hardwood tree, so named after the odour released when cut

Sukkel: 'struggle', 'toil'

Swartgat: abusive name for black South African, literally, 'black-arse'

Taal: 'language'

Tickey: name for obsolete South African threepenny piece, now superseded by five-cent coin; small coin

Tickey-**draai**: lively country dance

Township: area set aside solely for 'Coloured' or African occupation, e.g. New Brighton township

Vark: term of abuse, 'pig'

Vastrap: fast country dance, literally 'quick-step'

Vat jou goed en trek!: 'take your things and go!'

Vies!: 'angry!', 'disgusted!'

Vlenterbroek: 'torn trousers'

Voetsek!: rough command to go, usually to a dog, offensive to a person, equivalent to 'bugger off!'

Vrot!: 'no good', 'rotten'

Vrot ou huisie vir die vrot mens: literally, 'rotten little old house for rotten people'

Vuilgoed!: 'rubbish!', 'garbage!'

Vuka!: 'arise!', 'wake up!', Nguni (Zulu and Xhosa)

Waar die donner is . . . ?: 'where the hell is . . . ?', see also **Donner**

Waar kry jy seer?: 'where does it hurt (you)?'

Weg wêreld, kom brandewyn: 'go away world, come brandy'

Wie's die man?: 'who's that man?'

Witman is 'n snaakse ding: see **Haai!**

Woel: 'hurry', 'get a move on'

Yessus!: 'Jesus!'

The Oxford World's Classics Website

www.worldsclassics.co.uk

- Information about new titles
- Explore the full range of Oxford World's Classics
- Links to other literary sites and the main OUP webpage
- Imaginative competitions, with bookish prizes
- Peruse *Compass*, the Oxford World's Classics magazine
- Articles by editors
- Extracts from Introductions
- A forum for discussion and feedback on the series
- Special information for teachers and lecturers

www.worldsclassics.co.uk

American Literature

British and Irish Literature

Children's Literature

Classics and Ancient Literature

Colonial Literature

Eastern Literature

European Literature

History

Medieval Literature

Oxford English Drama

Poetry

Philosophy

Politics

Religion

The Oxford Shakespeare

A complete list of Oxford Paperbacks, including Oxford World's Classics, OPUS, Past Masters, Oxford Authors, Oxford Shakespeare, Oxford Drama, and Oxford Paperback Reference, is available in the UK from the Academic Division Publicity Department, Oxford University Press, Great Clarendon Street, Oxford OX2 6DP.

In the USA, complete lists are available from the Paperbacks Marketing Manager, Oxford University Press, 198 Madison Avenue, New York, NY 10016.

Oxford Paperbacks are available from all good bookshops. In case of difficulty, customers in the UK can order direct from Oxford University Press Bookshop, Freepost, 116 High Street, Oxford OX1 4BR, enclosing full payment. Please add 10 per cent of published price for postage and packing.